The Hill of Kronos

PETER LEVI

ELAND
London

This edition published by Eland Publishing Limited
61 Exmouth Market, London ECIR 4QL in 2007

First published in Great Britain 1981 by
William Collins Sons & Co. Ltd

Text © Peter Levi 1981
Poems by kind permission of Anvil Press

978 0955010 54 5

The photograph on the cover by Robert A. McCabe is from
"Greece: Images of an Enchanted Land 1954-1965"
published by Patakis Editions, Athens, and
Quantuck Lane Press, New York.

Typeset by Nick Randall
Printed in Navarra, Spain by GraphyCems

Contents

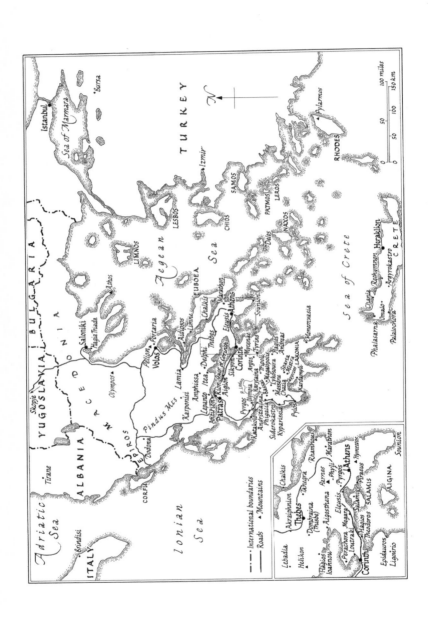

Introduction

I HAVE FOUND this book hard to begin because life has made me very happy and my own past history is becoming as distant as the mountains of the moon. There is too much to write about. Hungrier travel writers than I am often write better books. When I first went to Greece I thought I was discovering everything at once, five things a day. My hunger for the monuments of antiquity, for museums, for people, for light and shade, for mountains, woods, islands and seas, seemed to me insatiable. Indeed it has never been sated, but now I feel that I know Greece almost too well to write about it, and time meanwhile has washed away my footprints from those tracks. Greece has been the air I breathed and the life I lived, yet I can no longer easily recapture that young self to whom it was strange. Nor can I quite shake him off, and I am afraid that he will dog the reader through this book as he dogs me. Today I can answer nearly all of the naive questions he began by asking, but he is still asking questions and I have lost my shame about his naivete.

The best books in English about Greece, as a personal discovery, are by Patrick Leigh-Fermor, Lawrence Durrell, Henry Miller, Kevin Andrews, Dilys Powell. They have something in common, which I take to be Greek reality, not just a similar temperament, though most of them have been a close friend of at least one of the others, and a quality of the same generation marks all of them. The Greece they discovered was hardly born until 1930, and in the last ten years it has been transformed. There were earlier discoveries, by Wheler at the end of the seventeenth century, by Chandler in the eighteenth, by Leake and by Edward Lear in the nineteenth. There are Schliemann's diaries and Byron's letters. In all of them, the same, continuous Greece, what Durrell calls 'the distinctive form and signature of things Greek' can be recognised. Whoever discovers Greece today can hardly rank with Columbus.

Although I could not hope to rival what has already been so sharply and well recorded, and although I suppose this book that I have such a passion to write will be unlike anyone else's, if only because my life has been different from theirs, yet the continuous attraction of Greece for me has been something quite simple, and I am sure that I share it with many who will never write a book and some of those who have. It was the light, the physical sunlight. It was thyme-scented hillsides and plains of toasted thistles. It was the fragments of the marble architecture. It was spring at Pylos and at Sounion and in the Cretan mountains. It was the charcoal-burners in the pine woods and the donkeys and goats and anemones in the olive groves. It was autumn at Olympia, winter in the Arkadian mountains, the annual snowfall of wild cyclamen on the Hill of Kronos. But above all it was the people. Most of the best friends I ever expect to have are Greek, and we have fifteen years of our lives in common.

But I came late to Greece, at the age of thirty-two, in 1963. I had started to learn ancient Greek as a schoolboy, at a school where Greek was hardly taught. All I knew about Greece then was the Elgin Marbles, of which I treasured some sepia-tinted and forbidding postcards, and the fact that Oscar Wilde, who in the summer of my fourteenth birthday had just become my literary idol, said the Greek text of the Gospels was the most beautiful book in the world. So I demanded to learn Greek, and changed schools in consequence. From that time I have never ceased to study the Greek language. There were some ups and downs, of course. One of the ups was Oxford, where I was lucky enough to be taught some medieval and modern, as well as ancient Greek. There I discovered, like flowers on a slag-heap, the few wonderful Byzantine writers. And there I discovered George Seferis. I venerated him then as an immensely great poet; later I came to love him as a friend, almost as a father, and to respect and admire him more than I can express.

Coming so late in the day to Greece seemed at the time to be an impoverishment, but I take some consolation from hindsight. The terrible sufferings and the heroism and determination of the Greek people in their resistance to Hitler have transformed forever the way we look at Greece. Short of having known Greece before the war and fought through it in the Cretan mountains, as some of the English did, I prefer a Greece who knows herself and whom we know to all the privileges of pre-war Europe, and I am glad not to have lived through the disasters of the two anti-communist civil wars that followed Hitler's war. I am even more glad not to have lived in Greece or had friends there during the catastrophic mismanagement of the Cyprus crisis by Great Britain. By 1963 that was to some degree forgiven, though it was not forgotten. On the other hand, I did live through the seven nasty years of the Colonels, from 1967 to 1974, and I am glad I was there. I am a witness to what happened, to the dignity and obstinacy of the Greeks, to their gallantry and their decency in a period of nightmare and of darkness.

My work in Greece was that of an archaeologist of some kind. I took part in excavations, but I spent some years translating and annotating Pausanias, who wrote in the second century A.D. a description of all the surviving monuments of ancient architecture and religion; and then many more years working at a full commentary on his writings in the light of modern archaeology. I chose him because of his reality, and because by studying Pausanias I could hope to know Greece as I longed to know it. The commentary is still unfinished, indeed hardly started, but I owe Pausanias a loyalty deeper than that of scholarship. Through him I got to know landscapes and sanctuaries and villages and mountains I would not have seen otherwise. And work is peace after all; I have found it a resource in bad times and a pleasure in good.

The trouble was that my interest constantly spilled over, into the history of these same monuments in the Middle Ages, into the Greece of the first archaeological explorers, into modern and recent history, into the people among whom I was working, and finally into prehistory, which for years of obstinate stupidity I had resisted as an irrelevance. Perhaps the explanation was just that I had too many professions. From 1964 I was a priest, but a priest without local duties. I taught the classics in Oxford but I had to be abroad in winter, originally for reasons of bad health, so I took up classical archaeology. Yet the underlying condition and the force and momentum of my life were to be found in neither of these full-time professions, but in poetry. And there was still my unending love affair with the Greek language. I also had an average educated curiosity about birds, flowers and landscapes. As middle-age approached, the curiosity became a passion.

What I liked about Greece was not just poems and not just books, but the impressive force of the language itself, unconfined by dictionaries, spoken in the streets, in cafés, and in the country. Greek has a longer continuous history than most languages; its written records go back nearly four thousand years, and its alterations in that time have been gradual and seldom ruinous. Under the Roman empire, it was almost a world language. Under the Turkish empire it sank back into its own roots, and recovered what it had lost, the beautiful behaviour, the suppleness and bite of country speech. In the last generation poetry has been written in Greek as powerful, as memorable, and as individual as the best English or Russian poems of this century. The modern Greek language has hardly been charted, it can be learnt only by listening. It has an astonishing range of tones and resources and slowly learning and relearning to speak it has been one of the most satisfying pleasures in my life.

In the end I came to write poems of my own in Greek, not by choice, which would have been freakish and perverse, but when I had begun to dream and to think in Greek, and the pressure to write poetry had become irresistible. Those poems have no part, really, in this book, but I do not think they are worse than what I might write in English. I mention them because they represent the furthest point for me of identification with 'the distinctive form and signature of things Greek' without any loss of identity. The loss of one's national or professional identity in the pursuit of a love affair with a foreign country is always a mistake, I believe. There is something phoney about 'going native' anywhere in the world. Equally, of course, it is better not to amaze the inhabitants of another country with Bermuda shorts or a bowler hat, nor was I tempted to do so. I travelled in the wildest places I could find. I was a friendly bachelor. I drank deeply the wine of the country. But if ever anyone took me for a Greek, it was by chance, and only because so few foreigners speak the language.

After many years of study and of a monastic religious life, my first visits to Greece were like a delayed spring, a breaking of the ice. At one moment, I even thought or pretended to myself that I had fallen in love, but it was only a ballet of love. Since then I have known the real thing, which is a very different matter. But in 1965 I had just finished a long and often depressing course of training that had lasted seventeen years. It had included so many illnesses that the training itself seemed like an illness. Now the air glittered and smelt of leaves. I was both sophisticated and innocent, and I was very hungry for life. Greece treated me kindly. It was not a mythical or exactly a romantic place for me; what I was searching for and hungry for was reality. All reality is historical, I suppose; it always descends from history, and the history continues.

If I were to try to thank my Greek friends, and all the others to whom I am indebted and this book is indebted, the list would be terribly long. I once worked on a combined book with two Greek scholars and we thought of a note of thanks to the institutions which had tolerated us. That is rather treacherous ground. But I must express a more personal gratitude at least to Nancy and Betty Sandars, and to Philip Sherrard, who encouraged my first steps in Greece, to Patrick and Joan Leigh-Fermor who have been so good to me for many years, to Nikos Gatsos, Charles Haldeman, Takis Loumiotis, George Pavlopoulos, Takis Sinopoulos, Iannis Tsirkas, to Maro Seferis, to Vanna Hadzimichalis, to Joy Koulentianou, to Athina Kaloyeropoulou, to Amalia Fleming, to Jane Rabnett, to Francis Bartlett, to Niko and Barbara Ghika, to Constantine and Aliki Trypanis. No one has ever been better treated by life than I have been; no one has ever has so much more from life, or from Greece, than they offered it. But most from Deirdre, to whom I dedicate this book.

For Deirdre

1

A Taste of Greece

HEYTHROP COLLEGE was an enormous, four-square eighteenth-century mansion which had suffered lamentable alterations. It stood high up in the wind, its park was bald and ragged, and the Cotswolds heaved around it. Orchids and bluebells grew undisturbed in the more distant woods. Every prospect was a green desert. In summer you could hear the cry of vixens at night and in winter you could hear the snow falling. It was a walk of a mile or two across fields to the nearest country bus stop. The dullness of the theological lectures was beyond expression; it was absolutely unrelieved, and there were four or five a day, many of them delivered in fluent, incompetent Latin. But the worst enemy was the dampness and the cold. I was thirty-two and coughing my infuriated heart out.

The first summer I spent in Greece was not achieved without a skirmish. I had fluttered my wings in that direction as a Jesuit undergraduate at Oxford, in the middle nineteen-fifties, but every request for permission was met with well-phrased silences, and the journey never took place. I am glad now that I never went then, because perhaps if I had I might have got Greece out of my system too early. By 1963 I was very hungry for it. The fall of Constantinople in the fifteenth century was as real to me as the 1914 war. Homer was as powerful and as god-like in my ears as Shakespeare. I knew that George Seferis was one of the greatest, perhaps the greatest, of all the European poets of this century. It was time to go.

Things fell out luckily in the end. We used to translate the psalm *Beati immaculati in via* at Heythrop as 'Blessed are they that are not spotted on the way out.' I was spotted too often, and for this among other middle-aged delinquencies I was summoned to the Rector's office and told, quite kindly I must say, that my ordination as a priest, which ought to have been that summer, was postponed until I amended my irregularities. This made me an awkward figure to have around during everyone else's celebrations. In the atmosphere of sympathy always created by that sort of public disgrace among Jesuits I suggested they should send me to Greece. They agreed at once. There was a difficult moment later, when someone counter-proposed a Jesuit retreat house on the lake of Annecy, but I mustered such arguments against that as I blush to recall, and to Greece I went, planning my own journey.

It was June. The first sentence in my journal is: 'Thunder crumbling into rain. Enterprises and places having a dogged air.' But that was North Oxfordshire, which I was leaving. There follow some notes about poems, and the phrase 'lumpy provincial *chinoiserie*', which someone had used about Claydon. Then a few sentences from a Greek novel, meticulously copied out. It is not a novel I would recommend now, and the style of the landscape passage I copied is exaggerated almost to self-parody. But it seemed significant at the time; I suppose it was what I expected Greece to be like:

> A blue line over the soil of the earth, where there are trees, tombs, flashes of lightning written and extinguished, it drowns in the sea, beyond everything is the silence which is the final limit of the world...From the east, from the line of hills, the dawn star balancing over the bare earth of Anavysso like a hawk watching his prey.

When I did catch my first sight of Greece, it was not like that at all; it was like the poems of Seferis. But that was a resemblance I had for some reason never expected. I would prefer, as most people would, to live in a landscape of Edward Lear. I knew, or thought I knew, that classical landscapes were irrecoverable. In fact there still are times and places, which await those who need and deserve them, where Edward Lear's landscapes still exist in reality. Even the landscape of antiquity is not absolutely irrecoverable, though that demands a patient and scholarly dedication, and the rewards are rare. Greece has touches even of the landscape of my novelist, an old Athenian banker called Venezis who must by now be dead. Anavysso is no longer a refugee settlement, it has hotels and bungalows; there is nothing romantic about it. But I recognize the silence, and the star that hovers like a hawk.

My notes must have been written in a train, because just after them comes a query about the horse-shoe shape and the loud echoes of certain railway tunnels, and then something indecipherable about the leaves in Green Park. Every stage of the journey seemed easier than the last. The most difficult was getting myself driven from Heythrop to Banbury station. London, even so short a time ago, was a splendid and flowering city. Aeroplanes were new to me, and the fact that mine, which should have left at midnight, was delayed until a quarter to four in the morning, gave me romantic pleasure. I roamed around Heathrow in the hot air, gazing at red and green groundlights and at huge aeroplanes like mechanical beings without human purpose or animal instinct. Dawn was ragged and stormy, a wilderness of red far away to the east. There was fog in Italy; we landed at Milan and I spent a long, hot morning in a train to Genoa.

This being my first, and for all I knew my last Greek adventure, I was determined to see as much as possible on the way. The ship from Genoa called at Naples, and from Naples it passed between Sicily and Italy to the Gulf of Corinth. There are a lot of ways of getting from England to Greece; by now I have tried most of them, but the first had its merits. A quick break south is the beginning of wisdom, Genoa and Naples are not negligible, and the sea is the sea. I took the advice of an old central European exile: 'You must not descend on Athens for the first time from the air, like a gangster or a salesman of stockings.' Later, I came to prefer that long train that pulls out of Victoria on winter afternoons, the small ferry like a coal-scuttle, Joyce's 'mucus-coloured, scrotum-tightening sea', and dinner on the way to Paris. I liked dawn in the Po valley, looking back at the Alps and longing for coffee, and the old-fashioned luxury of a ship from Venice.

Venice is not exactly halfway to Greece, it is more like halfway to Byzantium. Once or twice I have taken the old route of the Oriental Express, overland beyond Venice through the endless length of Yugoslavia, with through-carriages from Calais to Athens. But that route always did involve resourceful shopping for food, wine and water, knowing where the hidden baker was near the station at Venice, and the smoked meat shop at Milan. It was always an exhausting adventure, and there is now so little to eat on that train that no one over twenty-five ought to travel on it. I remember a knife fight being narrowly avoided somewhere south of Belgrade between Greek and Turkish immigrant workers, and someone being taken off the train at night for attempted rape, and then being quietly put back a few carriages down. I once nearly died on the railway somewhere near Tito Veles, of severe blood-poisoning, contracted from a hasty injection in Athens and marinated in the sand and sea-water of an excavation on the coast of Libya.

The commonsense method with a car is either to drive all the way or to go south to the heel of Italy and take a ship from Brindisi. I have done this both by car and by train and both were arduous. There are only four advantages in the Brindisi route, which are the four cities of Rimini, Ancona, Bari and Brindisi. Rimini has the finest marble decorations of the Renaissance, Ancona is full of shadows and dramatic monuments, Bari is one of the strangest and most haunting cities in Europe, twin sister to Palermo, and Brindisi is where Virgil died. The flight of stone steps with the ruined columns above the harbour is where the Appian Way dropped at last into the sea. Horace once travelled there with Virgil and Maecenas on an embassy to Mark Antony; Brindisi fills the last line of his poem, 'the end of this long paper, this long road.'

The intellectual and the spiritual distances that separate our world from the ancient Greeks are terribly great. However close they seem to be, it is not really possible to know them by simple intuition, although as a schoolboy, like many generations of European schoolboys, and even as an undergraduate, I thought I could. I would read something for the first time or devour some piece of Greek drawing with my eyes, and all the centuries would seem to drop away. But each of those centuries has marked us. It is no bad thing to explore such a long historical gap through a long physical experience, and to move slowly towards Greece. The sea and the islands, as they first appear out of their distances, are still Homeric. That is some comfort.

At Genoa the sea was black, but the next morning it was a deep, brilliant indigo blue. I made friends with a young Greek sailor and two London Greek hairdressers, who shared the cabin I was in. The sailor was going home to Athens for a new ship, after an emergency operation for appendicitis. I recorded a few fragments of his conversation.

'I'm from Chios. All Chios men are sailors. Tomatoes? Best in the world. The Greeks can do nothing without a tomato. Seagulls, look at them. Seagulls are the company a sailor has.'

He sang himself an old popular song with a dialect word in it, the word for the twanging of a guitar-string. 'Sit and listen to this twang, on my own heart-string.' The tune was mournful and passionate, drifting away into a long eddy of notes. We passed Calabria, painted green and hung out to dry for a thousand years. The sun sank exactly behind us, and the ship sailed under stars that sparkled like sea-salt into the dark.

And for the first of many, many times I came on deck at dawn in the cold, while the ship was edging her way round the blue and grey silhouettes of rocks and islands, past the flashy white huddle of the port of Patras on the right, and through the narrows into the Gulf of Corinth. The gap must be less than a cannon-shot between northern and southern Greece, between low twin promontories, each with a tiny fort like a snail on a sand-spit, Rion and Antirion. All morning I was mesmerized by the coast of a wonderful inland sea as it widened, by mountains receding and advancing, by the walls of Lepanto like a diagram, by the tall rifted mountains to the south with their feet in lemon groves and almost in the sea, by the distant line of Parnassos to the north, with its monumental grace and bulk, by the ancient citadel of Corinth, which is a castle on an eyebrow of rock that has never been stormed in all its history. Then the lighthouse of Perachora, a sanctuary of Hera dug by the British before the war. Then the Corinth canal.

'It smells Greek,' said one of the hairdressers, 'now you can smell it, thyme and pine trees.' The other hairdresser wept, and put his hand on his heart. '*Les pins de la patrie!*' he said. The canal is a long straight slit between cliffs, two or three miles long, I suppose. It does smell very strongly of wild thyme and pine trees, at least in the heat of summer, but all that overpowering heat and clarity draw their resinous force at water level from one small pine growing out of the side of the cliff. It resinates the whole air. At the far end of the canal a priest was sitting under a vine eating olives. The whole ship cheered him.

My record of that day is meagre. 'The constant redefinitions of hills, mountains, capes. Itea in the mist, everything bluish.' And then: 'All these bare, exact words. Barren hillsides enmeshed with story-telling. Attica even more bare. Dusty and smoky Piraeus. The yellow akropolis marbles look as if they would crumble.' Seen from a distance, that must mean, from out at sea through the heat-haze of the city.

Now the factories and refineries on shore start miles to the west of Athens, now the inshore water around Salamis is crowded with old, rusted shipping, now you can smell the Piraeus smog an hour's sailing time to the south. The fumes crept up year by year from the docks and the industrial area. Twenty years ago they concentrated their power in a yellowish local haze; ten years ago they began to climb inland. Now there is no height in central Athens out of their reach. The ancient coastline near the city has disappeared under dumped rubbish and car parks that extend far out to sea. Many distant views of the akropolis where it was glimpsed between houses from a market garden or swam into sight from the Eleusis road, are seldom seen now, or seen in a livid apocalyptic light, when a ray of sunlight strikes downwards through the haze.

Sometimes I think modern Athens is a wilderness of monkeys living their busy and warm lives around the skeleton of some mighty dinosaur; yet I have come to prefer the modern Athenians to the skeletal grandeurs. Surely the akropolis, and the Parthenon in particular, is the noblest work of man. It has the restrained geometry, the impressive and deliberate size, the harmony and proportion and the splendid physical impact that we call classical. It has the animal, not only the spiritual, qualities of man. It has the peace and the subtlety that oriental buildings have. At the same time there is something naive and stark naked about that wonderful white marble. Is it white? Is it cream? Not a dead white or a salt white, but fresher than milk or cream, fresher than a white cloud, crisper than white silk. The marble exists because of the light, because of the blazing purity and strength of Greek sunlight. That light does still exist, more brilliant than the sun or the sea or any stone or mineral. The akropolis belongs more to the sky than to the earth; it is made of light and of white marbles, dark marbles, pillars, shadows.

On the night of every full moon, it used to be on the three nights, the akropolis opens until midnight. It was full moon on my first evening in Athens, and I first entered the akropolis by moonlight. It was an eerie, shadowy place. The pillars rearing above one's head glimmered slightly as trees do in the woods at night; they draped their heads in darkness and moon shadows, and pools of bright moonlight lay underfoot on the marble pavements. The marble was cool to the hand; in colour and texture it was like moonlight petrified. People, rather few in those days, appeared and disappeared out of a darkness disturbed here and there by camera flashes. The whistles of the guards made furious noises in the distance. The interior of the Parthenon was august and silent and very empty. It felt like a holy place.

Indeed it was holy, for nearly two and a half thousand years. When it was built it was the self-expression of the confidence of Athens, but it was not the most sacred building on the akropolis. It was partly a state treasury, partly a stone monument, a delight for gods and men; principally it was the house for a colossal new statue of the goddess Athene. On one great gable she sprang fully armed from the head of Zeus, on the other she disputed with Poseidon for the territory of Athens, and inside she stood roof-high with a marble snake rearing up beside her. The Parthenon frieze was her procession winding round the walls. But that ceremony ended at a smaller temple on the north edge of the akropolis rock. The holiest statue of Athene was an old wooden idol that lived in the smaller temple, where it shared its house with Poseidon and a sacred snake. The print of Poseidon's trident was in the rock over there, and the first olive tree that Athene gave to mankind, 'miracle born out of the living rock', grew nearby. The smaller temple, the Erechtheion, stood in the ruins of a Mycenean palace.

But the Parthenon was also a holy place. When it ceased to be a temple it was transformed at once into a Christian church, and that is how it survived so long. The last traces of wall-painting are still visible on the marble walls, and the outer wall at the west end carries a long Latin epitaph, almost illegible now, in Gothic script, and a simple thirteenth-century painting of the Annunciation, high up to the south of the door, below what is left of the Parthenon frieze. In the Middle Ages the akropolis was a fortified village. In the fifteenth century Italian princes held their court in the big range of marble buildings at the west edge, the state entrance planned by Perikles. When Athens fell to the Turks, the Parthenon became a mosque. When the mosque was destroyed by Venetian gunfire in 1687, a smaller mosque was built at once inside the pillars that survived. It was desecrated in the end by a stray Englishman, on the day of the Turkish surrender in the Greek war of independence. He rode his horse into the building and did all that the Turks had done in Greek country churches.

On my first night in Athens I would not have known all these details. They and many more have accumulated like dust from years of reading and of pleasure. The Parthenon has had strange visitors. Another Englishman called Francis Vernon, who saw it in 1676, a member of Christ Church and an early correspondent of the Royal Society, who was murdered for his pen-knife the next year in Persia, is the only witness we have to the design of its innermost columns. His travel diaries, which are full of the names of plants and sketches of fortifications, are still unpublished. Hugo Favoli, an imperial diplomat, produced at Louvain in 1563 his *Journey to Byzantium* in three books of catastrophic Latin verse. He mistook Dubrovnik for Epidauros, and he greatly admired the sober whitewash with which the Turks had smothered Hagia Sophia. On the subject of a long-bearded Gospodar in his cups, liveliness makes the low standard of the verses forgivable. But what excited him was Athens, an Athens otherwise unrecorded.

What he saw of Attica was devastated; there was little cultivation of the earth. Above the akropolis hovered a little swarm of glittering golden crescents. It might have made me angry, but I would like to have seen that. Visually, the Turkish period in Greece was more attractive than anything that has followed it. On that first night, and often afterwards, I dined in the courtyard of a rustic, tumbledown building of some dignity, high up in the Plaka, the old village Athens under the akropolis rock. It has been restored now, and I preferred it as it was, overgrown by jasmine and overrun by cats and children, and much visited by barrel-organs. The barrel-organs were owned by Greek refugees from Turkey; when the labyrinth of their squatters' huts was pulled down the other day, the last remnant of a dialect of the Greek language perished. The tavern was called the old university. It was once the first university of Athens, founded immediately after independence, with old peasant generals sitting on the same benches as their soldiers.

I was overwhelmed with happiness. I had never been in a world where a waiter in a café offers a cigarette to a client. I had never seen most of the business of a restaurant done by tiny boys who should have been in bed. I had never heard such dramatic voices, such quarrels and such affection. I had never known such grandeur treated with such familiarity, the ancient stones built into houses, and the akropolis with all its monuments like the local castle in an English provincial town. I had never seen pepper like gunpowder and salt like snowflakes. I had never drunk retsina from a barrel. I had never been so drunk. I had never been so clear-headed.

I find I have some notes of tea-time conversation at the British School of Archaeology where I was staying. It seemed all to be about the processes of change and decay. Greek dance music had never been any good since the thirties, those lovely old waltzes. No one can draw nowadays. The German occupation and just after it was the time to live in Athens, when there was no floodlighting of monuments, only decent moonlight. The old pure air and the famous sunlight and the starlight exist now only in Australia. 'I went to see if any of the tripods had died, of bronze disease … Not the old stairway but the one they use, or used to use, though that's abandoned too now, unless it's been quite eaten away, by the silver fish.' We argued about a stuffed white Athenian owl in a common-room at Balliol presented, I think, to Benjamin Jowett by the people of Athens. 'I don't think I would have missed a stuffed bird.'

The British School was a sympathetic institution, and by no means unfunny. Most of the work done there was everyday, scholarly hard work, but it had its eccentricities. Once it had been a Victorian marble mansion in a vast garden outside Athens, but the city engulfed it and new buildings have covered too much of the garden. Still, it remains an oasis of peace and greenness, and the library is big and cool and well-stocked. I am sure the tea must be as weak as ever, *The Times* as out of date, the bedrooms as bare and hot bathwater as restricted. Still, if the older archaeologists are still as kind to novices as they were to me, life is worth living. The summer was not a typical time at the British School. The students live there in winter; summer is reserved for excavations and the School fills up with travellers. I remember an aged schoolmistress who vanished one summer and had to be looked for by the police. She was run to ground in a tavern in the Piraeus, sitting on a sailor's knee and calling him a silly boy; she was quite in command of the situation. It was not an unfunny place.

Looking back on that first visit, I seem to have crammed an immense variety of things into a very few weeks: poetry and poets, museums, long expeditions on foot, and over and over again the sea, over and over again the streets of Athens. Most of my reading was in Greek; I had a Sophokles, a Homer and a pocket Pausanias. Apart from that concentrated nourishment I remember only Falconer's 'Shipwreck', a pleasant enough eighteenth-century poem which is not quite as good as I then thought it was, and of course the *Guide Bleu* to Greece, which begins with the harsh sentence, '*La Grèce n'est pas un pays de raffinement gastronomique.*' With that I disagree, but not as strongly as I would have done in the summer of 1963. Mediterranean food suited me. The fields smelt of rigani and the mountains of wild tea. I liked the cheese and the wine and the fresh eggs, and I was hungry. I liked the mullet and the lemon juice and squid and octopus and sucking pig. I drank enough retsina to know a range of difference between the best, which is fresh and appetizing and delicious, and the worst, which is like ship's paint from the Balkan war of 1912.

My journal was an excited jumble. It records more sorts of capitals of columns, more sorts of palmettes, and more tones and colours of marble than I could comprehend. I never pursued the formal stone flowers, either the palmettes or the capitals, but I wasted a great deal of disorganized energy over years in studying the sources of ancient stone. I came to no conclusions. The variations of marble inside the same quarry or in two quarries on one mountain can be so great as to confuse classification. Anyway, the scholar in any young person is often slave to an aesthete, and in my case the aesthete was satisfied without much scholarship. He was happy with the surface appearance of things:

Akropolis by moonlight, night of an eclipse, very strange misty and stormy evening. The thing itself is indescribable and incommunicable. Sweet-smelling white flowers grow on the base. Two or three cypresses.

National Museum. The gold death mask of Agamemnon reduces everyone in the way that the suffering of a servant or a peasant makes a whole society seem unreal.

Qualities of the Parthenon not expected: it is higher, stronger (consciously stronger, the pillars from the west are almost crowded), cooler; part of a complex of buildings and sanctuaries now perished. It utterly annihilates other buildings that survive. Creamy almost yellow marble.

Lemon and black butterflies on the hill of Philopappos. The last light on the west end of the akropolis. Apricot cream distant marble. The bright white broken thing and the bright blue unbroken sky. Heat. Smell of pines and sage and thyme. Creaking cicadas. Bright, warm moon and stars like woodworm.

Archaic painted snakes in the museum, tartan or striped black and red. Marble where some colouring has survived; it appears not so much coloured and faded, rather as if it had restrained its colours. Hair of statues as dense as foliage, like flowerless, unscented jasmine.

The Parthenon this morning seemed terribly scarred and battered. Creamy crags and apricot streaks and stains. Yellow butterfly blown over by the wind from Philopappos. One dusk an owl flew up from the trees under the akropolis rock. Athene's bird?

The mythology of the ancient Greeks meant little to me, at that time, unless it was a clue to the landscape, something that revealed a secret about daily life. And yet I see now that I was making my own mythical Greece. The blue-haired stone horse in the akropolis museum had for me a simple relationship with Poseidon and the blue sea, and the gate of Hades in the sea-caves of southern Greece where white horses were sacrificed from the cliffs. That was a piece of almost scholarly naivete. But there was worse. Every traveller has his traveller's tale, his weird experience, the confirmation of suppressed, extravagant expectations. Mine was the small white owl at dusk. For someone else it was a white-bearded shepherd in a white kilt, riding a white horse. I had a friend who sheltered from a thunderstorm in the ruins of Mycenae, and in the last dramatic edges of the storm found a shepherd looming above her who seemed older than Agamemnon. Another friend found a peasant in the mountains near Larissa who claimed he had met the nymph Calypso at a water-spring. Two or three times, he said. He had never read *The Odyssey*.

These things do happen. I climbed a hill in Crete once with an old man who told me the story of the Cyclops. He said it was a local story and he could show me the cave. Years later on Corfu, in the ruins of the temple of Athene, I came across a ninety-year-old nun, the great-niece of Capodistria, first prime minister of Greece; she remembered the excavation of the Gorgon pediment, which is now in the museum a few miles away. 'Six Kings came, and nine princes. Lemonades they drank in the convent. And ropes they brought, and took her away, away, away in a lorry.' That excavation was in fact visited by six monarchs and their children, on one of those royal yachting parties that still took place fifty years ago. The old nun offered to show me the tomb of the Four Brethren. This turned out to be the old stone altar of the temple rotting away in its field. 'These they did not disturb. These are saints.'

'What saints are they?'

'Saint Gorgo, Saint Athena, Saint Kerkyra, and Saint ... and another Saint. Four brethren.'

Kerkyra being the Greek name for Corfu, I wondered if she knew the fourth name.

'Saint Napoleon, that's it, Saint Napoleon. They were four brethren, holy martyrs.'

I was saved from all this pleasant craziness partly by an industrious habit of mind, and partly by poetry, an even more powerful and coherent mythology. The landscapes were those of George Seferis. The countryside was that of Nikos Gatsos, 'a little wheat for the festival, a little wine for remembrance, a little water for the dust'. And all over the south I charted the villages where old men told me in confidence of an ancient buried treasure. It was usually a golden sow with twelve golden sucking pigs. Occasionally there were only three or only seven. Once, in the hills behind Nemea, it was a golden duck with twelve golden ducklings.

I used to be fascinated by a monument on the top of a mountain between Argos and Arkadia: three great cairns of stones. Its ancient name was the Hermai, plural of Hermes, and a piece of an inscribed altar to Hermes was found there. Its modern name is Stous Fonemenous, the Murdered Men. Hermes is the shepherd of the dead, so speculation was tempting. But the origin of the name turns out to be a fourteenth-century romantic tale in verse that was popular in this part of Greece. Many local monuments are named after different parts of the same story: the Castle of the Beautiful Princess is where her father imprisoned her, and the Murdered Men are the graves of her suitors. If any readers should think this explanation unlikely, I assure them I have been shown at Kardamyli a ledge of cliff where the local prince used to drink coffee with Menelaus, and a stone on which Lord Byron, who never went there, played draughts with General Kolokotronis, whom he never met. In an eighteenth-century Turkish account of Greece, the Sermon on the Mount was preached on a hill near Nauplion and the temple at Sounion was a pleasure house built by Solomon for the Queen of Sheba.

The heady delights of these stories were no stranger to me than life in the street. I came to know every street market, every bazaar, almost every tavern. I wandered among smells wailing like saxophones, or rushed about in clapped-out American taxis, (they were bigger and more battered in those days) with their tyres screeching like gangster films. The shoe-cleaners still had boxes with glittering brass fittings. Shoe-cleaners came, for some reason, from Kephallonia. They looked like farmers from Normandy. The best cooks came from Alexandria, but an Alexandria that disappeared before my day. The businessmen had yellow, dignified faces as if they were all about to be seasick. In the afternoon you could see fishmongers layed out on their own slabs. Late at night, as café after café closed down, everyone in Athens who was still awake homed in on the same few tables, and conversations mingled. A film producer I had never met was wandering about looking for someone, anyone, to write an English script for a film called *Zorba the Greek*. We all refused; no one liked Kazantzakis.

Nor do I like him now, though I think that was his best book. His verbiage is too dense, his exaggerations falsify, he is too poetical, too rhapsodical altogether. The best modern Greek writing is as pure as lemon juice. It is also highly critical. I was not able to isolate all that was best at once. The language was still difficult, so I liked simple lyric poems, not all of which look so wonderful today:

> Eros
> the archipelago
> and the prow of his spray
> and the seagulls of his dreams
> on his topmost rigging the sailor whistles
> a song.

> Eros
> his song
> and the horizons of his journey
> and the echo of his homesickness ....

Those lines must be from an early work of Elytis, a distinguished writer at least as old then as I am now. I knew little or nothing about him, but it was not difficult to meet poets in Athens, since they all went to the same three or four cafés and bars. When I arrived I walked straight to Flocca and left a message with a waiter for Nikos Gatsos. He was in the café, and he came over. He was the most enchanting and unexpected friend I had ever made. His appearance is that of an elephant of brilliant intelligence and extraordinary kindness. In forty years he has moved cafés once, when the old one was pulled down, and tables twice. His smile is seductive, his shoulders hunch, his eyes are hooded but distinctly mischievous. His conversation, which ranges widely, is humourous and subtle, pausing like a river to take in any strange object that presents itself. He knows more about poetry than anyone else I have ever met. He is admirably mysterious.

He makes his living as a song-writer, which means that over many years the Greeks have had better-written songs than anyone else, and by translations. As a poet he claims to have been on strike for forty years, but his long early poem, 'Amorgos', named after an island he has never seen, is one of the master works of this century; and if ever I knew a poet, and a great poet, he still is one. He was the son of an innkeeper in what was then a remote village in Arkadia. George Seferis once said to me that the only person alive he envied for his grasp of the Greek language was Gatsos. There is an element of surrealism in 'Amorgos', like cold water so refreshing that it makes one gasp. But his language, the form of his speech, has a continuity with folk-songs. In his childhood that was still a living language:

> And because of this I would have you, young men,
>   to go down naked into the rivers
> With wine and kisses and leaves in your mouth
> To sing of Barbary as the carpenter follows the
>   track of the wood's grain
> As the viper moves out from the gardens of
>   the barley
> With her proud eyes furious
> And as the strokes of lightning thresh the
>   young

The translation I quote is by Sally Purcell. When I first came to Athens I had never seen a complete translation, and the poem itself was out of print. Now there are three or four. I wanted to make one myself, but I despaired and still despair of the freshness and sharpness of his Greek. I did write a poem of my own, dedicated to Nikos, which was meant to be a substitute, but it was a poor one. So distant an imitation is hard to class as the sincerest form of flattery. 'Amorgos' has stayed in my head and resounded through many re-readings for nearly twenty years. It never loses its freshness. It is like a new coastline, a new continent:

> How much I have loved you I alone know
> I who touched you once with the eyes of the
>   Pleiades
> And embraced you in the wild hair of the moon
>   and we danced in the summer fields
> On the stubble after harvest, and we ate the
>   cut clover
> Dark and great sea with so many pebbles round
>   your neck so many coloured stones in your hair

But this beautiful poem takes us too far. We are in Athens and I am a distinctly green young poet and novice archaeologist on a spree. Nikos is drinking coffee. 'Talent is nothing,' he says. 'We have hundreds of talents. What we need is something else.'

I spent much of my time in museums, teaching myself to draw a few details from Greek vases, teaching my eyes to see them. I remember as a theological student going to see Sir Maurice Bowra in Oxford, when I knew I was destined to teach there. I wanted to know how to behave, what sort of teacher to be. God knows what I wanted. He asked what my main interests were. I said literature, and within literature rather Greek than Latin, though both, and rather poetry than prose, but also Greek vase-painting. It came out in a sort of stutter. 'I see,' he said. 'Pots and poetry. Like me. Pots and poetry. No way to pay and promotion. No way to pay and promotion.' So between the notes about conversations in my journal come the drawings, and the ceaseless observations of light and stone:

Some days the stone seems not only hard but harsh. An unexpected window where you see harsher marble with sun on it; the sky with sun on it looks harsher. A deep blue tan. The gorgon is a grinning boy with his tongue out tying a reef-knot in a snake. *Convolvulus elegantissimus. Hermodactylus tuberosus* like a widow iris.

Where were these flowers? *Hermodactylus* actually is a widow iris. It grows wild in Greece and I have seen it high up on Mount Parnes in April. But in late June or July? On the slopes of the akropolis? Or in the Athens flower market? I wish I could remember. The only growing things I can still recall from that summer are trees, particularly the olive groves seen from above like the pelt of some healthy animal, and a little later the blazing yellow in the fields and the white skeletons of enormous thistles. I recall burnt and shaved and bare places, great rocks, very red earth, the shaded recession of trees.

In the journal, influences and conversations of friends mingle, and I think I was taught the rudiments of Greek landscape and how to look at it, also how to live with it, by Canon Bartlett, whose long passion for Greek travel made mine look feeble. He was the gentlest and most enterprising companion I could have imagined. We went together to Portoraphti, to swim by moonlight so bright that it lit up the floor of the sea. We ate fish soup afterwards which I remembered for fifteen years and put in a novel. And we went to visit the cave of Vari, high up on the far side of Mount Hymettos. The cave is full of strange ancient inscriptions by a shepherd who believed the nymphs had taken possession of him, with a crude, beautiful relief of the mother of the gods carved in stone. We wandered for hours in a hot wind among sage and thyme and young pine trees, and the Canon lost his straw hat or the nymphs stole it, but we failed to find the cave. I have seen it since, and it was worth the effort. The poor ruins of a small ancient farmhouse lie some distance below it; they were excavated a few years ago by British archaeologists. Perhaps it belonged once to the man the nymphs afflicted.

These were expeditions into Attica, into the countryside round

Athens. By now I was getting ready for something on a bigger scale. It was ambitiously planned, with little notion of the inadequacy of maps, or the real difficulty of some of the terrain, or the stunning effect of great heat. I had a huge haversack, an enormous pair of boots, and my father's old racing binoculars. I used an old British Naval Intelligence chart of the principal Greek droving tracks as they were in 1916. The difference of reality from that chart surprised me greatly. Almost the only one of my presuppositions that turned out to be true was the least likely. Walking alone in wild country is richly rewarding for an archaeologist in Greece. It really is quite easy to stumble across things. But only experience can teach you to recognize them. That came later: in 1963 as an archaeological reconnaissance my time was largely wasted.

It is easy to seek and to find, but you have to know better than I did what to look for. I was obsessed by caves, not the sea-caves of southern Greece, streaked with purple and silver, but the dark places of ancient religion, where Sophokles says that the souls of the dead rise up buzzing like swarms of bees. It is a simple fact that sacred and mysterious caves are common in ancient mythology and religion. Delphi had its chasm and Eleusis had its cave. Dionysos had his cave on Naxos, and Zeus had several caves in the Cretan mountains. Besides, I am fond of caves.

Before setting out, one great excitement remained. I had brought from England an introduction to George Seferis, and he was in Athens. From sheer nerves I arrived at the wrong time and on the wrong day. His house was blue and white and modern, with mermaid street-lights by John Craxton and a dolphin knocker. It stood high up under the pine trees of the old stadium of Athens, which was restored by an Egyptian Greek ship-owner in about 1900. Peace and quiet are hard to come by in Athens, but that was a perfectly placed house. It was approachable only by a long, dark flight of steps cut in the rock, or by an obscure cul-de-sac. When I rang, Seferis, like an aged tortoise in voluminous khaki shorts, came out blinking onto his balcony. He took my mistake in extremely good part, beamed a benediction and went back indoors to sleep.

Two days later I got it right. His conversation was memorable.

'My poetry,' he said, 'it has been hard dying. I have sometimes said that I owe my career as a poet to the fact that I do not play bridge.' And then, 'To be a real poet you must – you must be master of your language. I think I have mastered my language. But there are only two or three people in Greece, poets and myself included, and Nikos Gatsos is one of them …

'You remind me of the late Princess Marie Bonaparte, with your interest in caves. She was always telling us about them. She introduced Freud to Greece.'

It is amazing how much I understood, how early, from George Seferis. The charming playfulness, as well as the darkness and seriousness of his mind, and the sorrows of his lifetime, can hardly have been matched since the days of Aischylos. As a poet he belongs undoubtedly to the modern movement; he knew and loved the work of Laforgue before ever he met Eliot; but there is a power and directness in his poems unique in Europe, I think. Yeats is hysterical and Eliot is obscure by comparison. His mastery really is grounded in the mastery of his language. There is a sense in which he virtually invented modern Greek, both in prose and in verse. The brilliance and gravity of his prose, and the beautiful behaviour of the Greek language in his poems, both came from the same magical and powerful understanding. He is also the only person I have ever met who could wonderfully improve the expressions of a French writer in French and an English writer in English. But Greek was his kingdom, and the language itself owed him a debt.

He was like the Pink Panther, 'a groovy cat, a gentleman, a scholar and an acrobat', the grooviness being a youthful suppleness of mind he never lost, and the agility being rather intellectual than physical, at least when I knew him. On that hot afternoon in his garden he told me of the existence of Nicander Nucius, an exiled Greek from Corfu who travelled in England in the reign of Henry VIII, and fought in the war against the Scots under a captain called Thomas of Argos. The ashes of Thomas à Becket were shot into the air from a cannon while he was passing through Canterbury. I find now that George had already written about him in 1952, but no professional scholar has ever yet given a full account of his extraordinary writings.

He spoke of places one must go, things one must see, of Istanbul and the monasteries of Cappadocia. 'One must hurry. There are things unfortunately that do not last.' I asked him if he could introduce me to any young Greek poets, not great poets necessarily but decent ones near my own age. There was a pause, and a sentence or two of doubt. Then he said there was one, just one he could recommend, who worked in the offices of the bus company at Pyrgos, near Olympia. He was George Pavlopoulos, he led a lonely life down there, he was a very attractive character. Only last year I discovered that in that summer they had just met for the first time.

We talked about mermaids. He said people knew he had a passion for them, and sent him presents of mermaids. There was a mermaid of bread, I think from southern Italy, hanging against the white garden wall. It had been there three years. I said she was young, for a mermaid. 'But it is old,' he said, 'for bread.'

His wife Maro carried a small tortoise indoors from the garden. 'Look,' he said gleefully, 'it is going to make pipi on her hand.'

Next morning, I was off alone into the mountains.

2

A Journey

ATHENS SQUATS IN a plain among a few rocky hills, one of which is the akropolis, in sight and almost within sound of the sea. Not long ago the whole of that plain was cultivated, and even between Athens and the sea the traveller passed through vast olive groves and vineyards. Now Athens is vast, it overruns its hills, it has swallowed up its remote suburbs, and the infinite multitude of its houses laps the edges of the mountains. The furthest mountain inland is Pendeli, the source of the Pentelic marble of the Parthenon. It blocks Athens from the north-east; behind it lies the inland countryside of Attica, the best wine, the reddest soil, the most unspoiled of the villages and the medieval country churches. To the east of Athens is Hymettos, like a backdrop hanging against the sky. It was the last rays of the sun catching Mount Hymettos that told Sokrates the time had come to drink hemlock and die. A cold and a quenching drink, as the poet remarked. Athenians still call it Mad Mountain, Trellovouno, but that arose as a misunderstanding of Monte Matto, a Venetian attempt to pronounce Monte Hymetto. People have come to believe Mad Mountain is named after the riot of colours when the dying sun strikes it.

The Germans burnt down the forest on Hymettos to clear it of the Greek resistance. The Greek armed forces have shaved it flatter since then and installed radar. The third mountain is more tempting, Parnitha, the old Mount Parnes, the hunting forest and the natural barrier of the fifth-century Athenians. It limits the plain of Athens to the north-west and beyond it stretches the huge extent of the plains of Thebes. When Athenian boys attained to manhood in the fifth century BC, they did military service on this long barrage of forested mountain. It hides a chain of tiny fortresses, some of them still as well preserved as a ruined castle would be in England. My plan was to cross the mountains by the ancient track, which was guarded by the fortress of Phyli, almost in sight of Athens, in a fold of the foothills. Once in Theban territory, I intended to swing round towards Aigosthena, an ancient naval base that I believed the Athenians fortified on the Gulf of Corinth, and to make my way from there across other mountains to Delphi.

The first step was easy enough. I bought a large water bottle, a supply of ouzo and biscuits, and a walking stick. Then, to the amusement or resentment of the other passengers, according to their temperament, I humped my equipment into a suburban bus and set out for the foot of Parnitha. The bus route died out at the village of Chazia. No one knew anything about my track. I still remember clearly the feelings of heat, of foolishness, and of apprehension with which I started walking. But almost at once my spirits rose. I was in the gorge of the river Gouras, it was cool there, the track was very well defined, it was nearly a road. I met old men with donkeys and an old woman with two or three goats. She was dressed in black as if for a midwinter funeral in southern Ireland. She crowed, the old men grunted.

My first objective was a monastery called the Holy Virgin of the Gorges, Moni ton Kleiston. It was not hard to find, and my Greek map, which made up in lurid colours and dramatic little drawings what it lacked in precision, placed it clearly on the track that led to Thebes. It was a whitewashed, peaceful place. The air was pure, and everything smelt of rock and water and herbs. The gorge was awe-inspiring. I had some idea of visiting a cave of Pan higher up, but summer was the wrong season. The floor of the gorge was terribly overgrown and its sides were precipitous. I had no stomach for the unnecessary adventure of climbing down, and the fatigue of searching for one among so many crannies in the rock. Besides, I intended to cross the mountains that day. Vari had taught me a lesson about caves, and a shepherd I met underlined it.

'The cave of Pan? There is a cave of Pan. But there are many caves up there, many caves of the ancient people. Vari? Oh, you mean that of the Nereid. In the Convent is a very holy cave.'

We shared a biscuit and some ouzo, which was getting heavy to carry, being the same weight as a whisky bottle and three times as potent. I shared some more of it with two or three building workers who were sitting in their scaffolding at the monastery, roaring with laughter at the sight of me.

All the same, I regret the cave of Pan. Golden cicadas were found in it, someone told me, and it was the scene of the splendid picnic at the end of *The Difficult Man*, a comedy of situation and of character by Menander, which was newly discovered in 1963, and the only complete play we have by a writer of immense influence down to the time of Shakespeare and of Mozart. The critics took against *The Difficult Man*, but I can still read it with pleasure. I was pleased to see on the monastery gate a notice announcing that picnics and singing and blasphemies and drinking and dancing and high jinks were strictly forbidden. People are still inclined to the same delights that delighted Menander. Pan sleeps in his cave in the afternoons, and dislikes to be disturbed.

Beyond the monastery, its springs and its beehives and its wild garden, the gorge was sizzling with cicadas. The sun was now high. The track was a footpath. Then it was a choice of footpaths, winding about among pine trees and coming together again. Every hundred yards, the view became wilder and more impressive. Going became difficult. I was stung very gently inside the nostril by a bee. I began to have serious doubts about my route. The sides of the gorge were getting steeper all the time; in the end the path I was on diminished to a dry, slippery trickle between isolated pine trees being tapped for resin. It was hard to know what to do. I had come so far that I could see what might be the end of the gorge. It was a bald-headed, impassable crag. One might get round it but I was not equipped to spend that night in the open. It was now too dangerous to climb downwards, since the river was invisible, and the rock walls precipitous. Strange, beautiful moths flitted about. It was a world of silence except for the subdued roaring of cicadas.

I decided to climb upwards, which was not as easy as it looked. Soft-looking herbs between the rocks concealed the longest and sharpest thorns I had ever encountered. The thistles were formidable, admirable, unfriendly. My stick snapped in two. When I did reach the shoulder of rock where the mountain levelled out, I was little better off. The gorge was out of sight and nothing that I could see inspired any confidence at all. Wearily and shamefacedly, I made my way back to the monastery. It must have been four or five in the evening. I took off my shirt, which was soaked through with sweat, and washed it under a tap. A tall workman with a little dark moustache came bounding down from the scaffolding. What had happened? I confessed my folly and cursed my map. He looked at the map with an air of concern. 'Po-po-po-po,' he said. The track to Thebes is a turning off from the monastery road, about a quarter of a mile downhill. The ancient castle is there, easy to find, hardly half an hour's walk away. As for getting across the mountains, that was difficult. It would take me three hours, and I ought to have a guide. Tonight, where would I sleep? It was too late for the mountains tonight. I suggested going back to Chazia, and starting fresh and early the next morning. In that case, if I waited an hour or so, he could take me by lorry, when they all went home.

Of course I agreed, and spent the hour or so at the ancient fortress. There have been so many wars in Greek history, and so many walls abandoned or ruined, that even an experienced scholar can pass one by or identify it wrongly at first sight. I had already found at least one that morning I am still not able to date, and I was told of another near the top of the Gouras gorge which could equally well be modern or prehistoric. But the fort of Phyli is unmistakable. It was built in the early fourth or the late fifth century BC to replace an abandoned castle a mile away. Its stone-work is splendid and well preserved. That may be because its walls were among the first ever designed to resist the new destructive weapon of the wars of the fifth century, the heavy battering ram. The walls of Phyli are solid but thin; it must on occasion have been crammed with fighting men. The new device was that the walls were heavily buttressed from the inside, and the pavement on top of each wall where the men stood was carefully bonded into the vertical stonework.

My interest in details of that kind was amateur: I had little love of military engineering; I just thought the ruin very beautiful. It was the first undisturbed classical building in an undisturbed valley I had ever seen. I spent most of my hour bird-watching, and climbing about on the hillside among the last withering wild flowers. At other seasons I have found a kind of paradise on the slopes of that mountain. We once broke the exhaust off a car in an attempt to penetrate further, on a spring afternoon's expedition from Athens. Phyli is always unexpected, always the same. It has the small scale of local patriotism; it stands on the edge of wild country isolated like that imaginary monument in a line of Virgil, 'a white temple in a green field'.

I rattled down to Chazia with the workmen in the back of an open van. My friend, whose name was Sabbas, had decided to take me under his protection. There was no hotel, and in those days only one tavern, but Chazia did have an open-air cinema. First I was taken to his house in a back street for a wash and brush up. It was a tiny house held together by whitewash and enormous morning glories. He dressed in smart trousers and a freshly pressed, glittering white shirt, but when I was ready he surveyed me with horror. Had I no freshly ironed shirt? It was a disgrace to his house if I came out of it looking like I looked. His wife would wash and dry and iron me a shirt. How could I manage, roaming about Greece with no woman to look after me? Had I no family to come with me, to look after me? The shirt was ready in no time, since I had one that was clean but crumpled, though it was less snowy than his. We went out. His wife stayed at home, like everyone else's wife.

The square was full, and chairs were hard to find, but we drank an ouzo with an olive and a chip and a piece of cheese. I was introduced to old men with moustaches and exquisite manners, while they too drank or pondered their ouzo and ate their olive and their chip. The cinema was even more crowded. The sky was darkening. Someone in my row was holding a sprig of jasmine. At last the film started and we sat upright on our wooden chairs. It was called *The Bandit of Mani*. It was wonderfully, hilariously bad. The bandit pursued a complicated and dramatic vendetta which I was hardly able to follow. There was a lot of shooting with very loud guns. A girl was dragged along the ground by her hair. The whole audience cheered enthusiastically for the villains throughout.

Greek films in Greek villages used to be like that. Foreign films with subtitles add a special dimension. I saw *Gone with the Wind* once in Naples with the audience taking the wrong side, and an American western somewhere near Argos that started with a comic scene of an old-fashioned train, while the audience watched it stone-faced because to them it was a perfectly ordinary local train. Still, they did shake with laughter when the heroine met the hero at the station with a horse and trap, at the idea of a woman driving. Chazia is special all the same, as I was soon to discover.

We walked across to the chairs outside the tavern and installed ourselves again. This time I noticed a certain tension. I was being delicately but carefully questioned. What was England like? Was it true that bandits could kidnap a train and take millions of pounds? I denied this, not having seen a newspaper for days, and they nodded sagely. No doubt it was an exaggeration. Even in Greece one couldn't do that. But why did the English throw stones at the King and Queen of Greece? An intense silence followed, and I saw that other tables were listening. I floundered badly. If this had happened, I said, and I knew nothing about it, it was not the English people, only a few. It was an intolerable insult. But why? What few people? Did the police permit it? I searched for some excuse, any excuse. The grave faces waited while I stumbled over my Greek.

'It might be because Greece and England are distant. The English people love the Greeks. And maybe, quite mistakenly, those who threw stones did it because they love the Greeks, and believe, doubtless quite wrongly, that the King and Queen of Greece are tyrants. Maybe they did it for that reason.'

'But what are the English people like, politically?'

'They are freedom-loving and democratic, as I am also.'

Here I made an appalling mistake in Greek. I blurted out a word I had picked up, probably from a left-wing newspaper, without understanding its resonance. Literally it means freedom-loving, actually it means what 'liberal' meant in nineteenth-century Italy, and my friend Sabbas and the whole village assumed it was a euphemism for left-wing up to and including communism. The atmosphere altered utterly. First Sabbas, then all of our table roared with laughter, and as the joke passed from table to table the roar of laughter spread.

'We are all freedom-loving in this village,' he said. 'I was a partisan seven years in the mountains, and four years in prison. Eleven years of my life.'

People began to shake my hand. Drink began to circulate and an entire sheep was produced and cooked. It was one of the happiest spontaneous celebrations I have ever been in. Songs I no longer remember were sung. Nothing was too good for me. Today I can recall only the warmth and the feasting, none of the faces of those sweet warm-hearted men.

Sabbas took me home to sleep and we quarrelled over who was to sleep on the mattress. There was obviously only one. In the end we both slept across it, with our feet on the earth and our heads on pillows, side by side in the garden, which was also a hen-run, under a vine in bright moonlight. A cock crowed almost all night long. When we woke at dawn I was given a small very thick cup of black aromatic coffee, which stewing had reduced to a most powerful essence. It was brewed over a tiny fire in one corner of the cottage. Sabbas summoned my guide. I was not allowed to pay for my night's lodging, or the cinema, or anything I ate or drank in or out of the house, but I was told I might, if I wished, give a pound to the guide for his day's work, because he was a poor man. We set off at a fast pace.

'My name,' he said, 'Dimitrios, English is Jimmy.'

I was inclined to dispute this, if only to pass the time, but he had an unshakable argument, having fought in the desert with the Eighth Army, in which Jimmy was his name. He was a small lightly built, very friendly companion, but I soon stopped talking because he walked so fast. At Phyli we stopped for a drink from the spring. It was delicious water, as good as I have ever tasted. The ancient Greeks could tell the difference of taste between nine or ten different springs in these mountains, and so could Jimmy. I have sometimes imagined I could do the same, and I always liked the traveller returning to Attica in some fragment of a lost comedy, who knows where he is from the special tang of a water-spring.

I offered Jimmy my binoculars for a last look at the ruins of Phyli. They pleased him greatly. 'These we were having in the war. In the evening we take them up to a hill in the desert, and in the morning we make Bam! Bam! Bam!' He smiled at the happy memory. We crossed the mountains in two and a half hours. We met nobody on the way, except for two aged charcoal burners who beamed and waved as we passed by. When we came in sight of the plains I collapsed on a tree trunk, and Jimmy raced away homewards with his pound, even faster than before. Biscuits revived me, and I stalked downhill. It was not really a difficult route, though Jimmy had taken short cuts. I ought not to have needed a guide. But modern military tracks have confused the old simplicity, and I might well have got lost without him.

The truth is that I was dazed with hunger and fatigue. When I got to the first village, which was called Pyli, and which I have never seen since, I sat stupefied on the nearest chair, and all that I remember is a young horse without shoes or saddle or bridle, cantering down the main street on its own. His tail streamed, and his hooves thudded softly on the bare earth. No one chased him. My journal for that day is only a few lines written down later. It speaks of early dew and then great heat, and two Aristophanic charcoal burners, and mountain plane trees, which are as unlike to other plane trees as the lithest Athens cats are to old tabbies. It notes 'glistening and shaded olive trees', and 'many nameless flowers on the mountain'. *Cistus? Arbutus?* A bush with fragile pink flowers.

'By the time you get to Pyli the mountain is a distant brown and blue intensity.' I once remarked to a painter how helpful I found a remark of Cézanne, that the sky is not blue colour but blue light. He answered that nothing is a colour, everything we see is light. That is particularly true of Greek landscape. It might explain why Edward Lear's watercolours and washes of Greek landscape are so true and the finished oil paintings are so untrue. My friend was a watercolourist. I sat ruminating at Pyli for too long, until the sun was very high. I seem to have eaten five fried eggs, a tomato salad, and a lot of cheese, and then slept for a while in someone's bedroom. Then with complacent cunning I took a bus. It was old and battered and very noisy, made of grey tin with all its windows open. It took me ten or twenty miles over a spur of mountain towards the Gulf of Corinth. As it ran downhill down the last stormy track, engine roaring, the noise of the cicadas was louder than its engine.

It dropped me a few miles from the ruins of an Athenian walled hill town, I think Eleutherai, the home of Dionysos. Its circuit wall was elephantine grey, but all that it encircled was rock and bushes and burnt grass. As I look now at the map, I see that the bus must have surely passed by Panakton and Oinoe, and I do recall straining through the window at some enigmatic ruined walls, but I was hot and tired and I wanted the sea. Country monuments are fine, but they have all been charted and excavated, they rouse no explorer's instinct, and they are too numerous. I was heading for something better, and I knew that with limited time I must choose one way or the other where to spend it. The rest of the day was a long trudge to Aigosthena, which has the best curtain of ancient walls in all Greece.

You see them as you come down the hill, tall and beautifully ragged with towers still standing among the vineyards. The modern name of the place is Porto Yermeno. It is, or it was in 1963, a tiny resort with two taverns on the beach and a few fishing boats, tucked away under Mount Kithairon in an inlet at the extreme northwest corner of the Gulf of Corinth. Aigosthena belonged naturally to the hills behind Megara, which lies west of Athens, between the Piraeus and the Corinth canal. But in the course of the wars that shook the ancient world to pieces, it became, or so I used to believe, an Athenian harbour, defended inland by a series of strong fortresses. Without it, no Athenian fleet could be supplied from Athens in the Gulf of Corinth. Corinth was hostile, there was no canal, and the only way home was to sail right round the stormy southern capes of the Peloponnese. The way to Megara and Corinth overland from Aigosthena was a difficult mountain track. Even the Naval Intelligence Guide mutters ominously about the danger of using it in a high wind, and the near impossibility of moving guns. A Spartan expedition that used it in the fourth century had shields and baggage animals blown into the sea. Attractive as it sounds, I have never walked the whole of this pleasing path, though I have traced most of it.

It probably suffered the fate of tracks along the north side of the Gulf. My friend Sabbas knew every path in these hills, and he warned me my route was impossible, because the government had blown up and blocked the footpaths in their struggle with the partisans, in the civil war that followed the German occupation. I confirmed this by conversations at Porto Yermeno. The tempting alternative was to make an agreement with a fishing boat, and get myself landed further west, at some port or village where a track might still exist that led to Delphi. That was what I did, though it needed police permission. We agreed to sail at midnight, for the night fishing. I was left with a happy evening of the delights of Porto Yermeno. Its wine was famous in antiquity for sweetness. Now it has a normal taste, but still delicious. I swam about in the sea, and clambered among ruins and gardens and backyards.

Aigosthena is something of a mystery. No Athenian writer in the fifth century had ever heard of it; the local temple belonged to an obscure prophet called Melampous. Serpents licked his ears when he was a baby, and he knew all animal speech. He communicated with woodworms about the fall of a roof, and learnt the wisdom of vultures. His image was that of a small man carved on a stone. He cured madness, and gave his name to a kind of hellebore. He had some connection with Dionysos as a missionary, but at Aigosthena he was treated like a god. Even the impressive walls of Aigosthena are mysterious. Scholars used to argue that they dated from the early fourth century and the imperial power of Athens. Now it appears they were built a hundred years later or more, to resist artillery. If that is true, then Aigosthena survived the classical age much as I saw it in 1963, as a small, forgotten place. Its military importance would have come and gone quickly, with the ambitions of a Macedonian prince.

Late in the evening, the village is haunted by the light single cries of small owls. It was a relief after Phyli, where a lot of Albanian is still talked, to hear the sputtering noises of ordinary Greek. In the church I found splendid religious paintings of the eighteen-forties. The sea whispered on a fringe of pebbles and débris. There were three fishing boats, the *Lion*, the *Strawberry* and the *Saint Demetrios*. They were floating fish-holds really, with antique one-stroke engines hidden in their bowels. They had a mast which was mostly for looks, and plenty of room on deck, but no particular gunwales. Mine was the *Lion*, painted white, heavily picked out with purple and silver. It was a thing of beauty, like a circus horse, but solid and strong-looking. The engine was primed with a burning rag, and cleared its throat with a series of explosions, which worried no one else but terrified me. Then it settled to an even drumming, the shore receded and I went to sleep on deck, wrapped in an old blanket, with my head on a rope.

We fished for part of the night, and for a few hours I think everyone slept. Once I woke while we floated offshore under cliffs among several other boats. The whole deck was wet with dew. At dawn we were close to a cove called Hayiou Ioannou, where I was put ashore. It was six in the morning. There was nothing in sight but a track climbing away uphill between two tall cliffs. It was cold, and I have never felt more lonely. The village of Dombraina took an hour or so to reach; by then the sun was beginning to scorch, and people were about in the street. I was immediately taken under the protection of an old American Greek. He was kind but determined, and his view of what we had in common was extremely strange. He called his fellow villagers 'these bums' and told me I needed a good English breakfast, which was to consist of a huge piece of fried steak. He took me to the butcher's shop. We narrowly avoided a quarrel when I frustrated this plan, but he forgave me even for eating mere water-melon when I pretended my stomach was disturbed. 'It's the no good sanitation,' he said. 'These guys don't have no modern notions. I got a good house, all fixed up.'

Every Greek village has at least one of these old gentlemen. They work a long, tough lifetime in the United States, and then they come home to die in their own village. Sometimes they sit uneasily in their old backgrounds, their politics in particular being usually to the right of right, but from America they bring home only money and an idiosyncratic command of English. A friend of mine once climbed one of the wildest mountains in southern Greece. The village he set out from came in a body to beseech him not to undertake such fearful hazards. In a grassy place on the top he met an old, tanned, wrinkled shepherd in a cloak. 'Have you been here long?' asked my friend. 'A month or two.' 'Where were you before?' 'Chicago.' He had spent twenty years there, washing plates in a Greek restaurant, and never learnt English.

Dombraina, apart from its pink and remarkable wine, was a disappointment. I had not realised that the Germans burnt it to the ground because the partisans attacked a column there. The new village was three miles away from the site of the old; it was not very pretty. Dombraina and Thisbe are now one place. I did get to see where the old village stood, and all of the ancient ruins, but it took time. Being shaved in the barber's shop was a special interlude, and then, repenting my rudeness over the steak, I had lunch with the senior citizen. His grumbling was constant, about the village, about his family, about the government, about all things Greek. It was not my place to agree, but I did in the end sympathise. When you meet them in America, the Greeks seem indomitable. But working in a garage or a restaurant in the United States is no preparation for Greek village life. Maybe the adaptable ones never come home. I left while my host took his siesta.

My mind was still humming with Parnes and Kithairon. But Dombraina lies under Mount Helikon, a stark, grey rocky mountain trimmed here and there with green. In spring it is all wild flowers in deep grass, but even the famous valley of the Muses has always had a strong mountainous flavour. The Muses are wild women of the mountains, after all, and Apollo was a herdsman's god. The most annoying disappointment of Dombraina was that a search for advice about footpaths led me again to a police station, where I was shown for an instant or two the only excellent map I had ever seen of a Greek province. It was hastily covered up again, because maps are a military secret. The officer in charge assured me that no path existed, and even if it did, as I do suspect, I was forbidden to attempt such a journey through mountains alone.

All I could do was to take a bus round the edge of Helikon, to Lebadia, the beginning of the inland mountain road to Delphi, and start walking from there. I am not sure why I was so determined to walk. My old notes are confused. I was starting to pay much more attention to medieval and Turkish monuments, and to entertain some cynicism about the famous landscape:

Pappa Silenos on his donkey can be seen most days.
'Psst! Psst!' a cry to goats, the ancient 'Psitta! Psitta!'
Lake Haliartos cooking gracelessly in the heat. An eel stew.
Sheep clanging and running.

Kreakouti. They sell the loot of tombs from Erythrai. And Aliki
has a high local reputation for the sale of loot. In the bus I was
offered a fine bronze coin of Thespiai. Too priggish to buy it.

What makes people so conscious of poverty? Tourists? The
extremity of the experience? The combination of intelligence
with this? The heat? Centuries of oppression by the Turks?

Paradise is how to live happily in a sunny climate, and this can
be achieved.

We came to Lebadia at seven in the evening. It was a fine, cool
evening, but I thought Lebadia unpleasant, wrongly so I now feel,
and I set off walking at once on the old road to Delphi, which no
longer exists. It was a wild, frightful, stomach-churning motor-
road, narrow and romantic and dangerous. The ancient drovers'
tracks would have been better walking; one could see them
sometimes, but once a road is built the tracks decay, they are no
longer a coherent system. The road I walked on was substantially
the path Apollo took in a long narrative poem about his journey to
Delphi which is as old as the seventh century BC. But it was a foot-
track then: Apollo was the ideal young herdsman, he could outrun
horses, he liked undisturbed mountain springs, he hated main
roads. The old road to Delphi swooped and soared and circled like
the flight of a bird.

Bars of shadow streamed across the mountains. Herds of goats
of more than one colour passed slowly across the light, bells
clanging, whole hillsides of goats. Beyond the last villages,
Tsoukalades and Korakolitho, the Crow's Stone, I slept by the
roadside, but not for long. Something was licking my face,
something was growling. I was surrounded by a herd of grazing
goats and an indignant dog. There are worse awakenings. Later that

summer I met a Canadian boy at the edge of the woods under akropolis of Athens. He had slept out, and woken in the morning to find bees crawling over his face and mouth, and swarming on his sleeping bag. He was not stung, and I was not savaged. But it was certainly time to move on. I walked through the rest of the night under the blackness and wizardry of the mountains.

Not long after dawn a lorry overtook me and drew up. Did I want a lift? The men in the back were quarry-workers from Parnassos, earning less than five shillings a day, sixteen drachmas. The place where they found me was where Oedipus in the legend killed his own father, the 'split road', Distomo. One of them told me the old story, but in a mysterious version, a kind of folk-tale. Oedipus was half Absalom, and his father's name was David. I wish I had written it down, but some of the detail was lost in the noise of that rattling thunder cart, and the events of the rest of the day wiped away the fine edge of his phrases. They left me under the mighty face of Parnassos, on a footpath to Arachova.

Arachova is a high mountain village. It communicates with all that long series of mountains which form the backbone of mainland Greece. In the dark age and even in the early classical age, the shrine and oracle of Zeus at Dodona received most of its offerings from high up in the Balkans. Arachova has the same northern quality. The black wine of Arachova is easier to find in Evrytania, in the almost impenetrable mountains to the north, than it is in Athens. They mix it there with Naoussa, another potent dark red wine. The result is a delight, but admittedly very strong. Arachova is a white village, high up on a shoulder of the mountains. Its narrow roads, except for the main road, are innocent of motorcars, clean, unpoliced. They smell only of mountain air. Hundreds of feet below, the valley has begun which leads down past Delphi to the sea. Its long, winding, widening floor is a river of olive groves. Arachova guards the passes and the upper grazing grounds.

I arrived at Delphi in a cargo of water-melons; I hardly remember how or why, but not because of the black wine of Arachova, which I found for the first time that night in a tiny tavern. The village of Delphi was still small and innocent in those days. It was built at the turn of the century when the government turned out the old villagers from Apollo's sanctuary, and removed them round a corner of hillside, so that now the village looks down at the sea, and the ancient sanctuary is an artificial solitude. The road runs below it, dividing it from other ruins on the lower slopes. It was only by the existence of the village in its ruins that Delphi was so early identified. An amorous intrigue, I think in the fifteenth century, brought it to the notice of the Italian princes at Amphissa, not far away in the plains. It was still possible for foreigners to make mistakes about it in 1600, but Milton knew well enough where it was. Every early traveller left an attractive description of the old village, with its great bushy bay tree and its pure, abundant water. The tree died of frost in the winter of 1892–3. The excavation rights were more or less auctioned by the government; they were finally ceded to the French for an agreement to buy the Greek currant crop.

Delphi is splendid and terrible. 'In the beginning,' says Seferis in an essay on Delphi, 'was the anger of Zeus.' The sanctuary stands on the slopes of a high mountain terrace, hemmed in by flashing cliffs, hidden from the sea behind the last shoulder of the mountains. It was a holy place of the herdsmen of Parnassos, a water-spring bursting out of a split mountain. The Myceneans knew it in the bronze age, and their tiny striped statues of worshipping women or of goddesses were found near the threshold of Apollo's temple in the fifth century BC. The classical Greeks gathered them carefully together, so that few have been found since, and buried them on the slopes below the modern road, in a temple of Athene. In the dark age between 1100 and 800 BC, Delphi was almost deserted. By 700 it was a famous sanctuary, a great oracle, a place of pilgrimage and of wonders, a keystone of the disjointed unity of the Greeks.

A thunderstorm was growling away inland towards Arachova. Light rain fell on the olive groves in the valley and a light wind was combing their unbarbered hair. An eagle dropped swooping and circling out of the clouds. It was the first time I ever saw a free eagle; I asked an old peasant woman what it was, for assurance. 'A crow, my friend.' 'Not an eagle?' 'An eagle, a crow. They're all crows.' Just as they say of any flower, 'a flower, a wild mountain flower.' But everything has a first time. At the first modern Delphic festival, the beginning of the revival of classical tragedy in ancient theatres, they played the Prometheus of Aischylos. The performance was interrupted by a heavy storm with loud, re-echoing thunder-claps for twenty minutes. Out of the storm came an eagle, soaring and circling over the heads of the audience. No one moved, and those who were there still spoke of that day with awe forty years later. The festival was organised by a poet of hilarious dottiness and pretention, a kind of super-Yeats, called Sikelianos. Even the theatre is not classical; you must think it away to recapture the austere and pure beauty of ancient Delphi. But the eagles are genuine.

You must also think away the ruined columns of the temple of Apollo. They were assembled during the war, with a number of column-drums that happened to survive from different re-buildings of the temple. Still, they are acceptably impressive from a distance, and they give a necessary element of vertical scale to the whole sanctuary. Delphi was crammed with very tall monuments, craning like hollyhocks into the sun and the light. They were harshly handled by earthquakes, and the clamp-marks in the building-blocks show signs of constant rebuilding. As the pilgrim entered, he wound his way uphill past a series of monumental dedications from nearly every nation in Greece. Entire treasure houses, like miniature temples, sheltered the richest national collections of offerings; some of the finest early figure-sculpture in marble comes from their decorations. They show a rare combination of savage ferocity, childlike glee and spirit, and geometric subtlety, artistic mastery. The vigour and gaiety of these scenes of conflict was my strongest impression of Delphi. That and the mountain, which I climbed.

In so many years of Greek travelling, I have never got right to the top. Time at Delphi was always too short. I was too much mesmerised by the museum, which I hope I know by heart, and by small questions of topography, which perhaps nobody will ever disentangle. There exist ancient vase-paintings with Delphic scenes; they have elements of truth, but they are tantalizingly inexact. Once, exploring in the valley, I found a new site, a mud bank by a waterfall that leaked small pieces of ancient terracotta; it may have been a farmhouse I think, or a very small sanctuary. The pottery was fourth or fifth century. Once or twice I tried the mountain path again. Pausanias calls it 'tough going even for an active man', but he was old when he climbed it, complaining more and more about bad roads, and showing increasing interest in bird-watching and in the gods of healing.

Scholars were tougher in the old days. I knew an old lady who climbed Parnassos alone in the nineteen-twenties to see the sacred cave at the top. She spent the night on the mountain, keeping herself warm by embracing an enormous dog which befriended her. She also encountered a shepherd who made amorous advances to her up there on the heights. She waited for her moment, and shoved him backwards. He disappeared over a cliff. The Delphians are simple people. A Greek folklore scholar in the nineteenth century discovered in this area the belief that the monuments were built by an ancient pagan tribe called the Milordi; the Christian Greeks drove them away, so now their descendants return to worship their holy stones.

It must have been at Delphi I first discovered the thrilling relevance of Pausanias, and I see from my journal, rain-spotted in places, that here my drawing took a turn towards usefulness:

> Of these elements, grace, charm and imaginative power, one is lucky to come away from a Greek museum bemused by grace and not befuddled by charm. The third element is always present, but hard to talk about or think about, hard to see it.

It needs clear eyes. Even here, I believe, I was thinking at the back of my head more about poetry, ancient or modern, and more about my own problems than about what I was looking at. I noticed a young Greek woman at Delphi standing in front of the famous bronze charioteer. She was combing her hair in the mirror of his glass case where the light caught it.

When I first saw it, Delphi was more a single experience to me than it has been since. The lucid morning shadows and the deep evening shadows, the mountains and the tracks and whatever I read or remembered about the lost ancient world, had a coherence I can hardly recapture. I made friends with an old guard at the sanctuary. His lair was a little hut with pine-branches for shade, and a bucket for burning olive-wood if it was cold, and hooks for plastic bags of lunch and for dried herbs. He called the treasury of the Athenians the House of the Pythoness, but he also claimed that she lived in a lake where people could swim, with a snake in it that ate everyone. He assured me that snake-tailed women swam round the yachts at Itea below Delphi, but the sailors spoke of sharks, so the foreigners kept away and never saw them. He was a very jolly old man.

At night I slept in the temple of Apollo. I wanted the last light and the first light and the starlight on those stones. I did the same that year in many sanctuaries. There were fewer tourists then, and archaeological areas were only beginning to be fenced and patrolled. All that business of barriers had started after a summer when an American beat generation poet slept in the echoing tomb of Agamemnon at Mycenae, seducing a series of German girl tourists. Delphi was wonderful at night, absolutely lonely, with the loudest bird noises at dawn I have ever heard, echoing back from the cliffs. At about two in the morning I woke with words running through my head that nothing I was reading or thinking or dreaming could have put into it. 'I know more than Apollo, for oft when he lies sleeping, I see the stars at bloody wars in the wounded welkin weeping.' It was the brightness of the stars that woke me, and one in particular like a white diamond, terribly close. It was the biggest and the brightest and the most naively beautiful star I have ever seen. I fell asleep again at once.

Next morning they killed a snake near the place where I slept. The village was full of the news, which I heard in the barber's shop. It was an enormous creature, beautifully marked, long and strong, with a wicked head. The first guards on duty saw it coming out of the temple of Apollo and streaking away downhill towards the treasury of the Athenians. They caught it there, and people came out from the village all morning to see it. I had no stomach to do that, but I believe the descriptions. I have never seen such a creature in Greece, or met anyone who has, unless what I took to be a dead eel run over on the road last year was really a dark snake. I am inclined to think it was, but it was not a pleasant sight and once again I let the opportunity go by. The snake at Delphi was nearly two metres long and four inches thick.

Hanging about the sanctuary at Delphi taught me something about the Ion of Euripides. It begins, unusually for a tragedy, with a long lyrical aria sung by a boy. The boy is Apollo's bastard son, a temple boy unaware of his ancestry, at work in his father's temple. The play, after various melodramatic reversals, reveals his origin, and he becomes the founder of the Ionian race. Apollo's eastern Greek, Ionian connections were an important part of the power of Delphi, and Athens was an Ionian city, with Ionian festivals and tribal divisions. It may even be that the eastern Ionians set out as colonists from Athens in the dark age. Certainly the ambassadors of the peace between Greeks proclaimed for every Delphic festival travelled far and wide. What I felt that I understood for the first time was how the still and early morning atmosphere of the opening of the Ion, which is followed by an arrival of pilgrims much like a busload from Athens, was rooted in reality. I thought it a perfectly possible life, to be a temple servant in such a place, to sweep and to scare away birds, and not to know one's ancestry:

> Now the sparkling chariot
> and the horses of the sun
> glitter on the extended earth
> and the upper air on fire
> puts the stars to flight.
> Now the untrodden mountain-tops
> of Parnassos glittering
> take the touch of dawn
> for the race of men.
> Smoke of unwatered frankincense
> mounts into Apollo's roof,
> the Delphic priestess takes her throne
> at the tripod of the god,
> crying to the Greeks she brings
> the same words Apollo sings.
> Servants of Apollo, go
> to that silver spring below,
> fetch holy dew, Kastalian water,
> and enter to the Delphic shrine.

That is not by any means the only aspect of Greek religion or Greek poetry, nor is it the most interesting, but it does exist. Those silver tones and that solemnity, the pure atmosphere that Gilbert Murray liked (this is not his translation but mine), and the hush that something is going to shatter. Or one may think of Delphi under the Roman empire at a time when all its monuments were intact but marble surfaces were covered in inscriptions as crowded as the columns of newspapers. Fat old Plutarch, a local man with the privilege of a Delphic priesthood, an *homme de lettres*, biographer, philosopher, critic, sat among the official guides discoursing about the decay of oracles. One may imagine a much earlier Delphi, the huge, Irish-looking stone girls from Naxos with pots on their heads, the serpentine bronze pillar of twisted snakes with a gold tripod on their noses. What is hardest to imagine is the central elements of the religion of the place.

There are other puzzles. What appear to have been the greatest paintings of Polygnotos, the greatest and most original painter of the ancient world, were at Delphi. Nothing is left. They were wall-paintings. We can reconstruct from descriptions the whole of their subject matter, their tall shape, their suggestion of perspective, innumerable little details. But no work by him has survived. It is as if a thousand years from now we had verbal descriptions of the works and the influence of Picasso, but nothing at all that he painted, and we had to chart the nature of that individual energy through adaptations and imitations by his contemporaries. I have walked about on the upper hillside at Delphi, near where the painted walls once stood, growling with frustration at the loss of Polygnotos. If the descriptions and the hints were less enticing, one would mind less. To make matters worse, a few pieces of monochrome painted plaster have been recovered from the ruins.

The best works of art at Delphi, as at most of the oldest Greek sanctuaries, are probably the small bronzes, a foal suckling his mother or Odysseus escaping from the cave of the Cyclops by clinging to a ram's belly. The sculptor must have thought that was an impossible adventure; his Odysseus, a strong little man with an amused expression, is holding himself in place with a rope. At Delphi I found more variations and combinations of marble, an

Ionic capital in Parian marble glittering like fine sugar on a solid Pentelic column, and some dark grey stones I was unable to recognise. I contracted an affection for faded terracottas, and I kept taking quick glances at the masterpieces of the museum, as if they might betray themselves. The Delphic charioteer must have been a very high monument in his tall bronze chariot with its tall bronze horses. From the poor remnants, it is mostly the hooves of the horses that suggest that height.

From Delphi I clattered gently downhill to the harbour town of Itea. Behind me I left the awful cries of goats in a storm, the yelling and sawing of mules, the screams of hawks. Ahead the earth was as level as the sea. A ferry used to sail in the summer between Itea, on the north side of the Gulf of Corinth, and Aigion, on the south side. Today you would have to go round by Rion and Antirion, but in 1963 that would have been impossible; there was no road westwards along the coast. Blue mountains loomed across the Gulf. The last sight of Delphi was the crack in the mountain where the water is, and an evening mist on the hillside. At Aigion I meant to get a train that runs from Athens round the northern Peloponnese to Pyrgos, a little inland from the west coast, a bus journey from Olympia.

The ferry crossed at about six or seven; the train passed some time after midnight. I swam to cool myself, ate and drank and slept under a plane tree. The plane trees in the square at Aigion are huge and umbraceous, but the wine was pinkish-yellow and bitter and the water tasted chalky, the old springs having been disturbed by earthquake. About midnight I went swimming again in the deserted sea. Then the train came, not very late. A few years later, admittedly in the winter, I have known it be four hours late. I installed myself with the laughable illusion that I was going to sleep.

3

An Arrival

SECOND-CLASS journeys at night in summer on crowded Greek trains are a sort of nightmare picnic, an infinitely prolonged afternoon in a bored café, a sad and serious ritual of musical chairs without music. The conversation is one that a lonely traveller with a little Greek will soon know by heart. Where are you from? Are your parents alive? Have you brothers and sisters? How many? What do you do? What do you earn? Do you like Greece? Is it more beautiful than other countries? Is it true that there are no oranges in England? No grapes? No olives? How do you know Greek? It's the most difficult of all languages, did you know that? And the richest. It has ten words for a stone. I'll tell you them. Where are you going? What for? In relays, five or ten people in turn came to sit opposite me to entertain the stranger and be entertained. I started to answer with fantasies, but that made no difference. The same questions returned like mosquitoes. It was very hot.

We came into Pyrgos as dawn was breaking. As we stumbled up towards the bus station a cock was crowing, the sky was red and grey. I had the impression that whatever was not made of plaster was made of mud, and everything was painted white. The roads were like farm tracks. A boy of about seventeen came out of the bus station yawning, with a brush and bucket of whitewash, and white spots on his chest and shoulders. He had been working all night. He knew about the times of buses to Olympia; they started early in summer, and we were halfway there before I was well awake.

It was an enchanted early morning world of flowers in gardens, sheep in the road, old crones at their cottage doors, rich green valleys and simmering pine forests on the hills. Here and there cypresses stood up statuesquely above olive trees. Orchards of oranges overhung the road. I have travelled that road now on foot and in buses and cars, some hundreds of times. The road has been rebuilt and the villages have altered, but it would still be difficult to pass through those valleys without some quickening of the blood. After a night journey, or even a day journey through the long coastal plain of the western Peloponnese, the last miles before Olympia are what the early Christians hoped for when they died: refreshment, peace and light.

The village of Olympia was still tiny. Its museum was an amazing study in Bavarian neoclassic stucco, painted deep yellow. So was its railway station. Its only hotel, which at that time I was too ragged to enter, was the S.P.A.P., an oasis of pre-war calm with a mature, luxuriating garden, and one of the most impressive and harmonious views in the world. It was the only Greek railway hotel. Higher up on the same hill stands an abandoned country house of one of the early Queens of Greece. It was her doing that the whole of the ancient site of Olympia is overshadowed by enormous pine trees. It is also a fine place for wild flowers in their seasons and a refuge for songbirds and for hares.

Above Olympia stands the Hill of Kronos, a great cone of pine trees with the sanctuary of Hera and of Zeus clambering on its skirts. Kronos was their father, and Homer tells us how they first made love 'deceiving their beloved parents'. Kronos is Saturn, the king of a wonderful country, the god of the golden age. At his harvest festival slaves and masters enjoyed themselves together on equal terms. He castrated heaven, who was his father, and separated heaven from earth, who was his mother. He had the nasty habit of swallowing his children, for fear they might treat him in the same way, but his wife and sister, the mother of the gods, tricked him into swallowing a big stone, and the gods were vomited up alive. Zeus overcame him, but at Olympia, rather uniquely, they seem to be friends and neighbours. The Kronion, the Hill of Kronos, is just outside the sanctuary of the other gods, with the dignity of height. The principal event of the women's games at Olympia, which were held in honour of Hera, was a race to the top of the Hill of Kronos.

Travellers often think of Olympia as uncharacteristic, perhaps Italianate or too rich. That may be because of the pine trees. Lysias in the classical age called it the most beautiful and the most sacred place in Greece. It lies just inland of the great plain of the river Alpheios, where that mighty river makes its way to the sea. Olympia is locked away from the coast by a barrier of small hills; further inland, it gazes up towards the serious mountains of Arkadia. In winter and spring from the stones of the temple of Zeus you can see the sunlight flashing on their snowy peaks. That is where Alpheios comes from, with his tributaries. From the Olympic sanctuary you can neither see nor hear him, because Olympia lay buried for centuries under ten feet of Alpheios mud. When Richard Chandler found it in the eighteenth century, only a few stones showed. No one knows yet what lies underground between the sanctuary and the river, but something certainly does: streets perhaps and public buildings, a market place, a town.

The sanctuary was a sacred wood with altars and shrines scattered here and there among the trees. The temple of Zeus came later. Olympia was already famous for an athletic festival, with horse races and chariot races and a huge crowd. That took place on a wide semi-circle of flat land, created and defined by the Alpheios; the sanctuary is bounded towards the west by a tributary river, the Kladeos. The athletics took place to the east, outside the sacred wood, in a stadium and on the race course. Perhaps in the beginning this was another meeting-place for herdsmen, since it divides the upper, summer grazing grounds from the winter grazing on the lower Alpheios. The festival was in summer, when the river could be forded. When we first hear of it, most of the athletes seem to have come from south of the Alpheios. More than one of the settlements in the hills that overlook it from the south is very ancient.

Many scholars and amateurs wanted to discover Olympia, and to excavate it. It was identified by Richard Chandler, of Magdalen

College, Oxford, with the help of the local Turks, and first surveyed by a Yorkshire squire called Stanhope on behalf of the French Academy in the eighteen-hundreds. His curious career merits more attention than it has received. But the systematic excavation of Olympia has been the principal work of German archaeologists in Greece, and it has been triumphant. Work is still going on. In 1963 the new museum, which looks like a plastics factory, did not exist, and many of the most exciting bronzes were still underground. I think it was still unknown that remnants of an earlier, smaller, Ionic temple lie beneath the massive ruins of the fifth-century temple of Zeus. It was certainly still widely believed that the famous Hermes of Praxiteles, with its waxen texture and its brainless physical beauty was the genuine work of that master. I do not believe that any more.

Since then I have worked at Olympia myself. I even found a new piece of the Triton mosaic from the temple of Zeus, kicking about among loose stones, and a piece of the upper stonework of the training gymnasium, with a band of colour still on it, lying in the river Kladeos. It must have been washed down from the muddy cliff where the main car park now is. A number of the most desirable objects from Olympia, much more desirable than what I came across, were chance finds. They include a fine helmet now in the British Museum, and a priceless gold cup like a heavy flower, which is in Boston. But in 1963, seeing everything for the first time, I was content with the place itself:

It belongs now to lizards and ants. Crickets drowning the voices. The wrestling cloister, unexpectedly slim pillars, like the cricket pavilion at school.

Bushy pine trees as tall and green as elms. Dust on top of the Hill of Kronos, still hot two hours after dark.

Some of the fallen column drums of Zeus' temple are eighty-one inches in diameter.

What imposes itself at Olympia is the unalterable desertion of the place, the gigantic disarray, the earthquake.

The starting-marble in the stadium is cool to stand on.

The Hill of Kronos covered with pines, a more primitive house than they built for Zeus; it has outlasted his son's house.

To Zeus: the water and what is around it. Carved on a bull. The Alpheios is the tawniest, wildest and strongest river I have ever swum in. Great expanses and islands of sun-burnt sand and stones. Here and there a Greek boy or a gravel worker.

For days I wandered round the monuments, trying to learn them. At night I slept on the summit of the Hill of Kronos. In the heat of the afternoon I went to the Alpheios. The guards used to give me pears from some secret tree, and when finally I discovered the village swimming-place, round a bend of the river upstream and protected by a breakwater, the village children did the same. For lunch I used to eat tepid stuffed tomatoes in a tavern, and sweet, crisp, insubstantially heavy slices of watermelon. I find a note based perhaps on a misreading of Pausanias, that 'The local daemon, the preserver, the snakeboy, was fed with those drugged honeycakes on top of Kronion. I suppose the sacred snake of Athene was doped in the same way.' This must refer to a mysterious cult of the boy Zeus, who was also a snake. I am sure that by the honeycakes I meant *baklava*, which you could buy from a caravan outside the sanctuary. But the ancient world had infinite varieties of honeycakes. In parts of Spain to this day every festival has a different kind. 'Dust,' I recorded. 'Soft dusty dust and a strong smell of mint.'

The ruins of the temple of Zeus are terrible and beautiful. Its stones are so immense, its fallen columns so heavy and so disarticulated, the silver lichen on the dark grey seems so aged, that one can almost hear the thunderclap of its fall. It can never be restored; too many other monuments crowd around it. The temple was the house for a colossal statue, as the Parthenon was. The ancient Greeks when they saw it said that it was the god of Homer, and that it added something to human religion. It must have been awe-inspiring. It was by Pheidias, as Athene's statue was; but here, against every likelihood, his workshop has survived in the ruins of a Byzantium church, now ruined in its turn. Some of the moulds for decoration and some fragments of a glass palmette have been recovered there. Even less likely, a little Athenian wine-pot, slightly broken in antiquity, has the master's name scratched on the base. I doubt if it was used for wine; more likely it was an old, familiar possession, and he used it for brushes or small tools.

I was bemused by Olympia. I struggled with the statues, disliking the sleek thighs of Hermes but admiring his feet. I found the face of Apollo terrifying; he was too sure of himself, too arrogantly youthful, too blank-eyed. Years later, the temple sculptures began to move about in my imagination like the heavy elements of a dream. At first sight I found them technically perfect, admirable, but too hard, almost abhorrent. I was lonely, except at breakfast on top of my hill, alone among the Chinese trees. As the sun rose, four or five brown peacock moths fluttered around the clearing. I poured a little water for the dust. I returned again and again to the ruins of the temple of Zeus and the temple of Hera. The great altar of Zeus is missing. It was made of the accumulated, compacted ashes of centuries of sacrificial fires. In the end it towered up forty feet or more, like a miniature version of Kronion. But Alpheios swept it away long ago. I became obsessed by the temple, but on the Hill of Kronos I felt at home.

That was independent of mythology. I had forgotten, though I must once have read them, the strange verses Pindar wrote about Kronos. He was speaking of the dead. 'In nights like ours for ever, and a sun like ours in their daytime, the brave win a life without labour; they do not put out their hands to trouble the earth or the sea's water for an empty living. Close to the most honoured of the gods those whose pleasure was to keep their word pass days without weeping.'

The others carry
a burden that should not be looked upon.
And they that have endured three times over
life in this world
life in the other world
go by the road of Zeus

to the Tower of Kronos,
where the Airs who are Ocean's daughters
blow round the island of the Blest,
and the flowers are of gold
on earth blazing in bright trees
or water-nourished,
with these they twine their hands and these they weave:
severe Rhadamanthys is their Lord
whom father Kronos keeps
to be his counsellor,
near the almighty height of Rhea's throne.
Peleus is there, Kadmos is there,
the mother of Achilles took him there
when she by praying moved the heart of Zeus.

This was not a heaven to which ordinary people could aspire: it had a remoteness in time as well a mythical distance. It was set deliberately in heraldic terms, not those of everyday realism. To the ancient Greeks, who had never seen an artifical flower or a florist's flower, the golden flowers were magical and immortal, because gold retains its freshness. I find the company of Kronos in these verses immeasurably more inspiring than the 'life without labour' of the earlier part of the poem.

I left Olympia reluctantly, to go back to Pyrgos to the bus station and the railway station. This time I ran to earth George Pavlopoulos in his small office. Pyrgos was a small town of some twenty-five thousand people; from most parts of it you could catch a glimpse of the hills or the sea. The bus station, which was and still is always crowded, is used by everyone sooner or later. It is the thronging, suffering faces of old country people that make it remarkable. It stands in a busy street below the town square, next door to a down-at-heels neoclassic town hall. George has worked there most of his life. He had lived in a number of rented houses in different parts of Pyrgos, one in Captain George Street, one, which was a peaceful, quiet house, in Cemetery Road. In early middle-age, he acquired by good luck through a working men's housing scheme the house he now has, on a new estate near the Alpheios. In 1963 he lived in cramped quarters, and his wife was expecting a child. He shook hands, and we agreed to meet after work.

His smile was so warm and immediate, and his modesty and intelligence were so captivating, I knew at once I had made a friend for life. The Greek he speaks has a purity and simplicity I was already able to recognise. He is the best traditional storyteller I have ever heard in any language, and one of the best talkers. He has the calmness and seriousness of the provinces, and at the same time a perfect assurance. I came in time to see how much Seferis loved him and why. Over a period of years, I disentangled from casual conversations what I could of his remarkable history, and of the history of Pyrgos. His father kept a rather grand café and cakeshop with exotic bottles of liqueurs. A childhood illness incompetently treated left George lame for life. Prewar Pyrgos was a rich provincial centre, with splendid neoclassic buildings, dancing classes for the waltz and fox-trot, and traditional horse-races in the streets once a year.

Then came the war, the Italians and the Germans. George and his friends, a bunch of boys of about sixteen, went to the Bishop, a magnificent figure called Antonios with a bass voice in church like a Russian opera singer, to ask his advice. They wanted to know if they ought to start an intellectual magazine to keep up people's spirits. He gave them the Cathedral printing press. He himself went off into the mountains to join the armed resistance. In negotiation with the Germans he was fearless, wonderful, and very effective. He was dethroned for that, after the war, and sent to a penitential monastery. His body has never been brought home. I have seen the magazine, which was called *Odyssey*. It is better than anything my generation were turning out at that age. They went on to produce a series of plays: Pirandello's *Six Characters in Search of an Author*, and one they wrote themselves. All this in wartime Pyrgos.

There was a row about the play they wrote themselves. It was not so much the banners proclaiming 'Freedom or Death', which they explained away somehow. It was a long monologue, arranged by George, full of strong views about human freedom. He was summoned by the Gestapo to tell them who had written it. For a time he refused. Finally, as pressure increased, he said it was someone bigger than him. They insisted on the name of the author. With some pleasure and some courage he gave it. It was Victor Hugo. At this time, George's best loved cousin was in the mountains with the resistance. Towards the end of the war he appeared in Pyrgos at George's house, with friends on rooftops to cover his retreat, and a pistol under his overcoat. George was wanted in the mountains. His lameness made him reluctant to go; he might be more hindrance than help. They would find him a mule. They would look after him. They wanted him as a writer. George's father decided that his son must choose for himself, but his mother was upset at his going there and then, so the decision was postponed. That opportunity never came again, and when the resistance liberated Pyrgos George's idolized cousin was shot dead by a sniper from the Cathedral tower.

Terrible things were done at that time. Pyrgos had more to lose than most places; collaboration had provoked retribution, retribution provoked reprisals. When the last Nazi general left, he destroyed nothing, but the Nazi Greek militia remained in control of Pyrgos. The resistance came down from the mountains, and a surrender was negotiated. Unhappily, some of the militiamen had records so black that they dared not surrender, so that as the resistance brigade entered Pyrgos in peaceful triumph they were fired on from police or militia barracks. The battle that followed was a grim one, and Pyrgos burned for five days. Most of the best neoclassic buildings, which were unique in Greece for their beauty, perished at that time. The bitterness that was engendered took a long time to die away, if indeed it is not as I believe still smouldering here and there. It has not lacked fuel in the last thirty years.

George studied at the University of Athens. He has always seemed to me essentially self-instructed, as most poets are. He was poor, he could hardly afford either to buy books or to retain them, but had some experiences of a much wider world. He listened to music, he read widely and thoroughly, and he crouched in the bushes in the National Gardens to hear Sikelianos, a poet so Delphic that he sometimes sat in a tripod to receive guests, address a long, rhapsodical monologue in ringing accents to a tree.

Sikelianos really believed he was alone, if that makes it any better. George Pavlopoulos got a job in Athens, at a time when they were few. It was almost a civil service job, I think to do with the administration of Marshall Aid to Greece. But when the office closed, the job ended; there was no prospect of another. He returned to Pyrgos in some depression and after a time married a childhood friend; he has worked in the bus company offices for a pitiful salary ever since. And he has written his poems.

When we met, most of his poems were still to come, and so were most of mine. We had in common the paternal benignity of George Seferis whom he, of course, knew much better than I did, and many common passions. He has told me since those days that I seemed to him then a romantic, almost mythological figure, Odysseus fresh from his wanderings in a ragged straw hat. To me he seemed at least as interesting. Both he and his wife were descended from simple heroes of the war of independence. There was a great-uncle who had been a clan chief of shepherds, who came to Pyrgos once a year for his saint's day with gold-mounted pistols in his belt, and feasted whoever came for a week in his tents. At the same time they were modern, poor and touching. Of all living creatures they seemed the most deeply rooted into Greece, into whatever it was in Greece I most admired. Their manners and hospitality were extraordinary to me, like those of a Shakespearean hero and heroine in the woods. George's three childhood ambitions were to walk in a forest, to tread on snow and to travel in an aeroplane.

We took the bus that goes to Hayios Andreas, to what was then a tiny tavern called the Lyra, run by two fishermen. Its terrace, from which you could reach the seashore by some rough steps, had a gigantic olive tree and an even more gigantic vine for shade. It looked out across a deserted bay to a little island called Tigani, which means the frying pan, and beyond that to the sunset and the very distant ghost of Zakynthos. To get to Hayios Andreas, the bus took a journey across the sands of the long beach of Katakolo, picking its way between the swimmers and the sun-bathers. By such a route, said George, Telemachos in *The Odyssey* travelled to Sparta.

Hayios Andreas is his place. Prehistoric marble figures have been found in the tavern car park. There are ancient columns on the floor of the sea, and I have seen marble capitals washed up there. Tigani is full of the graves of the poor fishermen who worked this coast in late antiquity, and the beaches hint at how their city perished. They have black, volcanic sand. Above the Lyra, on a steep and over-grown hill called the Onion, stands a ruined medieval castle called Pontikokastro: Mouse Castle. I climbed up there once after rain, and saw that the hillside was leaking fragments of Mycenean pottery from one place, and classical pottery from another. If any reader of this book should be tempted to go there for the looting of ancient souvenirs, I am happy to assure other readers that he is very likely indeed to be arrested. Mouse Castle belongs to the Greeks; it belongs to George if it belongs to anyone.

I have only the sketchiest notes of our conversation. 'The sun sets full of dark bees.' That must be a quotation, but from whose poetry? 'Every morning I wake with a rock in my head. Inside the rock is a bird, not the bird that whistles in the branches, but the one that colours the sky.' That comes from a poem he wrote in combination with Takis Sinopoulos, another Pyrgos poet. It arose from a conversation in the early morning. I asked myself how it was that these Greeks, in stone once and now in words, could be so sweet and gentle without writing nonsense. Salt in the blood, bare rock, centaurs. A sparseness of life and energy. An almost childish delight and absence of shame. George spoke of Seferis, of how Seferis had deeply understood Solomos, the Greek Byron, and the Cretan Erotokritos and the folk-songs, and brought all these things together in a living speech that had not lost the mighty force of its origins.

'His language is like the ruins of the temple of Olympian Zeus … I respect the church only because it has preserved for us so many great things, and because there have been fine church poets.' Later, on the beach in the dark, he spoke again of Olympia. 'What men were they that made those mighty things? Whatever they believed, they believed it better than us. Our fathers made them. We do not understand how great our fathers were. We have lost our fathers.' He quoted or showed me a sentence he had written about Seferis. 'He ends always with an echo that spreads further, one feels, into the wide circles of another familiar voice; it drowns in the sea.' We talked about Mayakovsky and about Kavafis.

The Hill of Kronos

I was falling asleep, dazed with travel and sun and sea and the Greek language, and also with some of the best local wine I have ever tasted. I remember he told me the Greeks say dry lightning where we say dry thunder. We were watching great violet flashes out to sea. I noted down 'the innumerable places in which I have slept or fallen asleep and in which cigarettes have dropped out of my fingers since I crossed Parnes.' That night I slept in George's house, in a bed. I was wakened by a rhyming cry soon after dawn, in which *tomata* rhymed with *salata*. Breakfast was a bad moment, since George's wife had catered for what she knew of English taste, and instead of coffee or the bread and honey of the cafés or the oranges of the market, I had to consume a quantity of weak tea, several slices of dry cake, and an aubergine pickled in treacle. In the street someone gave me a carnation. A boy selling combs and socks outside the bus station told me that he made a hundred drachmas a day at this trade, from which his employer gave him thirty. That would be less than three pounds a week.

It seemed to me that the English were not really liked as a nation in Greece, though they were treated with great affection as a phenomenon, and a substratum of memories and friendships from the war was still real. Everyone remembered Cyprus, the Elgin Marbles, the dictation of Greek foreign policy by the west, and some tricky market diplomacy I never understood. In Greece at that time the ritual lamentation of old women over the dead was still a living art form; they remembered their wounds. Greece was like an old village woman lamenting her epic wrongs, but the wrongs were real and the sorrow was moving. I thought everything was part of the heat, and that it was also heat which imposed a democracy of clothing, speech, personal habits and technical inefficiency. I see now that both these views are superficial mistakes, but it may be useful to admit here what I naively felt then, in spite of my excitement and philhellenism.

'There is a certain sort of English person,' said George, 'who finds everything in Greece; it isn't romantic exactly.'

'I know that; I know some of them. There are a lot of English in love with Greece, not romantically but really. Byron began as the one and ended as the other. I love Byron a lot. He does raise questions about poetry, but poetry is a difficult matter.'

66

'Poetry difficult? You might as well say truth is difficult.'

I liked the roses. Everywhere in gardens fat, old-fashioned roses were blooming among orange trees and lemon trees. They had no Latin or English names that I ever discovered. They were simply left over from the nineteenth century or the eighteenth. One was the salad rose; it yields a special oil which mixes deliciously into the dressing of green salads. I have never seen it since. But this was the shadow of the Turkish moon, where attar of roses and fragrant tobacco and rose-petal jam are or once were the produce of villages. The railway station at Pyrgos was smothered and entwined in dreaming blue *convolvulus*. The Alpheios twinkled like honey. I saw houses on stilts, a colony of reed huts, fine horses. Today that seems a false picture. Greece has altered and so have I. Were there ever quite so many roses? Were the horses so fine? The reed huts were real, but they have been swept away.

At Kyparissia, in search of antiquities, I came to the right area soon enough, but it was unexcavated, and I saw only stones and pieces of pillar among the fields. At the back of a small chapel of St. George I was shown a marble left arm broken centuries ago, without hand or shoulder. It must have come from a life-size Roman statue of a standing woman; the hand had held something; maybe she was Artemis the huntress. She must have been lightly dressed, as her arm was quite naked, but she was never very beautiful and the marble had a horny texture. Her arm lay beside an ancient grave-stone with most of its lettering obliterated, and the left forearm of a more elaborate figure, fully robed. The police, I was told, had come to take away another inscription, with fine, clear lettering; they had left these poor fragments to live near where they were found. The most impressive piece I saw was the fluted drum of a column, still in use as the High Altar of St. George.

For what was left of the day I wandered about Kyparissia, which was a depressingly modern place. It had mostly been blown up during the war, but the rebuilt town has at least a seaside air and a sea-light. On the jetty one marble fragment of an ancient inscription has survived all the rebuildings. I ate stew for supper at a tavern called a wineroastkitchen, all in one word, and attempted unsuccessfully to negotiate a price for a taxi south the next day. That night I slept in the ruins of the castle, among old cannons, beside a broken-down commemorative fountain made of iron perhaps a hundred years ago. I slept badly and found the next morning I had been bitten in some twenty or thirty places by the mosquitoes that had kept me awake. The stagnant water in that fountain should have warned me. But Greece always offers some immediate comfort to the exhausted and affronted traveller. As I nibbled my biscuit, a rival taximan whose existence I had failed to discover the night before appeared beaming on the battlements. Greece is where high-spirited American cars go when they die. They are driven by reincarnated cowboys, romping in the Elysian fields. We rolled away southwards in an atmosphere of contentment and blue skies.

Pylos lies on a bay, almost a lagoon, blocked by the big island of Sphakteria, facing west where the southern coast of Greece breaks away into long, rocky promontories. Pylos is the last oasis of the lushness of the west coast; it lies as far south as the rock of Monemvasia on the east coast, the island of Milos in the Aegean, and Bodrum in Turkey. It was the ruling city of the kingdom of Nestor, an old man strayed from an earlier generation who makes long wise speeches in *The Iliad*. Nestor's kingdom, which Homer often mentions but never defines, seems to have stretched away to the north, perhaps as far as the Alpheios. His name occurs in some affectionate verses written in Greek on a wine-cup from Capri during what seems to be Homer's lifetime. 'I am Nestor's excellent drinking-cup. Whoever drinks of this cup, desire shall seize him at once for flower-haired Aphrodite.'

Classical Pylos was a low-lying, coastal town on the sea shore and on the island. Even Homer always calls it sandy Pylos, and Homer's Nestor gives a sacrifice to the gods and a feast to all his people on the seashore. Mycenean graves on the island were disturbed for the dead to be worshipped in the fifth century, seven hundred years or so after the burials, because they were thought to be the graves of Homeric heroes. Those scholars of whom there used to be many, and there are still some, who use Homeric poetry as a sort of guide book to Bronze Age archaeology, in defiance of the chasm of time which they believe his poetry bridges, made many attempts to identify the Pylos of Nestor. One of the favoured spots was a hilltop miles to the north, which I have examined inch by inch. So far as I could see, it was an insignificant encampment overlooking an enormous Roman villa. Another consisted of isolated tombs of the right date and of great magnificence, a long way inland.

The place which is nowadays conventionally called Nestor's palace is on a fine hilltop, miles above the sea. It was unknown to Homer and unknown to the classical Greeks. But it really was the administrative centre of a Bronze Age kingdom, and it really was a palace. Its situation above the olive groves and the vines, with the sea glittering in the distance, is how I imagine a film star's palace might be in California. This was in fact an American excavation. If you disregard Nestor's bath (so named because someone took a bath in his palace in the Homeric poems), Ano Englianou, now called Nestor's palace, is a brilliant, enlivening monument. In the fields around it I have found five different kinds of orchid growing at one time. But it is absolutely necessary to visit the museum as well. That is a mile or two away in the nearest village.

The palace was destroyed by fire, and its archives, which were scratched on clay tablets, were baked brick-hard, so that we have them now exactly as they stood on the day of destruction. They left Greece on the last American ship to leave the Mediterranean before America entered the last world war, and it was their full publication that made it possible for Michael Ventris and John Chadwick to decode what is called Linear Script B, the speech of the Myceneans, the Bronze Age form of the Greek language. More tablets found at Pylos while they were at work confirmed their decoding, and confirmed that this was Greek. They had thought it might be a language related to Etruscan. The message of these archives about the last days of the palace was grim. Invaders were expected from the sea; the army was not concentrated, but split into coastal watches. The social and economic organisation of the villages was chaotic.

This was a last bastion of the Myceneans. The styles and shapes of the palace pottery are a provincial version of what was used at Mycenae, a little out of date, somewhat poorly executed. Pylos away in the western provinces held out longer than more important places. There was a painting in fresco on the palace walls which I take to represent a battle between Myceneans and barbarians, though I believe it is a copy of a North African painting, just as the harbour with its crowded shipping at Santorini is a copy. But the Pylos fresco prophesies the inevitable end. No such kingdom could withstand forever the hostility it provoked. Personally, I owe Pylos a great debt: it was here, superficially at first but then more and more deeply, that I became possessed with curiosity about prehistoric societies, and in the end about the whole history of mankind.

On that first day I merely jotted down the marine motifs of Bronze Age decorations, with the note 'this is part of a subaqueous huge vase. Facts are drowned events.' I then ate fish for lunch in a tavern at the port of Pylos, below an elephant-coloured Turkish fort. I can still remember that the lunch, about which I made no note, was wonderful; it seems I was preoccupied by fifth-century history. The Athenians, who had command of the sea, besieged some Spartans on the island here. Slaves or serfs were promsied their freedom if they could swim out to the island under water with provisions. That invisible swim, coming up once or twice for air, must have been difficult, but not quite impossible, or so I thought. Being now of a maturer age, my present feeling is that I would not let any son of mine attempt it. But the Spartans live inland, and most of the people around them were their slaves or their serfs.

All over Greece, many of my notes are stammering attempts to record the same things: the glittering blue, sometimes as at Pylos the near indigo colour of the sea, the wild thick glittering olive groves, the damp, deep tresses of the vines. Vines are so changeable from one season to another they are hardly the same creature. The yellow leaves in autumn are so papery and fine, and underfoot so moving, that one could live and die in an autumnal vine-arbour. The pruning in winter is a vigorous moment. The first fresh leaves and tendrils offer a thrilling promise. But there is something to be said for summer, even in the heat of the Greek countryside. I set off that evening as the sun cooled, inland from Kyparissia. Pylos was a hit and run journey; I could not have afforded the time without a taxi. But now I tied on my serious boots.

I was making for Phigalia, an ancient city above the gorges of the river Neda, where I wanted to investigate a mysterious shrine. I must have chosen it more or less deliberately for its obscurity, and because it was so deeply buried in the mountains. Not far beyond it stood the temple of Apollo at Bassai, which locally they called the Pillars, Stous Stylous. The Bassai temple is famous, and its frieze is in the British Museum, where for twenty years or more it was never on show; when it was at last shown it was left unguarded, so that a passing tourist knocked off a head from it and escaped with his trophy. That was no doubt a part of the policy of saving these things from neglect by the Greeks and making them generally available to scholars.

Bassai is a very remote mountain temple, but ever since it was found in 1765 it has had a romantic attraction. Most tourists visit it. All I was doing was choosing what I thought a more appropriate way of getting there. I wanted not only the landscape but the feel of the place, and of course I intended to sleep there. I have heard of approaches more adventurous than mine. Professor Shefton as a young man is said to have arrived on a mule from Olympia, in the middle of the civil war, when all those mountains were swarming with armed men. Herr Bocher, who first discovered Bassai, was murdered there later on for his brass buttons, which the simple bandits imagined must be gold. The temple was first studied and pillaged by Cockerell, a neoclassic architect of some merit, the designer of the Ashmolean Museum at Oxford. He and a colleague of his called Haller Von Hallerstein hawked their spoils around the governments of Europe. Bavaria acquired the temple sculptures from the island of Aigina, but the British bought the Bassai frieze.

Cockerell was an appalling man, but jolly and clever. 'As we were sailing out of the port in our open boat we overtook the ship with Lord Byron on board. Passing under her stern we sang a favourite song of his, on which he looked out of the windows and invited us in. There we drank a glass of port with him.' When he visited Sounion, the ground around it carried a crop of barley. He camped there: 'We broughts kids of the shepherds, and when work was over for the day, there was a grand roasting of them over a fire of thyme branches, with native music, singing and dancing.' That is not the Greece I was looking for – I had hardly begun to read the old Greek travel books – but I recognise it in the Greece I found. At Bassai Cockerell found his frieze by investigating a fox's lair among the ruined stones. 'One may still trace on the marble the injuries done by the fox's claws.'

The temple of Apollo at Bassai belonged to Phigalia. It was Pausanias who excited imaginations about it, by maintaining that it was built for the Phigalians as a thank-offering when Apollo turned away a plague, and that the designer was Iktinos, one of the architects of the Parthenon. Scholars still take this attribution seriously, but in order to do so they are forced to argue that the temple at Bassai was designed and begun before the Parthenon and not completed until long afterwards. The niceties of Greek architecture fell into the hands of specialised architects in the lifetime of Cockerell. One can no longer intrude into their mysteries. I knew little about Bassai, which must mean the glens, beyond what Pausanias says. I had never seen the frieze, though I saw it by appointment soon afterwards, and sent a full set of photographs to George Pavlopoulos. I wanted to see it for its beauty, of course, but I was even more interested in the local connection with Phigalia.

At Phigalia there was once a statue of Black Demeter, which was worshipped in a cave. She was made of wood, sitting on a rock; she had a horse's head and hair, with serpents and monsters sprouting out of it. In one hand she held the dolphin of Poseidon, in the other the dove of Persephone. She was dressed in black. This statue was copied in bronze in the fifth century, when the cult was revived after a famine and a threatening oracle. 'This Demeter,' says Pausanias, 'was the principal reason for my coming to Phigalia.' He made the traditional offering of the fruits of the earth, grapes, honey and unspun wool, with oil poured over it. 'There is a sacred grove of oaks around the cave, where cold water springs out of the ground.' But already in the second century A.D. the cave had fallen in, and the statue lay somewhere smashed under a fall of rock.

Poseidon, god of earthquakes and the sea, had mated with Demeter in the form of a horse. Elsewhere when this story was told she gave birth to a horse, but at Phigalia she bore a daughter called the Mistress. She retired to this cave pregnant and ashamed, the crops withered, so Zeus asked the goat-footed mountain god Pan to find her. She was found and gave birth. Recent scholars have not been as lucky or as sharp-eyed as Pan; the place has never been discovered again. Sir James Frazer made an educated guess, which I thought worth investigating; I was determined to look for myself at the gorge of the Neda below Phigalia: who knew what I might find? Somewhere in the same valley there was once an oracle of the dead, where their souls could be summoned from the underworld to be questioned.

I set off in the cooling sunlight by a road which dwindled to a track. The distant hills were a dusty herd of cattle, then they were the blue backs of disappearing whales. The valley narrowed. I wanted to reach Siderokastro by nightfall, for an early start next morning and a full day at Phigalia. I was doing well enough, I remember shady trees and some water. Ponies grazed and the river beds were full of oleander. Twice I saw what seemed to be classical remains, but there was nothing to be done about them. They were only a stone or two sticking out of the shrubbery, and I must plod on. A few miles from Siderokastro I was stopped by an ancient, battered Bedford truck, carrying in men from the fields. I accepted a lift with relief, but progress in that truck was more painful than it had been on foot. It steamed, it clattered, it hit stones, it raised a tornado of dust. We had to stop at a watersplash and wash it down like an overwrought animal.

We travelled between big hills of *maquis*, and wild or half-wild pear trees and plum trees, groves of figs, little woods of cypresses, big woods of scrub oak or holly-oak. Siderokastro was admirably isolated. Its name ought to mean the Iron Castle, but it has no fortress, and I imagine Siderokastro is a corruption of Castle of Saint Isidore, who begot other place-names in this peculiar region. I was too excited about the prospect of tomorrow to take Siderokastro as seriously as it deserved. It was a beautiful and hospitable place, but I was hungry for the morning.

4

Inland

I HAD FORGOTTEN the date. It was the feast of Holy Elias, who was carried up in a flaming chariot to Heaven, a village festival in every small settlement in Greece that has a chapel dedicated to him. Many of them have these chapels, often on the top of hills or mountains where lightning has struck or sudden fire has broken out. This in fact is the survival of an ancient festival of Zeus. Holy Elias may thunder, but the lightning belongs to God. When lightning strikes at Arachova, where in the nineeten-hundreds they were still swearing 'by the God of Crete', they say, 'He has burnt up a devil.' In a story told on Zakynthos, God has a war against the giants and fights it out armed with thunderbolts, as Zeus did. On Chios, the chief of the giants in this story was Samson. I had meant to spend the feast of Holy Elias in some traditional place. The only Mediterranean village festival I had ever seen was in the hills above Florence. That consisted of a pilgrimage and a service at a neglected chapel, followed by a procession and a donkey race.

It was not much of a feast at Siderokastro. There was no particular service; as the sun fell, people milled about wistfully in the streets, small private parties were going on, but no one was drinking, there was no music, no dancing. The three bouzouki players of Siderokastro had emigrated to Australia last year. I walked up and down with the young people of the village, who had at once discovered my bushy lair half a mile away. They were no more interesting than other young people. I did notice that they smoked cigarettes out of doors, but never smoked or swore in the presence of their fathers, so they said, until they had completed their military service. I suggested they must be fed up with so many tourists. 'Yes,' they said, 'in this year already we have had two others.'

At night I ate a Greek family dinner as someone's guest. The wine was their own, and excellent, the bread was home-baked, but I recollect the rest of the food as difficult to manage, an enormous quantity of tepid pasta. Everything in the house was managed by two aunts. I slept out under a vine, by my own wish rather than by theirs, but the next morning I was asked, before offering, to pay for my night's lodging, and had to bargain about the price. No one minded that, and I left with my head heavy with blessings. They were just a little shocked that I had no camera; in those days poor people all over Greece expected to be repayed for their angelic kindness with photographs of themselves and their children.

That morning's walk was wonderful. The air was fresh and the sun hot, as if it were autumn. The valleys were full of stones and groves, and everywhere children were herding sheep. Rock after rock echoed with the disorganized clanging of sheep-bells. Small, finely coloured butterflies fluttered here and there. I never saw so many varieties of flowering thistles, yellow ones, pink ones and blue ones. It is only now as I write that I recollect something forgotten ever since. On that day I saw the princess of thistles, *cirsium candelabrum*, which grows to more than six feet high and four feet across, weighed down with flowering spikes. Its spire and branches look like green nineteenth-century ironwork, though nothing was left of its flowers when I saw it but shaggy tufts. Since 1963 I have sometimes searched for it, under the impression I had never seen one, but the memory of it came back with the memory and the smells of that hot morning.

At Platania, a village with the plane trees it was named after, I found enthusiastic volunteer guides, and as usual I discovered that my map was inadequate and the situation of the gorge, which by now I could see, with the elephantine bulk of Lykaon somewhere behind it, was not what I expected. The 'old bridge' had been 'destroyed by the Turks', but a footbridge, a *podoyiofyro*, would get me to Stomio, the cavern into which the Neda disappears underground. The river runs underground seven miles, and then streams peacefully for a last level course to reach the sea. The guides were young men just out of the Army, happy to have something to do. We were down in the gorge of the Neda almost quicker than I wanted.

It was a strange, haunted place. The river had plenty of water even in summer, but it wound along the floor of the gorge, making small waterfalls and rock-pools, as a French river might do through a wood. Tall trees grew in the gorge, including oaks and planes, but on either side the gorge itself towered up infinitely. We thought of swimming in a small pool, but a snake had found it first. It took fright and sped away into the stones. At once there was a snake hunt. They caught it under a forked stick and stoned it to death. It was a small adder. The place where the river disappeared was enthralling. The Neda may, I think, have lost some of its water through this or that crack before it arrives at this point; here it simply laps smoothly over the lip of a grey mouth of rock, a gaping dark hole into which it vanishes headlong. On the feast of the Virgin in August, the local people stand on the brink of the gorge and throw down offerings into it.

Or once they say people did so. Now they throw down stones. The foundation legend of the tiny church which nestles on a ledge six feet or so above the floor of the gorge revolves around a flask of oil flung down that landed unbroken. That ledge was Frazer's suggestion for the lost cave of Black Demeter. I believe now that this place was the oracle of the dead. Demeter's cave must have been elsewhere; no one had found it. I did explore the caves behind the church. No rock had fallen there. But the last cave, beyond where the church is, on the same ledge, gives onto an inner cave. One must crawl six feet or so, then comes a chamber like the opening chamber, another ten feet of crawling and after that a bigger chamber. It was full of mosquitoes, so I went no further.

Anyway, the day had become a riot, and I was falling into the mood of my guides. We splashed about, we ate fruit, we attempted in vain to plumb the Stomion, we explored the chapels and the waterfalls and the pools, we gazed up at the huge limestone cliffs. I thought it was the most beautiful place I had ever been in. I hoped then that it might be the sanctuary of the scaly-tailed lady Eurynome, another Phigalian goddess, but that, they told me, was higher up the gorge. She was 'a wooden idol tied up with golden chains, like a woman down to the buttocks and below that like a fish'. The people of Phigalia said she was Artemis. Her sanctuary must certainly be higher up the gorge, 'holy from ancient times, where the rivers join, inaccessibly situated in broken country'. Pausanias was furious at the idea of such a creature being called Artemis. I suppose she was a water goddess, like Thetis, who was immensely powerful once. Eurynome had an interesting relative or male counterpart called Eurynomos, a daemon in the underworld with a blue-black body and fierce teeth, sitting on a vulture-skin and punishing the wicked. The officials at Delphi said his function was to clean away the flesh of the dead, leaving only the bones.

The Arkadians had in antiquity the reputation of an ancient, mysterious and innocent people. They were lost in their mountains, as the Neda is, and some of their rituals were blood-curdling. Eccentricities and contradictions survived in isolated villages in these clefts of rock for longer than they would elsewhere. Lykaon was Pan's original mountain and a place of wolf-cults. In all their racial myths that ramified backwards to explain so many modern quarrels, the Greeks allowed the Arkadians to be aboriginal, the first race of mankind, born from the local earth, acorn-eaters, survivors of an earlier age of the world. Lykaon is not called the Hill of Kronos, but the river Neda rises there, and they thought its headspring gushed from the rock at the will of Rhea, when she was pregnant with Zeus. The timeless golden age that Virgil and the Renaissance set in Arcadia is another matter. For Virgil it was the country of Pan, he believed Arkadian Pallantion gave its name to the Palatine hill, where a statue of Pan stood in the cave where the Roman she-wolf vanished.

Regretfully, I abandoned my splashings and searchings under the cliff, and with one of my day's friends began to scramble uphill up a path I might never have found, to the village of Phigalia on the far side of the gorge. On old maps and in old travel books it was called Pavlitza. It was an idyllic place. Its water-spring, to my extreme amazement, still ran out of an ancient marble fountain into its fourth-century basin. The ring of great stones where the elders of the village sat in the evening under the plane trees consisted of a heavy fragments of ancient architecture. I noticed a fifth-century inscription in local script built upside down into a barn wall. It was only the letters of a name.

The museum was in the schoolhouse, but the key to its door was at Peribolia, another village some distance away, because that was where the schoolmaster lived. I hardly remember whether we found it, but I think not. At that moment I assumed I was coming back to spend several weeks at Phigalia. The priest showed me round the village. He was a splendid village priest as wild as a mountain goat, and as wise. He showed me with rueful pride an abandoned chapel with thirteenth-century frescoed walls, inhabited by a colony of scraggy hens. I asked him if he ever came across antiquities. That year he had rescued the knee and leg of a statue, and his wife had turned up a ring with a gem-stone engraved with athletes. When the Olympic games were a kind of village games, Phigalia used to do well at Olympia.

One thing the priest lamented. There was a book, an ancient text which he needed. He had never found it even in Athens. It would be a great help to him in his researches, and he thought it a most interesting and educative book. Would I have ever seen a copy of Pausanias? Only a year afterwards I was lucky enough to come across the only other copy of the three little pocket volumes I use myself that I have ever found, for ten shillings in an Oxford bookshop; I hope it reached him. He gave me lunch, an enormous lunch at half past three in the afternoon, fried eggs from the Byzantine hens, and a wine that tasted of rocks and bushes. We saw ancient pillars in a chapel that had become a house, and a faded wall-painting of Adam and Eve in a dusty, Hellenistic garden. And we saw the classical city on its hill, the ruins of its walls and shrines.

When Frazer passed this way in the eighteen-nineties, he had the luck to be present when one of the oldest of all Greek athlete statues came to light. It was a *kouros*, a tall naked youth with a bony, muscular stone body. He stands in the museum at Olympia now; he was an Olympic winner. He is too gaunt to be graceful, but he has some strength and beauty. In 1963, Phigalia was just on the point of getting its first public road and country bus service. The bulldozers were turning up big marble fragments. It is more surprising how much has survived than how much has been ruined. The Spartans and the Arkadians, the Crusaders and the Turks and the partisans have all fought battles over this ground. Lykaon rears up in the background, grey and tufted, behind the nearer, darker hills.

My route lay through Dragone or Dragoi, which I take to be the Tragoi of the eighteen-hundreds, a village apparently named after the ancient word for goats or for all I know some forgotten goddess of goats. It was an easy track, but the afternoon was mellowing into evening. At Dragoi I opened negotiations for a pony or a mule, and a guide across the disused mountain path to the temple. Time dragged on, the sun was falling, and all I got was a little old man with a happy, mischievous face and a white moustache. The pony or the mule had to be fetched out of the fields. It was a splendid white pony, it was a tall dark mule. We would have to cross in the dark, it was cooler and not very dangerous. We set off in the beginning of dusk and dewfall, and in the fields we met the mule. She was a diminutive, wicked-eyed, grey donkey, and it took him half an hour and many colourful curses to catch her. With obvious reluctance, she carried my pack. 'Mule,' he said, 'is our word for a donkey.'

By this time it was really dark, but we plodded on. We threaded our way over slippery and ankle-breaking rocks, with what seemed to be ravines on either side of us. The old man, who was called Nikitas, was unwilling to stop for me to get a torch out of the sidepocket of my haversack. Nikitas and the donkey knew their way. I did persuade him at last, after a particularly excruciating stumble, that I had to stop, and when I produced the torch he marvelled at it. He had heard of these, he said, but never handled one. With this we could cross all the mountains of Greece. Where would I like to go? We became close friends, and I gave him a drink of ouzo. If I could have afforded it, we would have wandered off for ever. His wife was a sour old woman, as he told me.

Nikitas and the donkey were dark shapes ahead of me, but the torch helped, and the ground improved. We seemed to be in a field, rising towards a sort of hedge. Below the hedge we halted. 'Water,' he said. The pale beam fell on grey marbles. A spring ran out between them, not much of a spring, but enough to explain the field. The marble was even more thrilling by torchlight than it would have been under the sun, and the water on that journey, at that time of night, as welcome as mountain dew or arbutus leaves would be to a flock of goats. Not more than a few yards beyond the spring we scrambled up the last slope of stones, and there above us, in the beginnings of moonlight, stood the pillars.

They were rough to the hand, an encrusted, starlit, greyish assembly. They reared up very high. I have seen them by storm light in the winter, when they were blazing greyish-white shapes, and by snowlight, when they were greenish-black and dripping. I saw them next morning, as the sky turned grey and then blue, and the shadowed mountains shared the transformations of the columns. Bassai is half a temple, half a mountain cairn. When it was found it was a vast cairn of stones, and at night it still belongs to wolves and foxes, although there are no wolves left so far south. Nikitas was as impressed as I was by the columns at that hour. We wandered about staring and feeling our way. The donkey grazing was the only noise.

We dismantled my pack and found the last of the ouzo, which we shared. The donkey's bridle snapped, so I offered a rope I carried for emergencies that never happened. It had a loop at one end and a toggle at the other. Nikitas pounced on it gleefully. 'Now I see,' he said. 'Now I see the cuckold how it works. Like this.' He put a noose round the donkey's neck and pulled it tight. 'With this I will get home, with this cuckold.' I tried to explain, but it was no use. He had jumped up on the donkey's back and they were trotting away into the night. He shouted back a few times. The last I heard was 'Mr. Peter, *Petraki mou*, I can see nothing at all.' I still wonder whether they did arrive home.

It is curious to compare that journey with the same track as it was travelled by Captain W. M. Leake around 1800:

We soon begin to ascend Mount Cotylium, which is therefore correctly placed by Pausanias at a distance of forty stades from Phigaleia; for though the temple is at least a two hours' walk of a man or horse from the ruins of the city, we may be allowed to apply the forty stades to the nearest part of the mountain on which the temple stands. After ascending for half an hour through pasture land, in which there are some sheep-folds belonging to Tragoi, we enter the forest of oaks which covers the summit of all these ridges. The path winds among the trees for half an hour, when I am suddenly startled from the indolent reverie which such a pleasant but unexciting kind of road often produces, by the sight of one of the component cylinders of a Doric shaft of enormous size, lying half buried in earth and decayed leaves.

It was daylight of course, and tracks were in better condition in his day.

I was woken by a crow's voice echoing from five mountains, then the barking of a dog and the tinkling of mule-bells or sheep-bells, God knows how many miles away. Poppies and asphodel and what seemed to be wild hollyhocks were growing here and there among the stones. I went back to last night's water-spring, the temple spring I suppose, and perhaps the reason for the temple's existence. The sun as it rose slightly silvered the columns and the rocks, but Lykaion turned black, and the further mountains seemed to be made of solid dust and shadows. I settled down to draw the temple, but despair soon overtook me. I picked a flower, noted a ground-plan, and scribbled a sentence about stone palmettes, sprouting ungovernably like wild lilies. Then the fact that the lizards up here were a rustier colour than in the coastal villages.

It was easy to see why people thought Bassai was by Iktinos. It was a miracle of proportion and loneliness, and its long, archaic shape and the slimness of its inner lines do breathe the atmosphere of great architecture. The morning was very hot, and the slow, satisfying geometry of light and shade moved among the eastern columns. I do not know why this temple was not oriented east-west, but the statue of Apollo stood against the west wall, facing the sunrise through a side door. I do not believe it was intended that the temple should face Delphi, although that has been suggested, and its long shape does imitate the old Delphic temple. Neither Bassai nor the Parthenon is a conventional Doric building. They have something else in common too. They both carried swirling continuous friezes high above eye-level, the Parthenon outside but in shelter, Apollo's temple inside the inner walls.

What amazed me at Bassai was the extreme daring, the inventive richness and the almost casual manipulation of forms in the interior as it must once have been. Every advance of design was a new transformation of the same stiff forms, in the fifth century. It must have been almost like the progress of some marvellous child with a box of nursery building bricks. The unyieldingness of the forms, the hardness of the stone and slowness of the techniques of handling it were essential conditions of that progression. Of all the crimes committed so wantonly against Greek art in the last two hundred years, I most bitterly regret the stripping and looting of these noble stones. But what can one expect? Already in the second century A.D. Aphrodite's temple on that mountain was roofless, the statue of Apollo had been moved to Megalopolis in the plains, inscriptions were unreadable and statues overgrown with ivy.

The temple caught every small breeze, but by half past nine in the morning the sun had melted a candle in the outer pocket of my pack. I had never seen a landscape look hotter, but it was misty as well, an angry, hard-biting heat. I ruminated ineffectually among some nearby stones which I believe have been excavated since. A naive and parasitical scholar of my kind without a permit to excavate or the time to be ever quite thorough enough is like a greedy man without a tin-opener. I took the mountain road down to Andritsaina, under mountains, I noted, whose size induced sleep. On my road I came on yet another spring with old marbles and a classic shape. Fig trees and flowers sprouted between its cracks. But here I learnt a lesson. It was inscribed with a cross and the date 1754, with the words, 'On the feast of Saint George (?) the spring of this land was constructed.' Why not, after all, go on using the same shapes and even the same stones?

At Andritsaina I ate cheese. It was better than any other cheese I had found. The retsina was a solid dark colour, with a full taste and a cold sting. Rain fell, obliterating the mountains, and the deepest toned thunder of a lifetime rolled and rolled among the peaks. I thought Andritsaina in the rain was 'a dull, small, unclean provincial town'. What a mistake. It was old-fashioned then, and it has hardly altered since. Now I think of it as the most unspoiled of all the small places I revisit. It has old-fashioned metal shops where shepherds match their sheep-bells; you can buy the pelts of mountain foxes; the tavern with the innumerable panes of glass in the upstairs windows makes the best bean soup in Greece. And most unexpected of all things, Andritsaina has one of the best public libraries anywhere in the provinces. It goes back to the eighteenth century; the books are thrilling in themselves, let alone as a collection. And the library contains an excellent museum of local antiquities.

But on my first visit I failed to discover the library. The sun did come out, and my jottings became a little less gloomy, but perhaps it is best to transcribe them here as they were written:

I broke walnuts in a porch and ate preserved cherries. Perhaps the sites Pausanias visited were like this, hens running in and out of the legs of statues, everyone asleep or disliking the season, the retsina good but the architecture smothered in wild figs, everything falling to pieces; roads, timber, cats, old men, statues, books. In this country people shit and sleep wherever nature overcomes them. But even about these things a certain discipline exists. And no one gets drunk. And no one ever abuses water. Kyparissia water is praised in Andritsaina. Phigalia water is famous for miles. So is the water at Bassai.

The truth is I was simply waiting for a bus. I noticed the languid, devouring weeds, and the deep pink roses in unkempt backgardens. I saw walnut trees the size of elms, and huge plane trees. But there was only one bus a day, and I ended by roosting for the night, on a rug I bought from a peddlar, on top of the bell-tower of the church. It was a free-standing, concrete structure made as it were from a Meccano set. I have seen it since, and it looks uncomfortable, but I slept on it like the most innocent of the dead. Dawn was splendid. It seemed to happen a great distance away, with no relation to the little town. The first thing stirring in the street was a boy to light the baker's oven, then a policeman, then the same boy washing at a spring, then two women to draw water. Then I was awake.

I have never had anything stolen in Greece except maps, and that only twice in fifteen years or more. The first time was in Andritsaina, waiting for that bus. The bus drove through mountains, by a roundabout route, across the young Alpheios and down the great gorge that leads to Karytaina. The scenery was more impressive than I could grasp in words: enormous hillsides, bright green pines, bottomless ravines. But I had to keep my eyes half shut, to pretend to be asleep. An old woman had begun to sing and the other passengers were telling her to be quiet; it was disgraceful in front of a foreigner. She sang a traditional lamentation for the dead Christ. She must have sung for an hour, all down that tremendous gorge. I could make out some of the words; they seemed to be late medieval, from that strange period when the influence of Franciscans in the Greek islands spread into vernacular poetry, and a western sweetness entered into the expressions of popular religion. I had seen one like it a year before; it had been lying unknown and unpublished in the Bodleian library until Dr Joachim of Munich found it there.

Her music was most weirdly beautiful. The rhymes and rhythms which had seemed so simple on paper took on strange counterpoint. I do not know whether that long lament has ever been written down; very likely not. Certainly the music was old and as free as folksong; it had been learnt by ear, it lived only in that old woman. The reason why she sang is that the laments for the dead, a traditional impromptu ritual form of words and music, were then almost the only popular and traditional art form that survived among women in southern Greece; but to sing such a lament for pleasure in a secular atmosphere would be bad manners and bring bad luck. To lament the dead Christ was just admissible. Those words were mated to that music long ago; it was a bold innovation in the late Byzantine world to celebrate Christ in the traditional form of laments for a dead young man; this was popular poetry, not church poetry. For mile after mile she sang on and on.

And Mikis Theodorakis, most famous and best loved of Greek musicians, learnt the elements of his art from an old church singer at Tripolitsa, now called Tripolis, which is also in Arkadia. That old man knew by heart every part of the ancient repertory of the church, and the whole corpus of secular, traditional music. He sang all day in churches and all night in taverns. Mikis was born at Pyrgos, and his childhood friend there was George Pavlopoulos. They used to sit on the edge of the square looking towards the sea at Pyrgos, by the ruins of the Byzantine tower that gave the town its name, and discuss their futures. Mikis was going to be a great musician and George was going to be a great poet. They were going to write an opera together. It would be a pastoral opera, and it was going to have real sheep. They were eight years old then. Now the square has been rebuilt, and the ruins of the tower have disappeared.

Karytaina is Gortyna, the fortified refuge of the Greeks from the ancient Kortys or Gortys, when that half-derelict town was destroyed by the Slavs. There is Slav blood in the Peloponnese to this day. The faces you see that look so un-Hellenic are Slav faces, not Turkish faces. The Turks on the whole kept to their own villages. There are even one or two of those that survive, and the Turkish music survives in them, with fifes and drums. They still keep to themselves, and they have few visitors. But the folksong of southern Greece, and of all the Greeks, has a lot of things in common with Serbo-Croat folksong, even with songs that go back to the Middle Ages, to the Serbian empire before Kossovo. So far as I know, this fascinating community of tradition has not been exhaustively studied. But when the Greek war of independence broke out, it was intended as a general rising of the Christian Balkans. That would have given Europe a different history, I suppose.

Karytaina has a formidable castle. It was built by Hugues de Bruyère, one of the Crusaders who overflowed into Greece in the thirteenth century. His son was the hero of a lengthy jog-trot historical poem in Greek, one can hardly call it an epic, the *Chronicle of the Morea*. It was years before I could acquire a copy of that, but I have found it makes excellent reading. It is a perfect combination of dullness and excitement, in an extended prosaic style lit up here and there by the poetry of what it touches. In fact it is like most medieval chronicles. Karytaina was bought back by the Byzantine emperor after a hundred years, but it still has an eleventh-century church with a French bronze bell. The strangest of all the Frankish ruins in Greece lies beside the Stymphalian lake, where Herakles murdered the water-birds. The lake is high up on a plateau in the mountains behind Corinth, a dreary place in winter but green and delightful in the spring. Beside it stand the ruins of a Cistercian monastery, built of ancient marbles.

In the plain beyond Karytaina I noticed very little. The castle on its fantastic crag receded, and even that seemed miniature. My eyes were mountain-scarred. I saw only scraggy vegetation, and hedges of cactus with yellow flowers like pitiable decorations. Today the whole scale of that plain has been altered by a vast new power station painted red and white, as impressive as the Didcot power station which looms in the same way above so many country roads. The bus dropped me at Megalopolis, the federal city of the Arkadians, built in the sixties of the fourth century BC. Forty villages and hill-towns were abandoned to glorify it, and its ruins are spectacular. There I met a tortoise, three Californians and an Australian. We wandered about together among the empty benches of the theatre and the overgrown senate-house. The marble was crusted grey and spotted with lichen. There were steely-blue thistles, mauve hollyhocks (can they have been mallow?), the silent circle of grass, and the tortoise.

Why, I wondered then, do we not consider the history of Arkadia more carefully? What a private rhythm it has. It ambles through the classical age like a peasant, out of step with the others. What did it ever produce but a few marvellous works of art made in it by foreigners? A mother-goddess with strange eyes or a horse's head or a fish's tail, a smell of goat attending on the gods, and then at the last moment this failed attempt at federal politics. A few good poets who wrote short, perfect poems like the dying notes of sheep-bells. Maybe their arts were dancing and music, which are quite lost now. That was what the Romans said. But at the mountain sanctuary of Lykosoura, once in every solar year, a man called the Wolf slaughtered a child, and the child was eaten. The man then swam away across a lake and lived out of sight like an animal for eight years. When his time was over he swam back and took human clothing. This appalling ritual was still celebrated a hundred and fifty years after the birth of Christ.

The gods of Megalopolis were only federal gods, never very terrible, never very holy. What is left of it now is mostly bases of statues and drums of columns too heavy to move, and painted terracotta that the reapers neglected. Looked at from here, the whole of Greek history was a strange and ominous cavorting. What did the tortoise think of the Californians? Flocks of brown and white pigeons were grazing by the river. A communal blanket-washing was taking place on the rocks in the shallows, and the air was full of the happy shrieking of crones. A middle-aged lady was sitting in the porch of her house, spinning wool. I sat down and read Sophokles with a new understanding. It was only an embroidered version of this countryside, and of peasant rhetoric and lamentation, things as common as bread, which have for us an exotic taste. Honey, dawn water, leaves, age. The everyday liturgy of old villagers.

From Megalopolis, another bus to Tripolis. From Tripolis, another bus southwards as far as Sparta. In the bus station at Tripolitsa I fell in with young soldiers. They were national service recruits; the young ones were making ten shillings a month, and they had to provide their own boots and cleaning things. Their necks were sun-baked, and hot air seemed to run in their blood. They were as cheerful as little boys, but friendly and protective like villagers. It is worth repeating that there were fewer tourists in those days, and few foreigners spoke any Greek. Mine was improving. After the long Arkadian plain we began to climb into more barren upland levels and higher hills. Just above the final pass an eagle flew slowly above the world, hardly gesturing, high up and moving fast. At dusk we came down under Taygetos, which has the wildest, the most coherently wild silhouette, of any ridge in Greece. I drew it, but the drawing was too sober. The rockface at dusk had the colour of a blue pig.

'Shall we go to the women?' said the soldier.

'Who has money?' said the other one.

'We can go together,' said the first, 'for not much.'

'Ach,' said the other one, 'I am tired. And money I have none. And what about tomorrow? The bus is early.'

'Mr. Professor,' said the first, 'let us go to the women.'

'I also am tired.'

'They are clean women.'

'But I have to sleep, and write, and read.'

'One must have holidays. It is good to break the much reading.'

'No.'

'Tomorrow I will show you Sparta. Each thing. Tonight we shall go to the women. The cost for two together is not much.'

By chance I met him again the next morning, waiting for his bus. He looked very tired indeed and I got scarcely a good morning. Was there really a brothel in Sparta? It was a dashing, prosperous county town, the county town of Lakonia, so perhaps there was. But it seemed a most properly behaved place. Sewing parties of women sat sedately in their dusty rose-gardens. The temple of Artemis was deeply buried in orange groves and lemon groves. The most interesting layers of ancient Sparta were still hidden in 1963, under the town football pitch. The ancient akropolis was discovered by chance, by a stray Russian army under Orlov that reached this valley in the eighteenth century, with the thought of attacking the Turks at Tripolitsa. The first serious classical visitor was even earlier. He was the crazy Abbé Fourmont, sent by Louis Quatorze. He smashed most of what he discovered, in order to spite his rivals and his successors. There can never have been so very much. Apart from its shrines, classical Sparta was not very classical. It was not so much a city as a congregation of villages. It was notoriously unwalled. The walls are late, and the river has eaten most of them.

The museum was fascinating; I filled page after page of notebook, and was first on the scene at a beautiful mosaic floor which turned up under my astonished eyes on a building site in an old orchard. It took just ten minutes after it was found for the archaeological inspector to take charge. Sparta has a strange history. The Myceneans in the Bronze Age were nearby, but not here, and in the Middle Ages when Sparta was a stony, unregarded hillside, life had moved to the monasteries of Mistra. Mistra is a whole hillside of churches and monasteries, within walking distance of the ruins of ancient Sparta, and of the modern town. I spent the afternoon there, and made friends with a serious German boy who was writing a doctoral thesis, if I remember rightly, about the art historical role of the pheasant.

Mostly I wandered alone. I found Mistra a terrible and beautiful place. The painted plaster, still largely unrestored, carried the scars of village magic and civil war, eyes gouged out of ikons, bullet-holes in walls, and everywhere the dust. All that was left of that labyrinthine sacred world were nine nuns and a bishop's palace. But the variety and richness of the surfaces were overwhelming; the gilt and indigo, the lime white and yellow, the scraps of painted flowers and the faded, ruined saints. White stains and green stains and deep blue stains streaking everything. My inmost desire at that time was embodied in Mistra: to live among classical ruins, disoriented elements, and paintings so old and so scarred that time itself became in them a kind of religion, paintings that annihilated everything but themselves.

I recall fine realistic paintings of flowers as well, iris, lily, anemone, and a flower I was unable to name. And the trees around the sepulchre of Christ had leaves of a strange, almost luminous green. But there was a mutilated face of Christ that entered more deeply into my thoughts; it was rotted and blue-faced, a Christ growling like a wolf. The hillside smelt strongly of catmint and rigani. 'Who painted them? This picture is not part of this building, but this building is part of this picture.' The wish to construct, if only a tenth of a life for ten monks. What monks attempt and imitate in their lives, in their hands, painters in their colour. This painter was both. The outrageous suffering of Oedipus is not different from the rhetoric of suffering of these pictures. That at any rate was how I thought at the time.

Yet Mistra is a luminous place. Apart from the grim fortification on the crest, Mistra is a kind of paradise. The blood of the civil war has washed away, the smoke has cleared, even though four thousand men died in one night. In the fifteenth century this was a beacon of intellectual liberty and light. It was more like a university than a monastery. This was the chosen refuge of Gemistos Plethon, a scholar whose influence on the Italian Renaissance was healthy and vast. Here he wrote in imitation of Plato. Here he compiled the first reliable list of the archaeological sites of the whole of southern Greece, with the modern vernacular name each one. Here he entertained Cyriaco of Ancona, and gave him missing pages for a classical text copied at Constantinople, and sent him out to visit site after site, to draw the monuments and record the inscriptions for the first time. But the mutilated Christ who was like Oedipus is not to be obliterated. We must understand every part of our history. That is a matter of life or death to us. Lord Byron sailed away, and Cyriaco was last heard of reading Livy aloud to the Sultan in his tent, on the nights before Constantinople fell. That building is still a part of that picture.

I stayed on at Sparta for several days, dining in state and sleeping in a small hotel. Notes about what I was reading became pedantic, even scholarly, but in the field 'they say the late city wall has been eaten away by the river. Wandering through orange groves all I found was the slim head of one Doric column.' Sparta was being buried under new buildings or being washed downstream at a frightening rate. Virgilian irrigation systems and Vitruvian cranes for drawing water were some consolation. Sparta has a lushness that most of Greece lacks. Vines straggled in the branches of mulberry trees. A cricket half the size of my hand perched on my piece of bread. Even the front windows of buses carried entanglements of artificial convolvulus, even the front wheel of a bicycle that had only one pedal was a riot of unlikely aritifical flowers.

I was reading about islands in the *Guide Bleu*. I was longing to see the sea again. '*A une heure en barque de Kapsali, île d'Avgo, avec grotte très bleue (phoques et mouettes)*.' Avgo is the Greek for an egg. I had started out with the intention of walking the last, toughest part of the Peloponnese, but all local advice was against it, and time was beginning to run out, and I was indolent. So I never saw Yeraki or Leonidion until years afterwards, and when I finally visited the Mani, it was by air from Athens and by taxi from Kalamata. That is another story. In 1963 I took a last bus to Monemvasia, the Byzantine Gibraltar of southern Greece, a tiny village nestling under a towering rock, and at that time hardly beginning to be ruined by development, as it has been since. All that I can remember of the journey is the dome of a church covered in what looked like tin foil, more dazzling at midday than the sun itself.

5

The End of Summer

IMAGINE AN autumnal or a late summer sea, a little Venetian harbour, a huge rock promontory hardly connected to the land: on its bald brow the ruins of a medieval fortress, abbey churches, the heat, the wind. Monemvasia means 'one way in'. Until 1910 the great gate shut every night, and a wedding procession had to pay to pass through it. The local people call that entrance the Albanian Steps, because their great-grandfathers remembered that an Albanian of the Turkish garrison was shot there in the eighteen-twenties. Monemvasia is also Malmsey. This is where the wine barrels set sail for England in the Middle Ages. No one knows any longer where that wine was grown. This was one of the last and greatest Byzantine fortresses. They held it even after Constantinople fell. At Monemvasia as at Constantinople the trumpets echoing from wall to wall and rock to rock answered the trumpets on the ships. And all that was nothing but an afternoon dream, a pleasure among ruins. The Venetian fragments, the Turkish and the Byzantine houses, and the classical antiquities existed at Monemvasia in a delightful farrago that invited the gentlest of musings. As for the trade with England, it has even stranger details. In the archives of Venice, a permission to sail has survived for three English galleys loaded with marmalade from Crete.

I slept on the Venetian quay, swam constantly, learnt one wine from another, grew used to coriander in the coffee, scrambled about the rock. The sea was deep blue and the sun was brass and the noise of waves came from several directions at once. Twittering squadrons of Alpine swifts soared and whizzed under the cliffs. A donkey peered down from the battlements. I had friends at Monemvasia, it was a kind of holiday. The Venetian and the Turkish monuments had come to seem as exotic to me as they did to the Greeks; they were sports of time. The green light in the great surviving church came from Venetian glass in the white dome. We spent days on beaches of fantastic sea pebbles or picking out the topography of obscure classical sites. My notebook filled up with Byzantine sea-monsters and strange fragments of folklore. There was a memorial service for two young brothers who died cleaning out their own wine-press, overcome by fumes. We ate funeral food, sweetened and spiced barley-grains and honey-sweetened bread.

Iannis Ritsos, the greatest poet of the left in Greece, and I suppose in Europe, was born at Monemvasia in a house like a Cornish fisherman's cottage. I had never met him then, and I knew little of his work, though some of his greatest poems had been published nine or ten years before. The reality of so many people's lives in the last forty years, so much Greek suffering, so much of the grit and gravel of everyday reality is in his poems; he has done more than a novelist and more than a poet for his country. A time was coming when I would understand Ritsos all too well. But not that summer. I left Monemvasia like a satisfied child, on an unromantic iron bathtub of a boat. We were ferried out to it, a moonlit cargo of old ladies and families and chickens and pots of basil. Sometime the next day we landed at Athens.

What was I to do? I luxuriated in European beds and restaurants, spent mornings on the akropolis, afternoons with Nikos Gatsos at Flocca, evenings in the remoter reaches of the Plaka. I read up in libraries things I should have known before setting out. I studied *The Bed-bug, its Life and History*, by Major Austin of the British Museum, but it was fleas that had plagued me, and it was not much use to learn that 'A portable apparatus for the destruction of bed-bugs by means of superheated steam has been described by Kemper.' I found myself unable to keep away from the Byzantine museum and the Benaki museum. The real Greece was taking over my imagination, and the classics were in eclipse. I began to prefer the travels of eighteenth-and nineteenth-century scholars and amateurs to any scientific account of what they found. I was reading 'Erotokritos' for the first time in years.

That extraordinary poem is highly resistant to translation. It was written in Cretan dialect by a Cretan with a Venetian name in the seventeenth century, when Venice held the island. Its plot is romantic and chivalrous, pre-Shakespearean, but the handling of the plot carries it a world away from Italian romance. 'And when the dewy night had put every man to rest and every creature sought a place to sleep, he took his lute and silently he walked, and struck it sweetly, sweetly, under the palace, his hand was sugar, his voice like a nightingale, every heart that heard him wept and poured tears.' Shepherds in Cretan caves still sing 'Erotokritos', all night if necessary. They know its thousands of lines by heart. Children are sung to sleep with it. Even though it has roots in European literature, even though it was published as a book four hundred years ago, it is an epic poem in its way: I mean only that it is used as an epic is used. The revival of modern Greek poetry in this century is founded on the rediscovery of 'Erotokritos' and the folk-songs in the nineteenth. Versions of it exist in Roumanian and in Turkish. The only known manuscript, ten years earlier than the first edition, was sold by a Greek from Corfu to Lord Oxford, the friend of Pope. The revival happened because of the fall of Crete to the Turks. The last survivors of Constantinople had taken refuge in Crete and in the western islands. The survivors of Crete moved west again. In Zakynthos and Kerkyra, or Zante and Corfu, in the eighteenth century, old men sang poems outside the wine-shops such as no one in those civilized islands had ever heard. Solomos, nobleman of Zante educated in Italy, a friend of famous poets, a poet himself in Italian as well as Greek, the admirer of Byron and the national poet of Greece in the war of independance, understood what Greek poetry should be from those tavern singers. 'Erotokritos' has been epic poetry for the Greeks in this also: in the transmission of their language. 'His voice was sugar and his sword was Death.' The word for Death is Charos. Charos is not Charon the ferryman, but an adversary who wrestles with heroes on a marble threshing-floor, as the angel wrestled with Jacob.

I travelled to Aigina, to the sea port and the mountain and the temple of Artemis among the pine trees. It has been struck by lightning since then, and heavily fenced. But on that evening, in that dawn and during that night it was perfectly, tranquilly beautiful. I could have built a nest like a crow and lived there with columns for company. It was a real difficulty about these temples that they were so beautiful. Everything combined to make them so, landscape and height, breezes and trees, the journey and the sea and the air. It was hard to take anything so beautiful perfectly seriously. The savage lines of a fishing boat or the chewed-up remnant of some single column, a thistle even, spoke to me more clearly than these placid and wonderful shapes. I had no appetite to reconstruct the temple on Aigina in the early fifth century, or to categorize its every detail and its every variation. I was more interested then in George Seferis than I was in Pindar. Greece as I knew it in 1963 taught me more than I digested at once. I have been back to Aigina and to Pindar.

So I left the columns in their morning mood of gravity and simplicity, climbed down through the pine trees to swim in the sea, and walked in a few hours across the island to take the ferry-boat home. I must not burden my reader with every museum, every church, every symptom of my restlessness, but I liked the little church at Palaiochora with a notice saying, 'Do not whitewash the frescoes, do not write names on the wall.' Certainly everything else on that island was whitewashed. But the purest whitewash was to come. I was planning a visit to Patmos, an island far to the east, not far from the coast of Turkey. I was not going entirely for religious reasons, but because of the fabled monastic library with its manuscripts. If I meant to be a classical scholar as serious as I then imagined I was going to be, I ought to get some further experience of palaeography, a subject I had neglected for three or four years. And there were things I wanted to see.

In the margin of a manuscript at Patmos someone wrote a small note in the fifteenth century: 'Today the ship came with the Genoese from the City.' That must be the fall of Constantinople to the Turks. When the siege drew towards its inevitable end, only a company of Genoese of all foreigners elected to stay on. They were posted in a tower, and when the city fell, on the night when the Emperor knew it would fall, the tower of the Genoese held out. They held out alone for several days, and at last they negotiated their own surrender on conditions. They were allowed to take their ship and sail away home. That note in the manuscript is the last of Byzantium. For a time the princes clung on in southern Greece, there were still Greek monasteries in the islands and in the mountains. The language never died out. The Aldine press at Venice was a Cretan enterprise. There are Cretan tragedies with the grandeur of Marlowe and a pastoral with the grace of Tasso. But I am glad we have that note about the Genoese.

Patmos needed some preparation, not only some delving into the old catalogue of manuscripts, but a permission from the Ministry of Education to work in the library, and a letter of introduction to the Abbot. While I was waiting for it I spent a happy week in Euboea, on my own at first among the classical sites and in and out of the sea. The sea at Chalkis is tidal; it flows up and down through the arches of the bridge that joins Euboea to the mainland, at a rate of knots. Contemplation of this interesting phenomenon, which is unique in Greece, is supposed to have driven Aristotle to despair and suicide. All that worried me was the sharks. I have seldom seen anything so ominous as those cruising fins you see sometimes from Greek beaches. I saw my first fin off Euboea. I need not have fretted, since ninety per cent of killings by sharks in those waters take place in very shallow water, when the animals are crazed with hunger. A dead shark hauled in by sailors that season had a newly chewed military boot in his stomach. There used to be no sharks in the Mediterranean; they came in from the Suez Canal, following the food thrown overboard from ships.

I recollect so little of Euboea, except the pine woods and the museums, that my journal surprises me. I seem to have dined on octopus, goat cheese, and a tomato salad smothered in onions and salt. I noted that the local retsina suited this curious feast. At night landaus, with jingling bells round the necks of horses, parked for supper outside the tavern. That was in Eretria. I burrowed on hillsides for unregarded monuments, took incompetent notes about a moth, blackish-blue with white spots, and slept on the beach. It was the beginning of the vintage. I visited the Amphiareion, the most lost of oracles, hidden among pines and small hills on the mainland, a little way inland from the sea. Amphiaraus was a prophet whom the earth swallowed up. In certain villages he was a god. He was the arbiter of dreams. Those who consulted him sacrificed a ram and slept in the ram's fleece. His ruined sanctuary is very pretty indeed, and I flung a coin into his holy spring, as the custom used to be. From that spring he is said to have risen up as a god.

People were not well off in Greece in the sixties in places like Euboea. The young despaired at their own mediocre education. 'We don't know letters. You don't say so, but you know it, and I say it isn't a good thing. We don't know our own language. We don't know books.' Fish on the quay cost four shillings a kilo, and with one middleman about seven shillings in a town shop. Olives, with three or four middlemen, moved up from ten or eleven pence a kilo to five shillings or more. As for writers, even a famous poet of less than international reputation, one who had written seven books, would be lucky to sell seventy copies. He might print four hundred, but two hundred would be given away. Prose was in the same doldrums. The girls in the gardens and the dark boys in the sea were growing up in a curious emptiness. The churches were full of glorious deep noises on a Sunday, but none of them had a big congregation that I ever saw. The classics were studied in translation, but it was forbidden by law to translate the gospels into vernacular Greek.

For a week I stayed with friends in a little colony of English houses at Limni, higher up the coast. What pleasure, and what friends. From there I walked away northwards, through olive groves and peach orchards, along the beaches and over the seacliffs to Aidipsos, at the north point of the island. At Aidipsos I found a ferry to Volos, an industrial port on the mainland of unbelievable squalor and beauty, both altered now, where a train ran along the main street. The smell of coal, of filth, of rotting peaches, old fish-crates and fresh roses was something I shall never smell again. It was left over from the nineteenth century. I was in Volos for the museum, with its unique collection of painted gravestones. More painting on flat surfaces has been discovered since, but at that time the tomb of the diving boy at Paestum had not yet come to light.

Even the first of the great Macedonian painted tombs was still unknown and unpublished, and the small archaic paintings from a cave near Corinth were still locked away among the inaccessible secrets in the cellars of the National Museum. To Volos one had to go, and I have never regretted the hours and hours I spent there. It must seem as odd to an outsider as it does to me that original evidence for these immensely influential beginnings of European art is so thin on the ground.

I climbed Mount Pelion, to a village full of plane trees and rushing water, and another near it where the bells in the church tower were a gift from the Greek leather workers of Odessa in the nineteen-hundreds. Never until I read Solzhenitsyn did I understand how many Greeks there were and still are in southern Russia. Hunting on Pelion for the cave where the centaur Cheiron was once worshipped, and where he was supposed to have brought up the young Achilles like Tarzan or the boy Mowgli in Kipling's *Jungle Book*, I learnt a newer, finer repertory of wild flowers and shrubs. On one of those walks I came across an old man and a boy on their way to a village festival. He was a famous clarina player, who walked forty or a hundred and forty miles from one festival to another. We sat by a spring under a tree, and he played for me. The clarina is a pipe with a reed in it. Its range is extraordinary, its music improvised. If the springs in the mountains had a voice, that is how they would sound. It has mobility and a resonance, like that of the loudest bird notes before a thunder-storm, but more so.

From Volos I took a hot, crowded train to a town near the Meteora, a cluster of monasteries on the top of inaccessible elephant-coloured columns of rock on the edge of the Pindus mountains, in a cranny above the plains of Thessaly. That was as far north as I ever got in Greece until 1978. I had no great wish to visit Athos, the holy mountain, where Roman Catholic priests were not viewed with friendly eyes, and no appetite at all to go there in disguise. What was worse, I was rather on the Greek side in the quarrels of Athos with Rome, which it seemed hardly decent to admit, and I had Voltairean reservations about Greek monastic life, so that my friendship would be feigning, my loving mere folly. As it has turned out, I have never found any Greek monk passionately opposed to the Roman Church, except on crazy grounds. The usual objections have been which shoulder you should touch first in the sign of the cross, and why the Catholics take only half an hour to say Mass. These are matters of limited interest.

I went to the Meteora only because they were nearby, and because I liked the idea of a place which you had to reach by being drawn up in a basket. Unfortunately, in 1963 a road had just been built, but I scorned it, and toiled up by obsolete footpaths. All the time I was at the Meteora it seemed to be five in the afternoon or five in the morning, my watch having blocked up with dust during the climb. I found out later that the path I took was that of the founder in 985 A.D. The ikons and the frescoes were fresh-looking and impressive. The crags were all I could wish. Nightfall was thrilling and dawn a revelation. The unrhythmic rhythm of the wooden rising-bell must be one of the subtlest inventions of mankind. Isaac and Jacob on the walls walked in a wild paradise of unearthly pomegranates. But the effect of the whole monastic warren in working order was quite different from that of Mistra. I felt more recognition, more observation of how life might be, fewer deep disturbances.

Down in the plain, old peasants still rode to market on ponies and in national dress. Their breeches and jackets were made from a tough, hairy, dark blue cloth. They wore white woollen leggings and blue kilts. Hats were skull caps; the aprons of women were embroidered in lighter blue on a dark blue-black. The tea was made of mountain herbs freshly gathered and dried for just a few days. The Greeks use more than one kind of herb for tea, I have tasted ten or eleven, but have been told there are sixteen, all of which used to be available in the covered market at Chania in Crete. I never found them all there, and the same herb on different mountains often has a different taste. I have always meant to write a monograph on the subject, or an appendix to a book like this, but I never got to the bottom of it. I do know that the commonest mountain tea is a sovereign remedy for everyday illnesses. Aspirin, after all, was discovered from a willow tea brewed once by village women in England.

In the train back to Volos I travelled with a holy ikon from the

Great Meteoron. So many of the older ikons in Greece have been hacked or burned or mutilated by the Turks, it is small wonder that they were gathered in, or as the legends say, they flew away to monasteries of refuge. There is an air about their intensity and their scars that comes from long years of embittered and secret worship, like the Jewish worship of the Middle Ages. This holy ikon was encrusted in silver in 1907. Once a year it revisits its villages. People crossed themselves in the street when it passed by, and when they saw it in the train, covered up with a cloth, they came to it and gave it money. At Volos there was a fair, with a motorcyclist on a Wall of Death, whom I watched. He seemed very bored. Outside, an old woman was trying to wash three sheep in the sea.

More days in Athens, more city life, night cafés, slices of melon, conversations. My notes on the museums grew shorter but more pungent. I was charting out several lifeworks for the next few years: annotated handlists of sanctuaries, medieval uses of ancient buildings, studies of rituals and dances represented on ancient monuments, the stone palmettes like an infinite desert of flowering thistles. At nights I dreamed about the stars and about sea-caves. Athens was full of a plague of sandflies, imported into the city by an international meeting of boy scouts at Marathon. The hot wind, the Meltemi, had begun to blow. In the British School of Archaeology, people spoke reminiscently of a summer so hot that the Director's wife on an excavation had baked meringues in a tin trunk by simply leaving it out in the sun. Someone told me that grass-snakes smell through their tongues.

My ship to Patmos was called *Marylena*. She pointed her sharp nose to sea and she sailed, with fifty or sixty terns hunting beside her like a pack of beagles, low over the waves. My last drawing was the cape of Sounion, with the temple like a marble toast-rack, as we went by. Sounion is the last or the first point of Attica, and the swell of the big sea begins or ends as you pass it. The temple that survives is Poseidon's, though Pausanias thought it was Athene's. Probably he never landed there; it was a remote spot, and infested with pirates. Falconer found refuge there after his shipwreck, but his ship was unlike ours:

embalmed with orient gum above the wave
the swelling sides a yellow radiance gave.

As a ship, it inspires admiration and nostalgia rather than a sense of security. *Marylena* churned her way solidly along, threading through the islands, imperturbable. The sun sank, the last coloured light drained away after it, the sea darkened to oil. We arrived at Patmos in the darkness.

For the last few hours of the journey I had been passing the time in conversation with two professional strong men, Iannis and Andreas. They were not young, but their whole life was spent in travelling about from island to island, and village to village, breaking chains, bending iron, and lifting one another up in chairs with one hand. Iannis was a serious, melancholy, sententious man. 'Good people make funny faces,' he said. 'They offer you a coffee.' He asked a lot of rhetorical questions about life, its nothingness, the speed of age. He was as sweet-natured as he was philosophic about all those dusty answers. He greatly admired Andreas. Andreas was fiercely devout, he sang church music with passion, he thought of being a priest. He knew scraps of seven languages and he made jokes. 'But this is a holy place,' he said. 'People should tremble, they should weep; faith is a crying, a weeping; people should sing on the roads in this island.' Andreas made endless grotesque funny faces, he proved the existence of God out of Aristotle, he was the sadder of the two, I thought. They were unmarried, they loved each other but they were not lovers. They were small men with huge muscles. I saw their performance later, and it was astonishing.

What imprinted them so deeply in my mind, of all the people I met on that journey, was that later, in the library, I was reading a manuscript of proverbs and witty sayings and moral quotations, some of them ancient but mostly from the late classical world. They were exactly like the philosophizing of Iannis and Andreas. Even some of the jokes were the same. 'And I say this to sum it up: whatever there is useful in the world, whatever keeps the world together and makes rational beings different from mindless animals, it is all the gift and the glory of winter.' Planudes said that; so did Andreas. 'How long should a man live? Until he sees that death is better than life.' Aristides is supposed to have said that. So did Iannis. 'We shouldn't stir up our language with anger, we should calm down our anger with language.' Aristippos is supposed to have said that, but I have heard Andreas say it.

Patmos is a small simple island of plain physical beauty. It has an upper village clustered around the monastery, and a seaport where no very big ship could anchor. There was no hotel, though there were two or three taverns in the port. I went at once to one in a back street, which was probably the poorest, certainly the quietest. They all had the same food, which was entirely a matter of the catch and the season. The people of the tavern found me a room immediately. It was in the whitest of white houses; I slept there in the marriage bed, and when I left the owner's wife gave me a present of her own embroidery to take home to my mother. On the first evening a little boy asked me how I got to Greece. 'In a ship,' I said. 'I know,' he answered, 'chutt, chutt, chutt,' imitating a motorboat. 'What is London like?' asked a bigger boy. 'Terribly dirty and noisy,' I told him, 'Ah yes. Just like Leros.'

The monastery was in the grip of some sort of power-struggle. It hardly affected me, except that the most formidable and youthful of the senior monks resented my permission to use the library. Mostly, I dealt with charming, very old men, who beamed and chuckled and encouraged me. One of the manuscripts I wanted was bound up in one volume with a work of Saint Gregory. This pleased them greatly. They asked me how old it was. When I told them they clucked with horror at all the dead centuries and took to banging the book to remove its dust, so that I had to rescue it. I worked in a small room on the monastery roof, which I shared with three or four Greek scholars from Athens, who were making a new catalogue. The work was absorbing. I had not set out to make any new discoveries, but I did find an unrecorded, longer version of one of the apocryphal accounts of the childhood of Christ. It was in a late medieval manuscript; I thought it fascinating that those unlikely tales were still being elaborated at the very end of the Middle Ages.

What got me into trouble later was the manuscript of Reader's Digest witticisms and pithy moral remarks. Some of these sayings were attributed to great writers; for all I knew, one or other of these attributions might even be genuine. In that case, since the manuscript had never been published, I might be reading stray unpublished lines of Menander or Euripides. I was morally bound to tell some experienced scholar that this treasure existed, however suspicious I was of it. Someone would have to notice it in print. Alas, the letter I wrote was compressed by justified modesty into ambiguity, and was misunderstood. After one or two warning thunderclaps of correspondence, I received a cloud-burst, the most furiously angry and effectively crushing letter I have ever had; 'Never again,' it said, 'until we see once more the learning of a Wachsmuth or a Reitzenstein, shall we ever begin to understand the complicated history of these manuscripts. And for yourself is it not time that you turned your attention to some small task within your capabilities, by which you might in the course of many years make some small contribution to classical scholarship?'

But that was in the future, it was the voice of the grime and fog, the Oxford mid-November in which even Zeus has bad dreams. Life on the island was cheerful in late August. I have never lived for so long on so small an island. At mid-afternoon the hills were green and stony, in the evening they turned yellow and the sea glittered darkly. Samos appeared on the horizon in a milk-white mist. In the evening the harbour was a string of warm yellow lights. In the morning at the top of the island the wind and the sea gave the whole place the sensation of the bridge of a petrified ship, but at mid-day it was like two or three hills from somewhere like Chipping Norton towed out to sea and abandoned for thousands of years. In the dusk, people paced around the square with the deliberate patience of zoo animals. That was where Iannis and Andreas gave their performance, to the whole population. It was a great success. Later at night, under the street-light outside my tavern, two or three sailors danced. Then a tall saturnine man took over, dancing alone with dignity and passion, as fluid and as dark as a shadow. He was a ship's engineer. No one knew him, but whenever he called at Patmos he danced under that light.

There were three cars on Patmos, all of them taxis, but I used to walk twice a day between the monastery and the harbour, by a stone-paved donkey-track that took a simpler route up the hillside, past the cave of the revelation of Saint John. 'I, John, who also am your brother, was in the isle that is called Patmos, for the word of God, and for the testimony of Jesus Christ. I was in the Spirit on the Lord's day, and heard behind me a great voice, as of a tumpet.' He was in exile, that is, where he could do no harm. Classical and Roman Patmos have left almost no trace; they can hardly have existed. The cave is a great grey sea-cave halfway up a small mountain. For most of the year the whole island is isolated in a circle of mist or haze, as if only this island and a few others existed, as if the light here were the only patch of sunlight in the world. In the early morning and at nightfall this light is dramatic.

The cave is full of flowers, like a conservatory with canaries in cages. It opens to the east, and before it was levelled it must have been a wild place. But it looks down at the sea and the harbour channel. Nowhere else on the island is so peaceful. There used to be a French hermit in a cave somewhere on Patmos, whose only books were the psalms of David and the works of Rimbaud. But this was a big cave, and it must always have been near whatever life there was on Patmos, and the Revelation of John, magnificent as it is, is not a wild book. Inside his cave, they show you a hollow in the rock where they say John lay to sleep, and a crack in the rock-face they say was left there after his vision. They also show you runnels in the floor which everyone on the island agrees ran with sharp-scented water like rose-water or lemonflower-water until thirty years ago. I found out later that travellers spoke of that in the seventeenth century:

'They add more, that as he was beginning the Works, there happened a great Thunder and Earthquake, whereupon, looking up to Heaven he spake those words; In the beginning was the Word. Besides, it is a most confirmed Tradition, that the Cavern, which now goes by the name of the Holy Grotto, was made by the Rupture of the Earth, in that Earthquake.' There were stranger stories still. A fig tree nearby had the word revelation written in Greek inside every fig. A stone basin near the cave was the font where John was baptized. He did battle with a magician called Cynops, which was the name of a mountain on Patmos. A man let down into a cave on that mountain was drawn up dead. 'The name of Cynops the Magitian, is known to all the People to this day; yea, not without some very improbable circumstances of the Story, that St John should cause him to jump twice into the Sea, and the second time to be turned into a Rock, which now bears his name.'

And yet I was convinced by that holy cave. I could understand that book written in it. 'From before whose face earth and heaven fled away, and no place was found for them. And I saw the dead, the great and the small ... and the earth that was has passed away, and the sea is no longer.' I could understand the wailing of the merchants at the fall of the great city, and the bitter denunciation of it by the angel that 'cried mightily with a strong voice'. No one can understand the ancient world who neglects the Revelation of John. Patmos is a very innocent island. It has three thousand inhabitants; in 1963 there was only one wealthy holiday house, and that was discreetly tucked away. In the early morning old women carried incense to churches where there was no service. In the afternoon a fisherman lay down to sleep on his own nets in the shade beside his three-year-old son. Basil grew everywhere in pots. The countryside was swarming with tiny lizards. A young lad told me quite casually in the square that the face of John had been seen to appear in the sea-hollowed hole where he used to sleep.

'It was there for about ten days.'

'When?'

'Oh, two or three years ago now.'

'Who saw it?'

'Oh, we all did. He did, I did, all of us here.'

One morning we were disturbed at work among the manuscripts on our rooftop by the very loud ringing of the monastery bells. An English ship, a destroyer or maybe a frigate, called *Surprise*, was paying a goodwill visit to the eastern islands of the Mediterranean. She dwarfed the island. On board was the British Ambassador, and here he came, in a procession of all three taxis, to see the monastery. I won a bet with the Greek palaeographers as to which of the figures he was. The naval officers wore elegant uniforms, and for such a state reception as this they were convinced the Ambassador would wear the grandest clothes of all. He had a pink bald head, an open-necked shirt, and trousers of a gentlemanly antiquity.

That day the island was full of young officers. I rescued some from a donkey-man at the cave of Saint John and offered them dinner by the harbour. They were extremely courteous and friendly. One of them asked if we might have a drink of ouzo, which he had always heard of but never tasted. He had been three years in the Mediterranean. I was asked back to the ship for a gin and tonic the next day. While I waited I became an agent for some fishermen in trouble. They owned a big, white fishing boat that worked these waters, and its engine had broken down. It needed a new exhaust pipe. They had the pipe, but there was no machinery for cutting it on Patmos. They would have to make Leros under sail, or maybe Samos, unless the British warship could help them. In negotiating this, I got to speak to some sailors on an hour or two of shore leave. Of course they would help. But did I know anywhere they could buy some of the ouzo the Greeks drink, in as big a bottle as possible, to smuggle it on board? Boatload after boatload departed with its bottle.

I came to hate the idea of leaving Patmos. There was hardly a lemon on the island, and honey had not come into season yet; you ate and drank whatever there happened to be, which was not much. But the ikons in the monastery were the real thing at last, formidable and sophisticated works of art such as no museum in the world possesses outside Russia, I suppose. And there were the manuscripts, there was swimming in the sea, which was deep in the harbour channel, there were evening conversations. There were a few Byzantine ruins, a few Venetian doorways. In the country sheep and goats ran together with their bells jangling. I had fallen into a routine in which one could live. But the year was getting late. The vine leaves that the light parted were yellow and brown, as if the leaves and the sun itself were melting. The last boat in the season was due, and I had to take it.

She was called *Kanaris*. She arrived several hours late after a rough passage from Samos. I had spent the day as usual; then in the evening I sat outside the cave of the revelation, drawing the landscape, and rode down the hill on a gentle bay pony called

Astroula, Little Star. The sun was slipping away. The wait for the ship was endless, and at the last moment I was suddenly arrested by the police. What had I been doing at the monastery? Had I been buying manuscripts from the monks? My sack was emptied and I was carefully searched. What was this notebook? If it was a journal, why did it contain writing in Greek? No foreigner can write Greek. This dialogue or monologue continued for so long that I very nearly missed *Kanaris*. I think I was released only because of the bore of holding me. I was driven out to *Kanaris* in a police launch.

Even in harbour she wallowed. Further out the sea was rough and starlit. The hot wind seemed to be lifting the old boat without any action of the water. I was travelling on deck, but there was no room. The main deck was completely carpeted with people, some of them groaning, some smoking, most of them seasick with green faces and blank eyes. On the quayside I could still hear an old woman screaming. She was losing her grandson, who was going to serve as a soldier. She rolled about on the ground, she tore her hair. Her family watched her respectfully. Some of the performances of the old ladies I was stepping over were almost in the same class. Two of them were fighting for space. One of them, having settled her considerable bulk, was unpacking a picnic on the chest of her neighbour. I made for the rusted iron ladder which led to the upper deck.

By that time the main deck was sealed behind me. People had closed ranks and settled down. The ship was under way. As the first terrific lurch sent a shower of spray high into the air like fireworks, I emerged at the top of the ladder. The upper deck was worse overcrowded than the lower deck. There was one place I hoped might be empty, and it was. I climbed with difficulty over the superstructure of bars that might in balmier days have supported a canopy. The next morning, I was not able to see how I had done this, nor am I now, but it got me to a lifeboat, and sure enough, between the boat, which rested on the deck, and the edge of the ship, there was room for one person to lie down. There was no railing of course, and the sea was heaving considerably, and unfortunately, to make the lifeboat easier to launch, this bit of the deck sloped downwards towards the water.

I contrived to tie myself in place by knotting a stray rope from the lifeboat round the feet of my sleeping-bag, and tying the upper part to a rail with my shirt. It was a most fearful night, but I slept. The worst moments were when the waves broke right over the ship, and I woke with my face full of seawater. God knows what it was like on the main deck, but whenever I woke I could hear the groaning. It was a bitch of a sea, like the flood by Tintoretto. Dawn had a fearful beauty, as you might expect, but it found us far from anywhere. There was nothing to eat on *Kanaris*, not even coffee, and we were now eight hours overdue. It was the Meltemi, the end-of-season wind. The sun blazed, the sea heaved, *Kanaris* rolled and tossed and pitched. There was nothing to be done about it.

My supplies consisted of a small block of Kendal mint cake and a big mug of water, and it was a quarter to seven in the evening before we got ashore. The last straw was docking at Athens. There was a crowd waiting, and a wire barrier, which was moveable. We docked in the usual place, but one of the gangways would have been outside the barrier. The police insisted the ship should move. The captain insisted we should land. The police maintained one gangway was not enough. The captain maintained they should shift their barrier. This argument lasted for one hour and three-quarters. I have forgotten how it ended; I think the captain won. I will say that the Greek passengers behaved perfectly. They were ironic, a little caustic, and to one another friendly and polite. They were not bored. They treated the quarrel as connoisseurs of such quarrels, grinning judiciously over all its aspects.

All the same, they do lose their tempers in that wind. Later that evening I read in the papers an account of an incident that occurred that very day in Athens. A young policeman had been on guard in one of the Ministry buildings in the middle of the city. They close at twelve, but someone always wants to get in at the last moment. With a lot of trouble he had just managed to get the reception area cleared. He had physically pushed the last clients out of the glass doors, the doors were locked, he was on the inside running his finger round his collar, and they were on the outside shouting and knocking. At this moment a full General arrived outside and ordered the policeman to open up. In Greece the police have or had to take the orders of the Army; they are part of it. So everyone got in again. A deputy minister came down the stairs and observed this. He was furious. He asked the policeman his name and stormed across to a telephone to complain about him. The policeman shot him dead, and then five more times for luck. It was an extremely hot day. They gave the policeman a sentence of three months, and then transferred him to somewhere cooler.

It was my last week in Athens. I spent it sitting in the coolest places I could find. The Hilton, where the air-conditioning can give you a cold, had not been built, and anyway it was not my style. Flocca was the only air-conditioned café, and there I sat day after day with Nikos Gatsos. Late at night we sometimes met again for dinner, but you could feel the Meltemi out of doors even under the branches in the oldest garden restaurants. The house where George Seferis lived was cool, and I saw him more than once that week. He told me about the funeral of Venizelos, the liberal prime minister who did so much for Greece between the wars. He was buried in Crete, the ship was hung all over with black cloth, and all the small boats that went with it in the early morning light seemed like a Venetian argosy. The soldiers lining the road stood to attention with tears streaming down their faces. It was spring, and the whole island smelt of spring. People had given the lemon blossom and the orange blossom of entire orchards.

My archaeological drawings were a little more selective, a little more precise, and the unanswerable questions jotted underneath them were at least worth asking. At Kaisariani, a spring that Ovid, of all people, made famous, in the ruins of a monastery on the lower slopes of Hymettos, I thought I spotted the fragments of a Hadrianic temple. Looking at the drawings now, I imagine these marbles must have been carved six hundred years earlier, but I still have no idea what building they come from. Fine decorative stones were prized and built into later buildings in every century down to the nineteenth or the twentieth. Sounion was easier; things may have moved away or broken or got lost, but nothing has arrived there from elsewhere since the end of antiquity. At Sounion I was pleased with the discovery of a marble Hadrianic lavatory seat sticking out of a cliff. It was also at Sounion that I first encountered a sea-cave which had to be approached by swimming. And it was there I found scraps of fifth-century pottery, that inimitable glistening beetle-black, on an unexcavated mound which is supposed to be much later.

There are places I went that I have not mentioned at all. There are many where I determined not to go because I now knew, with absolute certainty, that I must come back. I had a horror of overcrowding my head with too many impressions. I had seen plenty of Byzantine Greece, plenty of classical Greece, plenty of countrysides, an island or two and a number of small, neglected places. If I had taken on Mycenae and Tiryns and Epidauros and Corinth and Delos and Crete, I would have lost credibility in my own eyes. At Rhamnous and Marathon and Eleusis, all of which are close enough to Athens for a day-trip, I did little more than ponder among fragments, asking myself questions that only long and thorough research could have answered.

Already I was more and more drawn into the permanent life of the city of Athens. It was no longer just exciting; I had a number of friends, mostly writers and artists and musicians, much as I had in London. Their conversation taught me a lot. For one thing, their Greek was at least as subtle and motionable as French or English or Italian, and I soon found out that it was by no means as easy to hold one's own in Greek in an Athenian café as it is among shepherds or young people in the country. To say I was suffering a tension which underlies all modern Greek literature is to put it too high. I knew too little Greek. At the end of that summer I could only just survive a conversation in Greek without delaying it. The hardest test I set myself was an hour alone with Manos Hadzidakis, the composer. He has or used to have a thick Piraeus accent and very few teeth. At the same time he is extremely clever, easily bored, and talks fast. I thought I passed this test, but I never dared ask what Manos thought.

Later, year by year, I had a recurring experience which perhaps I ought to record. The first time it lasted two or three days, but every later time it grew less, until nowadays I scarcely notice it. After a few weeks in Greece, I had an afternoon or so of deepening depression, paranoia and despair about the language. The first time I went home from Flocca and wept. That night I sweated with nightmare, but towards morning I began to dream quite calmly and easily in Greek. The next day I woke happily, and decided to write poetry in Greek. For a time I never showed these poems to anyone, but when I had enough confidence in them I did show them. They usually contain mistakes of some kind, but in principle they are just like the poems I might write in English. Later, I tried translating one, and it came out easily in English as if it were a poem by me, not like other translations I have done.

But in that August I was not writing poetry in any language. I was learning a new style, or I thought I was. I learnt it mostly from Nikos Gatsos, but the whole of these journeys contributed. What surprised me when I got home to England and started to write was an obsession with the sea. I had seen a lot of it, here and there, that summer. I suppose I knew the sea already, in England, in Wales and in Scotland. The sea was a childhood friend and an adult passion, if any passions are adult. But even though I was not conscious of noticing it very much in Greece, it had touched something deep.

'The Meltemi has dropped.'

I heard it as I walked down from the akropolis for the last time. I took a taxi to the Piraeus, which by now was as familiar as Victoria Station, and went on board my ship. She was a Russian ship called *Litva*, bound for Marseille. I had seen that day the National Museum, the Parthenon, and several other monuments. *The Times*, which I took on board with a copy of *Huckleberry Finn*, was cock-a-hoop about a new British archaeological triumph. They had discovered a rutted Roman cart-track somewhere in Kent with sandal-studs still sticking in it. Sir Maurice Bowra used to say that British archaeologists are the only ones in the world so virtuous that they actually prefer to dig where they won't find anything.

The *Litva* sailed, the hammer and sickle floated, and I started on *Huckleberry Finn*. The ship was full of French trade unionists on a package tour. They had discovered that the waitresses, who were Russian students, were not allowed to speak to them under any provocation whatever. The result was an orgy of bottom-pinching during every meal. The ship's bursar attempted to convince me that there were no angels and therefore no God. But the worst thing of all was the banality of the piped music. I got so bored with that ship I deserted at Naples. The last notes of my journey are about fish in the Naples aquarium. One called *Loligo vulgaris* has eyes in his behind and can move sideways as well as forwards. The Russians ought to use them as waitresses.

6

Begin Again

I<small>T WAS A</small> difficult winter. The snow fell as it always does. The journey in Greece, and the houseparty and the mushroom-picking in the autumn in France that followed it, diminished into a vision, something hardly related to my less real life in north Oxfordshire. One evening in October, I think it was October, I went into Oxford to an evening of subdued social grandeur and there, as she came down the stairs, I recognised the love of my life. We recognised each other. But it certainly never occurred to me we would one day be married, as now we are. I thought simply and suddenly, there is the only woman I have met I could love for ever and might, if things had been otherwise, have married. But I was still determined to be an acceptable clergyman, and in that course I persisted for fifteen more years. This story is, strictly speaking, irrelevant to what I have to say about Greece, but its omission would leave to much of what is relevant unexplained. Or so I see matters. If my life had no unconscious driving force in those years, then this book has none.

I started again to write verse. As a five-finger exercise I began 'Thirty ways of looking at the sea'. The title was a parody of Wallace Stevens' 'Thirteen ways of looking at a blackbird', but the plan was to write a little poem a day for thirty days. I stumbled on something serious, the poems took over, and they were finished in much less than three weeks. Meanwhile I had also begun what became 'Pancakes for the Queen of Babylon', dedicated to Nikos Gatsos.

That took two years. It went terribly slowly. In whatever sense one poem can be more experimental than another, it was an experiment, but it was not an adequate equivalent of the 'Amorgos' of Gatsos, which is an incomparable poem:

> That is how the grape goes dry deep inside the pot and the apple turns yellow in the bell-tower of a fig tree
> That is how in a tawdry cravat
> The summer is breathing in a tent of vine-leaves
> That is how quite naked among white cherry trees my darling sleeps a girl unwithering as the branch of the almond tree
> With her head at rest on the crook of her arm and her hand on her golden coin
> On its warmess in the morning, when quietly quietly like a thief from the window of the spring comes in the morning star that shall awaken her.

It was 1965 before I got back again to Greece, first in the summer, having somehow conquered four of five weeks on the way to an excavation in Libya, and then in winter for three months as a student at the British School of Archaeology at Athens. Every winter after that for ten or twelve years I worked in Greece. My self-appointed task was a translation of Pausanias with a long archaeological and topographic commentary, and to learn as much as I could about my subject. Of course this vast undertaking altered greatly as it progressed. The scale of the commentary grew and grew. I became enthralled by the earlier travellers, first by Frazer, then by W. M. Leake, then by the obscurest of writers and the most unregarded crumbs of information. Meanwhile I began to explore Athens and Attica more thoroughly, until that in itself looked like a lifetime's work; and to spend a week at a time at every spot where Pausanias raised a problem, all over southern and central Greece. In the library at Athens I wanted the better libraries of Oxford; at Oxford I wanted Greek museums and Greek sites; in the field I wanted books, and among books every avenue led to more travelling.

The work proceeded sideways as much as forwards, and in fits and starts, like the progress of a drunken crab. At the end of five years I was back at the beginning, knowing better how to begin, covering the same ground in different ways.

Sometimes there was a gift of chance, an unregarded inscription or an ancient road, the hint of a lost sanctuary, and once an unexplored ancient city, lost on a shrubby hillside not far from one of the main railway lines of southern Greece. The ideal time and the ideal conditions for the sort of archaeological survey I was attempting were the years and conditions of William Martin Leake. He came to Greece younger than I was, as a British Artillery Officer to advise the Turkish governors on the defences of what was then European Turkey against the French. He was clear-headed, well educated and professionally capable. Pausanias was his guide-book. He travelled where he chose, on horseback with an escort of soldiers, and spent what time he chose on his researches. At the age of thirty-three he was back in London with his pockets full of careful journals and a pension of six hundred pounds a year from a grateful Britain. His publicly recorded career is fascinating, but his papers, which have survived in some number, add enough to make it astonishing.

He was born in Mayfair in 1777 and lived to be eighty-three. His father was Chester Herald and a member of the Commission for auditing the public accounts. His grandfather was a Captain Martin of the navy who adopted the name Leake from his brother-in-law, a distinguished admiral under whom he fought and whose heir he became. Young Leake studied at Woolwich; he was sent out to Constantinople at twenty-two to instruct Turkish gunners against the French and took the opportunity to explore classical sites in the Levant. In 1801 and 1802 he worked on a survey of Egypt with W. R. Hamilton, secretary to Lord Elgin. They sailed homewards from Athens with the Elgin Marbles on board. Their ship was wrecked off Kythera, and it was Leake, pistol in hand, who saved the lives of the crew by suppressing a panic. It was also Leake who sent down divers at once to rescue the marbles. His own Egyptian notes were lost, but Hamilton's were saved. Leake was twenty-five years old.

On his second visit he carried secret instructions from Canning and an order to British ships signed by Nelson aboard *Victory*. From February 1805 to February 1807 he worked in southern Greece, but

Turkey then entered the war, and Leake was imprisoned in Saloniki. He escaped and made a secret rendezvous with Ali Pasha somewhere on the western coast of Epiros, where he negotiated the withdrawal of Turkey from hostilities. Leake was thirty. He then served two years as British resident at Ali Pasha's court at Ioannina, completing his northern Greek researches and his collections of coins and inscriptions, and no doubt at the same time his survey of naval timber in Greek forests. He left Greece at thirty-three. His last employment was in 1815, which he spent as British adviser to the United Swiss armies on the French border. He had just published his first book, a study of the modern Greek people and their language. He was thirty-six and his active career was over. For the rest of his life he lived at Nottingham Place in London, producing books of growing authority, the best of them in his fifties. Edward Lear and Matthew Arnold wrote to him with gratitude and deference. He was covered with honours. He published his last work on Greek topography at the age of eighty, *A Study of Disputed Questions.*

Much of the evidence available to Leake's generation no longer exists. Where it does exist he is still quite often the best guide to it. The authority of his work is almost undiminished; he was very seldom wrong, but his arguments are so clear that nothing he claims needs ever to be taken for granted. Unfortunately, soon after his lifetime, a brilliant school of younger German scholars with little field experience of Greece set to work on Pausanias from a different point of view. Their presupposition was that such a late writer must be unreliable, he must have been merely repeating the opinions of others. That accusation is as true of modern classical scholars as it is of Pausanias, but his German critics did succeed in disentangling many of the debts he owed; my experience has been that there are more to be discovered. Still, Pausanias had the advantage over Leake that Leake has over us. He had seen the antiquities of nearly all Greece in a far better condition than anyone has done since. He had roads, horses, cities, libraries and friends. Leake's line of interpretation was fundamentally right, and modern archaeology, which is concerned with realities and not romance, has confirmed it substantially.

If only Pausanias had not told two lies in his very first paragraph. He approaches Athens by sea, and the first thing he passes is Sounion. There on the promontory, he says, stands the ancient temple of Athene. The same temple is still there, but excavation earlier in this century has shown without a doubt that the real temple of Athene at Sounion, which had stood just out of sight of the sea, no longer existed when Pausanias sailed past. It had been moved stone by stone, and re-erected in the centre of Athens. I suppose that Pausanias never landed at Sounion. The place was very likely dangerous, and perhaps that was why the temple was moved. It was not the only provincial temple to be shifted bodily into Athens under the Roman Empire. You can see the Roman lettering on numbered blocks of a fifth century marble building that seems to have come from Acharnai.

The second lie is easier to explain and needed no excavations to establish. After Sounion, he says, you pass the silver mines. But in fact the mines lie far inland, and the best approach is not from this coast at all. The solution to this problem is that Laurion, where the silver mines were, was a district, not a place. It had no official centre with sanctuaries and political rights, because its workmen were almost all slaves. It would be possible to get to the mines from the coast near Sounion. An abandoned jetty from modern mine-workings still exists there, and high up the mountainside of the Pente Vigles, the Five Watches that stand behind Sounion, I have seen slag from the ancient mines that must once have dropped from the back of a mule. I spent a lot of time round and about Sounion; so far as I know no other ancient landscape has left so many traces of itself. There are the remains of watch-towers, little fortresses of rough stone, an ancient road like a drovers' track which survives for a mile or two, and a number of ruins of fortified farms. By the fourth century BC a farm was often called a tower. It is easy in that landscape to understand why.

In the countryside I was often alone. I stayed in a series of strange hotels, went to the pictures in flea-pits, got to know the language and the life of the provinces, learnt what every traveller learns about himself, about police stations and bus stations and markets and bureaucracy. The bureaucracy was worse than the hotels. The Greek archaeological service is understaffed, comtemptibly ill-paid, and ridiculously over-extended. I can remember a time when one man with no car had to cover something like a quarter of the Peloponnese, which included two huge Byzantine settlements, some important classical cities and sanctuaries, and many isolated monuments. He was also in charge of all museums and all excavations in his area, including rescue excavations. He was responsible for every period of archaeological interest from the Stone Age to the nineteenth century. He was also expected to write and publish. Jobs were few and the service was highly competitive. The most active members of the service die young of heart-failure.

Things have got a little better, but it is small wonder that organizations like the British School, which has not always been wise or tactful or decent, are often to be found groaning with frustration over bureaucracy. Its members are a series of new brooms from privileged universities. Its directors are a series of grandly constructed experienced brooms. As the preoccupations and the techniques of archaeology alter, they have their first effect in the cupboard of new brooms. In this broom cupboard, Greek as well as English, I learnt a great deal as time went on. One can learn more about archaeology than about most subjects from conversations and journeys and a reading-list that is always too long. In specialised libraries one learns a lot from the scholar at the next desk.

But *homo academicus* is an eccentric species. There was the hammer and tongs lady. There was an ancient baldheaded expert who looked like Alastair Sim and spoke mostly in ironic whispers. There was a girl who wept quietly over folio pages of medieval Greek, which no one had taught her how to translate. There was a young man of ferocious learning with a handlebar moustache, whose three passions were Bronze Age war, Viking war, and the true history of the Wild West. But his underlying dedication was to accuracy and his career has prospered. Then there was the boy everyone loved who plunged into the Greek countryside like a dolphin into the sea, who had the most Greek friends and spoke the best Greek, who had not a talent but a genius for his subject, but who could never finish any piece of work. He was too busy helping other people with theirs. He was saved at the last moment by an unlikely stroke of fate, and found the perfect job.

Having Greek friends was certainly the key to a happy life. My own spread out in circles from Pyrgos and from Flocca. The chief Pyrgos friends in Athens were Takis Sinopoulos, a famous poet who worked as a doctor in a poor district, and Takis Loumiotis, a lawyer with a Dionysiac laugh, both childhood friends of George Pavlopoulos. I loved Sinopoulos as one can only love that kind of friendliness and directness, and such a secret volcano of intellectual clarity and passionate disturbance, but also as one loves one's doctor. The literary politics of Athens are ferocious, and I had no wish to take part, but I observed with awe the stamina and enthusiasm of the readings and discussions which I sometimes attended with my new friend, and the force of the animosities. It was a world away from Gatsos and Seferis. Those two were like Chinese sages under pine trees on their own mountain. This was like a Soho of poets replanted in a more generous soil, flowering as that withered garden never flowered before. It was funnier than Soho, but just as frightening.

With Takis Loumiotis I travelled everywhere. He was the most courteous and thoughtful friend, the most obliging and loving that I could have had. Wherever we went, he had a client. On arrival, we divided up for him to see his client and for me to spy out antiquities. We met again for lunch in whitewashed taverns perched on mountainsides, for experiments in the finest and obscurest wines in the Peloponnese. We drove where no track was, we bumped across fields, we jumped like goats from rock to rock among ancient fortifications. We tested routes, we improved on the map, we followed our noses. We found a peasant breaking up a pillar to make a salt-grinder, a hoard of prehistoric pottery tumbling out of a hillside, and an early walled town where no one had noticed it, a little inland and uphill from the late classical town that looks towards the sea.

That was at Sikyon. It was the only time I ever danced in Greece. We arrived late in the afternoon, two days before I was due to leave for England. I was determined to see Sikyon, but something had delayed us and the sun was falling. Takis spotted the local policeman walking out from the village towards the ruins and the museum. We stopped and offered him a lift. He climbed in happily and lit up a cigarette. He was on his way to close up the monuments for the night. A little early, but with so few tourists at this time of year what did it matter? Of course we could see everything. He would show us round. Or he would sit on a stone and wait. Sikyon is a beautiful, uncomplicated place. Dark grey stones lie like a ground plan in symmetrical order among flourishing grass. The city was built all at once, to a single plan by a Hellenistic prince, and the buildings are placed just as Pausanias describes them. The museum is full of small exciting terracottas from a cave in the mountains. We walked out in the sunset to a field above the antiquities, where the deeply coloured grass of spring was thickly scattered with wild grape-hyacinth. Its proper name is *muscari commutatum*, but the villagers call it 'bulbs'. It tastes like a sour onion. I had never seen a whole field before of those dense and fragrant blue spires.

Back at the village we sat outside the only tavern and offered the policeman a drink. He was allowed outside, but not inside. As it grew dark we moved inside to find something to eat. But now we must be his guests, so he moved inside too. The wine was not all bad, there was nothing to eat, so he sent a boy out for some lamb. The tavern began to fill up. We exchanged life histories, cigarettes, English snuff, jugs of wine. Everyone was laughing. Someone turned on the juke-jox. Dancing started, then everyone was dancing and laughing at once, some of them with cigarettes in their mouths, some with glasses in their hands. Plates and beer-bottles flew and smashed under the feet of the best dancers. This is a tribute: they dance on among the fragments unperturbed and you pay for your breakages. At that time it was already an illegal custom. Wine-drinkers accepted beer from other tables, beer-drinkers accepted wine. The whole village was crammed into one room. I danced for three hours without halting. It was all very innocent, but we drank the tavern completely dry.

'Let us go now,' someone said, 'to the bouzoukis.' 'To the night-club of the tourists.' 'To the hotel on the coast.' 'To the women and the bouzoukis.' 'Let us all go.' We roared down the hillside in one small car containing nine people. When Takis saw the road he had driven next morning and remembered his speed, his face turned paper-white. The bouzoukis were appallingly noisy and inexpert, and I think it was out of season for the dancing women, or we went to the wrong place. We got to bed at two, in the policeman's house, and we could hear his infuriated wife telling him off as we went to sleep. When we woke at ten she was still telling him off. They gave us walnuts and honey for breakfast, a good remedy. My head felt like a football. I needed a very long walk. That was how we discovered the ancient walls, and the fields full of early Corinthian pottery. For a year or two I used to exchange Christmas cards with that adorable policeman.

Takis brought me very good luck. He soon knew as much as I did about what to look for and where to find it, and I learnt from him how to proceed in villages. We seldom ran across illegal excavation or illegal trading in antiquities, though we did observe it here and there. Simple people are often pathetically eager to get rid of an old stone to a foreign expert who values it. There was an old lady in Crete who wanted to give me the head of a statue. I made the usual explanations about the law, and about these things belonging to the Greek people, but she said, 'It's only an old stone.' I said, 'It looks beautiful in your garden.' 'Take it, have it in your own garden. I am too old for it.'

'If you really don't want it, you should give it to the police.' 'They don't want it.' 'To the museum.' 'In the bus? I am too old for the bus.' I hope it is still where I first saw it.

Once we missed by a fortnight the evidence that might have pinpointed a lost sanctuary of Artemis. I was looking for that sanctuary, about which there are many opinions but no certainties. Pausanias visited it, and everyone knows the general area where it must be. When Takis and I arrived, we heard that an old woman gathering herbs had found a bronze statue of a deer, about two feet from nose to tail, and sold it for a pound to someone in the village. A fortnight ago the illegal buyer from Athens had made his regular visit, and the bronze deer had disappeared in the direction of the international art market at a price of three pounds ten shillings. No one will ever find the old woman, no one will ever identify the spot except by chance. When any archaeologist, myself included, claims to have discovered a new classical site, he usually means that he asked a shepherd on the mountain or a labourer in the fields or an old man at night in the tavern.

Sometimes you can get to know a village very well, almost become part of it, by living there for a time. But the bush of friendships and village connections has to be watered to flourish and survive. A few years later the whole climate and social geography may have altered. Unfortunately for me, I was always having to move on. The rewards of sitting down in one place were astonishing. The first place I remember them was Ligourio, near the great shrine of Asklepios at Epidauros. Asklepios was a god of healing, of miracles and dreams and holy snakes. His sanctuary was an elaborate marble rotunda standing on a hidden stone labyrinth, surrounded by temples of grandeur and beauty, and a stadium for games. His miracles were inscribed on stone by those who were cured. It is hard to separate sleep and dreams from anaesthetics and surgery, but surgery certainly took place at Epidauros; the instruments have been found there.

The life of Ligourio in my time there was simple and agricultural. In the morning the animals went out to graze and the mules and the donkeys set off into the olive groves. I was woken every day by the sound of flocks and of bells in the main street. At evening as I came home the animals and the family processions were winding inwards to the village from every direction. I came to know the shepherds on every hillside. The landscape was full of them, each one with a huge umbrella and a transistor radio playing music in the rain. There were three cafés in the village, one for shepherds and socialists, one for monarchists, and one, more dismal but more solid, for Greek Americans. Exploring the countryside hill by hill I came across site after site, most of them uninteresting to me, but some startling. There was an inscription, which someone has published since, to Zeus, master of the Fates, and there were well preserved ancient roads in a mountain valley leading down towards the sea. I still have my notes of all those places, written on the flyleaves of a novel by Simenon. But I never published that sort of observation, partly because it would all fit somewhere into Pausanias, partly because it seemed so easy to do, and my sort of survey is always incomplete, and also partly because publication encourages looting.

A day came when I had seen so many surprising places that I feared imagination was outrunning science. So I set off for nothing but a walk. It was a hot winter afternoon, the ground was dry and the sun had come out. I took a chance path over a hilltop and saw with some pleasure that there was no trace of classical or prehistoric antiquity in any direction. I sat down to bask in the sun and read Simenon. I pulled off my jersey. As I did so my hand touched the dust of the mule-path I had been following. It felt peculiarly hard. Idly, I pushed the dust around a little. Just under it lay a Roman or late Greek mosaic pavement. I scrabbled, still with my fingers, at an object that seemed to break the evenness of the surrounding earth. It was part or for all I know the whole of an elaborate terracotta lamp. At that stage panic overtook me. I covered everything over, and disguised it as carefully as I could. I did tell the archaeological service, but nothing happened. I dare say someone will find it again one day.

Nothing but a complete excavation could decide whether it was or was not the little sanctuary I had been looking for all that week. It was called the Hyrnethion, and in the days of Pausanias it stood among olive groves. It was sacred to a heroine out of mythology who died a tragic death. 'Those who founded the shrine of the divine heroine gave her this honour among others: by established law no man may take into his house the broken boughs of the olive trees that grow there, or any other tree in that grove, or make any use of them, but they leave them there to be sacred to Hyrnetho.' She was a pregnant woman buried in an olive grove, murdered in a conflict between men. I would like to know more about her cult. Was she a local goddess of the trees? Was she a goddess of women giving birth? All that remains is a story about violence and about a grove of trees. That recalls an epitaph George Seferis told me about, for a hero of the late Middle Ages, who was cut down at the white rock, by the black water. Such places and such verses are what one remembers best in later life, a few flowers on a bank, the women at work in the olive groves, a few thistles as yellow as the sun, a place where someone was buried once or there was a battle once, or a bronze bell dropped from the trappings of a horse and lay for hundreds of years until you found it. Archaeology is a kind of surgery, a selective operation into the extensive humus of ancient life. But its best reward is not its scientific result or a single object in a museum or any fulfilment of ambition. It is the sense of place, I think. It is the rhythm and form of villages that have survived, imposed on the unexhausted soil. It is the olive trees and the mountainsides and the traces of the dead.

The landscape of Seferis, like all landscapes intensely imagined, gives an impression of absolute truth and permanence. That is an illusion, of course. He once had a nightmare in which the Parthenon was auctioned to become an advertisement, every column a gigantic tube of toothpaste. The Athens of his poems is full of strange, muttering characters. He must be the only poet to have written with affection of the splendidly unromantic Syngrou Avenue, which I in my turn came to love as Athenians love it, because it leads in two tidal waves of asphalt to the sea. But even Syngrou is by no means what it was. Perhaps a poem is like an old-fashioned plate photograph, perfectly precise and true to detail, as if all time had led up to it, but then at once timeless and permanent. Only the fact that the photograph itself or the poem itself ages prevents it from being false:

> Here we anchored ship to repair the broken oars, to drink some water and to sleep.
> The sea that had embittered us is deep and unexplored and spreads out an infinite calmness.
> Here among the pebbles we found a coin and played at dice for it.
> The youngest won it and was lost.
> We re-embarked with broken oars.

The landscape of this poem is the same few rocks and pine trees repeated again and again, with an abandoned shrine, a square building buried in whitewash, over and over again up to the sky. It is and is not characteristic of Greece. The pine trees have been burned. This is a kind of nightmare, a place of despair. There is hope and there is courage in the poetry of George Seferis, but the hope is no higher than the heads of the grass, and the courage is most obvious at the moments of worst tragedy, for instance at the fall of Crete to the Germans. It is not only his own language but his country and its history that George Seferis understood better than other people. His meditation was more profound. He was conscious of the Furies, the avenging demons. We are talking of a very poor country, and what was once a good and simple people, under the burden of an intolerable history. During my early years in Athens that history was taking a new, appalling turn. As I began to sink a little deeper into Greek life, disaster was imminent. At first I heard of it only in anecdotes I could hardly piece together: a rigged election, the screaming from the prison island of Makronisi that could be heard at certain villages on still nights. But people did not on the whole reveal the worst about their experience of life to an Englishman. I knew that Nikos Gatsos had sold his books in order to live, during the great hunger. I knew about the lorries that the Germans sent round every day to clear the streets of the bodies of those who had died of starvation. I knew about the gambling on the pavements, the two civil wars, the strong conservative government, the intrigues. The first fresh political rumour I ever heard in a café was about the death of a left wing member of parliament at Saloniki. He was said to have been murdered by the army or the police.

The attempt to cover this gruesome assassination, combined with a quarrel between Karamanlis and the royal family, brought down the government. For the first time since the nineteen-thirties there were genuinely free elections, and old Mr. Papandreou became prime minister. Most of my friends were cock-a-hoop. In the British School old heads nodded dubiously. He was a liberal veering through socialism towards the left for support. He stayed in power for less than two years, but in the country they were years of somewhat breathless optimism. George Seferis was not optimistic; he maintained an angry and formidable withdrawal from political affairs, and some of the things he had to say in private about the politicians were hair-raising.

At that time I made two new friends, one at George's house and the other at a New Year party at the house of the Director of the School. Through George I met Iannis Tsirkas, an Egyptian Greek novelist with the sweetest and saddest eyes and the most serious and humorous face I have ever seen. We met at lunch, and when I said later to George how much I liked this man, he was delighted. 'I hope you will be friends,' he said. 'He will be a good friend for you. The other writers do not accept him easily because he used to be left wing.' I am certain George knew much more than he said. The style of Tsirkas in his novels is terribly strong. He is as readable as Graham Greene, with the range of Malraux and the subtlety of Proust. He was born in Alexandria, where he was a friend of Kavafis; it was the study of Kavafis in his historical background that made Tsirkas a great historical novelist. His books about Kavafis are not novels; they are sharp and brilliant literary biography, still unacceptable both to conservatives and to those critics who value Kavafis mainly for his homosexuality. I imagine that it was over their reading of Kavafis, which had something in common, and over their experience of wartime Egypt, that Seferis and Tsirkas must have become friends.

Iannis Tsirkas was, unless I am mistaken, formally denounced by the communist party when the first of the three volumes of his masterpiece, *Ungovernable Cities*, was published in Athens. The trilogy of novels moves through the whole Greek Middle East, Jerusalem, Alexandria, Cairo and in the end Greece itself. In the inter-relations of persons and of worlds, in its deadly portrait of a political commissar and its painful exposure of the many ways in which the common and decent Greek people were betrayed, it shows as only great literature can do the history of his times. It was years before I read those books, at a time when I needed badly to enquire into the past in order to understand the present. At first, Iannis was no more to me than a brilliant and fascinating friend, whose conversation was full of unexpected knowledge and surprising memoirs. But the day was soon coming when I was to turn to him.

That is true of several friends I was proud to know at that time. As the crisis of the whole country became worse, friendship in Athens became a game of musical chairs. Those who thought alike and trusted one another were drawn closer and closer together. They met more often, but in fewer houses. Acquaintances became deeper friends; at the same time others dropped away. Some went to prison or into exile; some became compromised, undesirable. The conventional hypocrisy of ordinary social life ceased to operate. I was lucky to have known those to whom I later felt closest just in time, a year or two at least before the deluge. In 1966 the political crisis became irredeemable. Papandreou as prime minister had prosecuted the case against the Saloniki assassination with indiscreet vigour. The right wing mounted a counter-scandal against him, which was a piece of utter nonsense, a libel against his son. He reacted high-handedly, by removing the minister of defence, who was appointed personally by the King; Papandreou was willing but unprepared to destroy the organization that threatened him. He was removed from office, and Greece was governed contrary to its constitution by minority governments for many months.

The other friend I made in time was Gustavo Duran. He had been a musician, the pupil and friend of De Falla, and a close friend of Lorca, before the Spanish civil war. He fought in that war on the republican side as a general commanding a brigade, and finished by conducting one of the last heroic defences. Songs are still sung about him in the Spanish countryside, and Hemingway, who loved him, I think, mentions him in *For Whom the Bell Tolls*. He was never a communist, or even an anarchist, just an upperclass Spanish patriot. He married an American, joined the State Department, served in Batista's Cuba, about which his stories were grotesque and very funny, and rose high as a servant of the United Nations. At the time of the Congo war his new career was suddenly and utterly blasted, through no fault of his own. He was relegated to administer United Nations' aid in Greece. He had not been there long when we met. He was only starting to learn the language, and his world was one of diplomats and bureaucrats and official receptions. But Greece had already bitten him. It was the nearest equivalent to Spain, where he could never return. And a few afternoons with Gatsos and some musicians brought back even sharper memories. I recall an afternoon at Flocca with Gustavo, Nikos, Manos Hadzidakis, and Lorca's surviving brother.

With Gustavo Duran I got to know the Plaka. As the ruins of a village I already knew it well. I knew the district of the barrel-organs, the cavernous old taverns with the trees, the sudden view of the ship's figure-head in a backyard, the traces of ancient topography, where to find game in winter, where to catch a breeze in summer. Gustavo's pleasure was the grander evening bars where there was genuine music. His wife had suffered an amputation, and her crutches made it impossible for her to negotiate the crumbling alleys and the stone steps. I was sent out with him so that once a week he could enjoy an Athens for which his soul thirsted. He hunted out places I would never otherwise have known: a Spanish bar with Flamenco music and dancing he recognized at once as the real thing, and a big comfortable bar with the best Greek singing I have ever heard. All those places closed under the Colonels or changed utterly, and the Plaka became the hideous parody it now is.

The disadvantage of those pleasant, lengthy evenings was that they were always on a Saturday. It was often very late when we got home, and at seven in the morning I had duties at the Cathedral, which meant getting out of bed before six. I tried buses, but they were too much worry. At one time I had a red, uncomfortable bicycle, which I used to tether to a tree outside Flocca. On the whole it was better to walk, and to see the yellow winter dawns breaking behind the Parthenon. On Sundays the whole of Athens goes on excursions far into the country. The sight of them arriving there, buying every loaf of country bread in sight, consuming every fresh fish, and falling on barbecued lambs and goats at half-past eleven in the morning, is a fearsome one. The worst are the women, busloads of them spreading out in battle order over entire hillsides in search of wild salad. And at stripping an archaeological site of its irises and anemones they are more damaging than the most voracious herd of goats.

The students of the British School sometimes went on Sunday excursions. There are so many places of archaeological interest in Greece that we had to take every opportunity to visit a new one as it arose. None of us had a car, and the only other bicycle was so superior to mine that competition was unequal. Mine did very well around Athens and the Piraeus, and I noted every two or three stones of the famous Long Walls as they appeared or disappeared in the continuous earthquake of rebuilding, but that was all it was good for. Somewhere I have a photograph of what are now distinguished archaeologists posed once in fantastical wonder around the first wild flower of the year, on a snow-stricken January Sunday in the mid-sixties.

Gustavo used to spend Sunday morning drinking sherry out of silver cups with the American First Secretary, a slow-moving, amiable mid-westerner who spoke a dozen languages. Into each one he had translated a book. He spent the war in Iceland, and Arthur Miller in Icelandic is his memorial. His wife was a Mexican of grand and Spanish lineage and Catholic convent education. Gustavo derided and adored them. But one weekend saw another side of Gustavo. There was an earthquake in Evrytania; a Canadian expert and someone from the Greek Home Office had to be taken to see the damage. Gustavo had to arrange what help he could. Would I like to come? Perhaps I had never been there? I might be able to help if I knew Greek? Of course I accepted.

We left Athens a little crowded even in that superbeetle of a limousine. Gustavo sat in front with his perfect chauffeur, and I made what conversation I could in the back. Gustavo was excellent and witty in English or French or Spanish, but the agronomist was English Canadian and knew no French, let alone Greek, while the Home Office man knew no English and rather little French. That caused trouble, since it was due to this man's position that everything said in Greek had to be translated into the opaque medium of his French, and nothing much said in English. But in the end it had its advantage, because this was almost the first field experience the Canadian expert had ever had, and his lack of French or Greek made it possible to cut short what might have been arguments of stupendous tedium.

We drove northwards as far as Lamia and then began to climb into a very wild country of mountains and pine forests. The principal and only town of that province was Karponisi, and the only road was the one that took us there. We transferred to jeeps and moved out at speed onto cart-tracks. The civil governor of the province had not slept for thirty-six hours, and hardly slept during the few days of our visit. Gustavo's heart was not healthy, but he showed an energy and a stamina I would not have expected even from a much younger man. He did have a heart attack, at least one. He got out of his jeep and leaned on the rough wall of a house to drink brandy. His face and his fingernails were blue. Of the earthquake itself the most unforgettable impression was a village conference in a hut after dusk, by the light of one lamp, with those exhausted, lined, unshaven village faces crowding round a single table. We had been told these people refused to be moved, in six months time, to a new village beyond the mountains.

'Would you move? Are you willing to go?'

'Where can we go? This is our land.'

'If the government builds you another village?'

'Where can they build it? We have not seen it.'

'But if they do. If they do build it, will you go?'

'Yes.'

It was a dark, solemn rumble, unanimous and profound. The terrified demoralisation that follows earthquakes is hard to describe, but we knew enough by that evening to feel the voice in the roots of the tree. The earth shakes herself like an old pig, she splits open, a few houses crack, a few villages crumble downhill in a landslide. In this case there were eight dead, but most of the village had gone to a festival across the valley. They looked back and saw their own houses carried downhill and breaking up. One man got back in time to see the arm of his own child sticking up out of the landslide as it went past him. Above another village, we saw a gap that had opened in the earth. It opened a little more every night. Yet the people had not abandoned that village. Where could they go?

The government was building prefabricated houses as swiftly as it could. Until Papandreou, the corrugated iron roofs would have had to be imported. Even now there was only one factory that made them. The difficulties of organization were almost unbelievable. The entire operation took place among spines of impenetrable mountain and thunderclouds of forest. Powerful rivers roared in the gorges. The bridges were still, since the civil war, guarded by armed men. Any section of the tracks through mountainous forest that did duty for roads might be blocked or flooded by rain. The civil governor had a staff of about four reliable assistants; I have never seen a man work harder or more effectively. What he wanted of us was food, wheat. But the only wheat available as aid was in America, and that must by American statute travel in American ships; it must wait until they became available. These people needed bread now.

What about the Greek government? I remembered the head-shaking in the British School over Papandreou's subsidy to Greek farmers to grow wheat. Was there not now supposed to be too much wheat? Yes, but that was needed; it was an essential bargaining counter to obtain foreign currency. But it existed in Greece? Yes, in silos. Then might not the Home Office consider using it now on condition they got the assurance of American aid, and replacing it with the American wheat when that arrived? Ah, that was a possibility, Yes, it might be a possibility. Gastavo laughed mirthlessly. We got our wheat.

In the last months of 1966 things got worse. At that time, having refused to join committees or to sign statements, George Seferis published one of his most powerful essays, the *Conversation with Fabrice*. It dealt with the comparative usefulness and decency of public involvement, and the vocation of a poet. The Fabrice of the essay is the novelist Theotokas, who had just died. 'I feel obliged to remain in the middle of things,' he wrote to me. He remained in the middle of things until the end.

'As for me, I began to sense my alienation from Greek party politics quite early on; from the end of the 1935 revolution. I underline the word party. Since then, I have given myself completely, body and soul, only for two events in our history: the last war and the question of Cyprus. Both times I saw great awakenings, and both times I had to swallow a certain number of bitter experiences. And now that I have passed an entire lifetime ravaged by military revolutions, dictatorships, political upheavals, risings, calamities and despair, after I have lived through all that, I can speak from close to the bone when I say, as a public servant, that I find it a heavy and sorrowful thing as the years go by that I must end in the conclusion that we have not made one inch of progress in these matters. And when a country does not show progress in the course of forty years that means it is in a headlong decadence.'

As Greece slid almost lightly from crisis to crisis, the words of this shattering denunciation were constantly in the atmosphere, a forgotten element. Nikos Gatsos was ironical and withdrawn about daily events. There was a strike of composers, because some music of Theodorakis had been forbidden on the radio. It entailed some farcical excitements, and Flocca was crowded with journalists. Nikos complained to them that as a poet he had been on strike for forty years and no one had noticed. When I asked him about Seferis, he said, 'He is right, of course.' The levity was among the politicians. I heard a rabble-rousing speech by Papandreou that would have done discredit to the fourth century BC 'They have called this the noise of a mob: I say it is the voice of the Greek people. Let them hear it in the palace.' The roar that followed did indeed sound like a mob. In early spring each side had threatened the other with civil war, and rumours of a military coup were buzzing like an angry swarm of bees. When I left Greece, the elections that the King had so long deferred were due to take place in a fortnight.

They were bound to be a landslide victory for Papandreou. People were infuriated by the flouting of the constitution. The Greek monarchy was imposed and more than once reimposed by conservative Europe. It had reached a low point of unpopularity. Besides, any kind of liberal government must have clashed, as Papandreou did, with an entrenched and sinsister force which had existed in the shadows for many years, and was not to stalk out into the daylight. The Greeks knew much more about all this than an uncommitted, curious foreigner could easily discover. They knew just where their shoes hurt. They knew how they were governed. When I returned to Oxford, a number of friends asked about the Greek crisis. I told them as impartially as I could how the cards were now stacked and what was possible. But I had no idea what was going to happen, I had not accepted the conclusion. Yet when the Colonels entered Athens three different people telephoned to say how exactly I had foretold events. I had done so ignorantly and innocently. I could believe no evil of the Greeks. I could not accept the disaster that I could see before my eyes. It was, to be fair, the first military coup I had ever experienced personally, and I was utterly shocked by it.

7

Another Hand

IT WILL BE BETTER to state briefly what happened in Greece in April 1967, although at the time no one I knew quite understood the whole story. At the end of the civil war, when the remnants of the left were executed or imprisoned, Field Marshal Papagos set up an organization of officers which by the early sixties controlled all military promotion. Indeed the meetings of its governing body had become virtually equivalent to general staff meetings. This organization proposed to the King a military coup before the general election, but it was decided to postpone the coup until the result of the election was available. At this stage an officer of lower rank in the central office of Greek military intelligence was sent for by a general and told that the ball was at his feet. This was Papadopoulos, a fanatic with no brains but some cunning and enormous self-confidence, whose speeches sounded like Charlie Chaplin's imitation of Hitler. His necessary ally was a tank commander, Pattakos, who was a sadistic buffoon.

The tanks entered Athens, stopping correctly at every traffic light. They wakened an old English resident in his hotel. He was greatly alarmed, and pattered over to the window. Then he went back to bed. 'It's only a coup,' he thought, 'the fifth I remember.' They arrested the King and most of the politicians. On the same night they swooped on houses in every province of Greece. Many thousands were taken, most for years, some for shorter periods. They were sent to concentration camps on the islands. But the lists were old, and the police searched houses that their victims had left ten years ago; they even enquired for the dead. People were hidden by their friends. Athens was full of ill-kept secrets, hasty arrangements, sudden arrests. After three days, the King broke his coronation oath. Against the advice of the British Ambassador, but in accordance with that of his American colleague, the King swore in the Colonels as a government. As a government they were like the Marx brothers without the talent, and there was something venomous about them that recalled Hitler, and had its roots in the Nazi period in Greece. Their police were a poor man's Gestapo. They lasted seven years.

Personally, I was not conscious at once of the extent of this disaster. One of the first ways in which I noticed it was that the excavation of Lykosoura was abandoned. A Greek friend of mine, Vanna Hadzimichalis, an archaeologist who was for some reason a member of the French School at Athens, was deeply involved in the Lykosoura expedition. The money was being given by the owner of the best liberal newspapers, and the excavation was going to be, among other things, a summer spent together by friends. Vanna belonged to the old-fashioned Athenian upper class. She spoke excellent German and English and perfect French, she was married to a talented architect who was on the verge of great success. He was the warmest, most romantic and loving of men, and extremely amusing. They were not very rich, but an afternoon or an evening in their house was always a delight. It was like living through an act or two of an opera by Mozart.

But the newspaper proprietor was on the wanted list. He hid for a few weeks, but they caught him, and for many years after his release he was not the same man. It was a pity about Lykosoura. The marble statue of the goddess Demeter from that sanctuary is a fourth-century monument, but the hem of her swirling stone cloak carries a strange series of decorations which seem to be copied from an earlier design. They are animal-headed human dancers. The religious cults of Lykosoura were certainly very ancient. A single early terracotta statue of a man with an animal's head was published after the Lykosoura excavation sixty or seventy years ago, but in the preparation for the 1967 excavation, the one which was to answer a hundred questions and which never took place, Vanna was allowed access to the guarded cellars of the National Museum. There she found two unopened crates, sent to Athens from Lykosoura and never examined. They were full of terracotta statues of animal-headed dancers; some of them still had earth on them.

That summer I had an excuse to go back to Greece. I needed to take a great number of colour slides to illustrate some lectures in Oxford on the antiquities of Athens. It was another move in the crab-like progress of a commentary on Pausanias. August was a month of heat and dry air. I find it difficult to take photographs at the same time as doing anything else; the camera distracts one's eye, or concentrates it in a special way. But the pleasure of the heat, the smell of herbs, the unexpected flowers, the coolness of the shadows, and the day after day of luminous marble architecture were all somehow intensified by the simple physical task of taking an endless series of photographs. I became cunning with the ruins, I stalked them and lay in wait for them and sprang out when they were least expecting it. At night I stayed with friends in a district called Metz. From the pillow of my bed each morning the Parthenon appeared in reflection in an old Venetian mirror.

Metz is named after a café, or a tavern, which must have been a pro-Allied restaurant during the 1914 war, when the King of Greece was pro-German. Before that the district was called Yefyria, the Bridges, because it was approached from Athens by a series of ramshackle wooden bridges across the Ilissos. Now that once proud river, which flows down from Kaisariani, has been tamed, and its water stolen at the head-springs. In my time it became a drain and was covered over, like the secret rivers of London. After the 1914 war, Metz became a place for painters and Bohemians, then a red light district. It decayed and became beautiful. Some of the last old houses of Athens used to stand there. It had an old neighbourhood tavern with little room and almost nothing to eat, and the best wine in all Athens. Metz huddled under the southern shoulder of the stadium, below the First National Cemetery. It was surrounded by pine trees in almost every direction. Most of its roads were gravel tracks, and the others were flights of steps. It was a place of refuge.

The two unregarded wonders of Athenian life are the cemetery, an enormous wood of pine trees thickly undersown with neoclassic marble monuments, and the rocky proletarian hillside at the back of Philopappou, where at a certain season of the year the sky is full of hundreds of kites. The great kite-flying day is Clean Monday, the first day of Lent, which has characteristically become in Greece a day of holiday and celebration, when families in the open air indulge in all those delicious foods not forbidden in Lent. There used to be a fair then, at which one could buy strange puppet-like monkeys with mouse-skin bodies and painted silver heads with pink and green feathers, and those glistening serpents of coloured beads which are made and sold by convicted prisoners. At least they are more humane than mail-bags.

The cemetery became one of my favourite lurking places. The heroes of the war of independence lie there, in a wilderness of other monuments, and the first Greek aviator, and by now a number of my friends. The neoclassic marbles run riot, they reflower as rococo, they burst out into sunblasts of baroque. My favourite tomb is that of Makryiannis, the peasant general of 1821 whose memoirs, written with a purity and force that has no parallel in Europe since the sixteenth century, are the foundation documents of whatever is best in Greece. They were recovered as wrapping paper from a butcher's shop, and it was George Seferis who first pointed to their profundity and their value. During the 1939 war they circulated in typescript; the Germans put a price on the head of rebellious Makryiannis. Under the Colonels, people left red carnations at his monument. His face on the bronze plaque is consumed with rage and suffering; he has the face of a starved prophet. In his old age he wrote a long and bitter series of letters of reproach to God. He was imprisoned, tortured, virtually starved to death, under the early monarchy. I am constantly moved to tears by his writings.

In the summer of 1967 we had a car. The swish of air through its open windows, the speed of it on the big roads, and the places it got us to are still a vivid memory. It was then I first saw the Ptoion, a comparatively small archaeological site in Boiotia which has no road. We raced north from Athens and made our first raid on a barn near Tanagra which was an archaeological storehouse for local antiquities. My friend was a Byzantinist, we had both tried more than once to get into this fabulous barn, but on this occasion we managed it. We never achieved it again, but on this day we made friends in the village and had access to the treasures for an hour or two. From Tanagra we travelled across the Copaic lake, which is now rich earth. In 1967 the reed huts of semi-nomadic peasants were still a common sight. There were several attempts to drain the lake; the French had failed, I believe, and its return to agriculture was achieved by a British company before the war, that left behind it a curious colony of English-speaking families who played tennis and gave tea-parties and exchanged visiting-cards. Alas, I never knew them.

The route to Ptoion passed Akraiphnion, with some fine-looking fourth-century walls and the tops of columns re-used in the Byzantine church, smothered in gold paint. I see now that Ptoion is only three or four miles away, but I remember it as much further. The road was a cart-track, it forked once or twice without signs, and I dare say we got lost. The place was magical. It was a small, green valley. We stopped the car under a tree beside a deserted chapel and gazed across at green terraces picked out with lichened, ruined stones. At the top of the ruins spring-water still poured away through the mouth of an ancient stone animal, the stone troughs were still in use, a few brambles and bushes sprouted here and there. Behind the terraces rose a curtain of rock. Apollo's hawks wheeled and screamed around his abandoned oracle.

Lightheartedly we sprang up the boulders and began to scale the rockface. That was a mistake for two reasons. Firstly the rock-face, like most rockfaces, was harder than it looked, or at least I found it so. Secondly, the hawks had a nest somewhere in a cranny of that warm cliff, and their attentions became unpleasant. But we found at the top what we expected, a cult-place of some kind, with a litter of ancient pottery, mostly rather late and rather crude, which must have rested there undisturbed since the last worshippers abandoned the decaying shrine. It had been rich once. The Athens museum has big, archaic stone statues from the terraces, and an entire farmyard of small bronze animals. Kroisos of Lydia gave dedications in gold to the Ptoion. Nothing is left there now but the hawks and the rock and the watered valley. As we came down, a herd of more than two hundred black-fleeced goats wandered through the ruins. They had eyes of a wonderful wickedness.

On that visit to Greece I had determined to keep an open mind about the Colonels. We saw few people, so it was not difficult. Already the conversation in all public places had become laconic or discreet. The only evidence that I came across of the impact of the new régime was the disappearance for ten days of one of our favourite taxi-drivers. He came back with the marks of someone who had been badly beaten up, but he refused to talk about how or by whom. The aeroplane I was taking home was three hours late leaving. I spent the time in the sea, and then had lunch at a seaside restaurant, out of doors. An old gardener came and watched me.

'I see you are a foreigner,' he said. 'You know how I see it? You don't eat bread.'

'I did eat a little. I've had enough to eat.'

'Ah, that's the wisdom of foreigners. A little and not too much. It's like democracy. People need a little but not too much. Do you agree?'

'It's not my place to disagree. It's your country. In England I am a democrat.'

'Ah, but here they need the stick. They need the cutlass. No more strikes now. No more strikes on buses. They come on time now. Do you like our government?'

'Not my business. I'm glad to hear you do.'

'You tell them that in England. Tell them the working man likes this government.'

'Did you dislike the other?'

'Those pimps! Those pathics! Do you know what they did to me after the war? Those communists?'

'No, what?'

'Broke my fingers. All my fingers. Look at them.'

'What on earth did they do that for?'

'Because I fought. I was only a soldier. Because I fought for Hitler, as a volunteer. Hitler was a good man. I wish we had him now. He was all right, was Hitler.'

'I can't quite agree.'

'Well, you tell them in England, about the bread and about the democracy. You advise them. Hitler understood that.'

He was the only spokesman for the Colonels I encountered. Those I have met since have not offered any improvement on his arguments. I did have an American friend who was pro-Colonel, but that I put down to a certain arrogant eccentricity. He was obsessed with the corruption of Athens and hoped to see it purged by the provinces and the lower middle classes. It was a complicated, almost a brilliantly wrongheaded theory, and it put a strain on friendship as time went on. It is difficult to remember now that bitter feelings between old friends did not arise at once. They were cumulative, and it was only after a year or two that supporting the régime became unforgivable.

In the first years George Katsimbalis was rather on their side. The ageing Colossus of Maroussi was a figure of whom I stood in awe. He boomed like a battle-fleet, he crowed and roared and gasped, he stood no nonsense. He was Maurice Bowra with the glands of a goat. He loathed communists and left intellectuals and liberals. He was extremely funny, absolutely uninhibited, and the best story-teller in the world. He made western European gossip columnists sound like great-aunts at a baptism. Katsimbalis met Henry Miller in the thirties through Gatsos and Elytis. Henry Miller had wandered into the Brazilian coffee bar wearing a Hubba-Hubba cap and engaged them in conversation.

'What do you read in Greece? What American literature?'
'Oh, this and that, you know.'
'You read Dos Passos?'
'We don't like him. He's too wordy.'
'You read Hemingway?'
'That is not really for us, you know. Too much machismo.'
'Raymond Chandler?'
'A kind of parody.'
'Steinbeck?'
'He's all right, still developing, still limited.'
'Who do you read then? What do you like?'
'There's a writer in Paris we like. He's just written a book we thought interesting. He's called Henry Miller.'

He was speechless with pleasure. All he could do was point his finger at his chest and say. 'Me, me, it's me.' He became so excited that he wanted a brothel.

'Elytis and I do not know much about those things. We will introduce you to Mr. Katsimbalis. He will know.'

There was one limit to the uninhibitedness of Katsimbalis that deserves to be recorded. He once took my Byzantinist friend to see his old mother. It was the end of a long uproarious lunch. But as the taxi got closer, Katsimbalis got quieter. When he entered the house he was whispering. He tiptoed into a big, cool room with its blinds down. There he knelt and kissed the hand of a very old, very quiet lady, and withdrew. As the taxi drew away he began to talk louder; at the centre of Athens he was booming like a foghorn. Once in the early days of the Colonels we ate out of doors somewhere in the Plaka. He had been defending the government with some inconsequent argument or other, then suddenly he turned to attacking them.

'Do you know those shits are opening our letters?'

'Quiet, George.'

'Shits they are and shits I call them. They are shit-bespattered.'

'George, for God's sake, someone will hear you.'

'Waiter, tell them from me. Katsimbalis says they are shits.'

'For heaven's sake, George, don't do that. They'll arrest you. You know they arrest people for talking in cafés.'

'Know? Of course I know, but they can't arrest me. I am the only bloody supporter they've got, and I say they are shits.'

All the same, life was altering greatly. People ceased to go out. A Greek lady archaeologist who had been kind to everyone I knew for a generation resigned her position. She was the secretary to the archaeological service and editor of its journals. She put in her resignation formally, it buried itself among a mass of papers, and it was not noticed until it was too late. There was a Colonel in charge, since there was now a Colonel in charge of everything possible and many things impossible, and even more chaos than before. He sent for her to an office high up in the National Museum.

'What do you mean by this?'

'I have resigned.'

'You have tricked me. You have been deceitful.'

'If you will just say that once more, I will pick you up out of that chair, and throw you out of that window into the garden of the Museum.'

'Never has any woman so addressed a Greek officer!'

'Then it is high time, and I am proud to be the first.'

In the provinces, archaeological exploration became more difficult. I had spent some time trying to solve the problems of a valley disputed in antiquity between Argos and Sparta. As usual, at the beginning of such a problem, there seemed to be too many place-names recorded by Pausanias and others, and too few sites, most of them in the wrong place. But as usual, some days of walking over the ground produced too many possible sites, all in plausible places, with too few place-names to fit them. The question of identification depended on distances, and therefore on roads. I was curious to test one route in particular 'that no one uses now', from an ancient town to the next valley. I climbed the path, which was mostly excellent, occasionally overgrown, among the fantastic bush colours and rock colours of late autumn. It took all day, and at the top of the mountain the world went mad. A raging storm of wind and rain had climbed up from the sea by the opposite route. Trees were blowing down. I was soaked to the skin in spite of my anorak. It was Beaufort Scale 9, I was told later.

I ran down the far side of the mountain as best I could until I got in shelter of olive groves. A storm among olive groves is a strange sensation. It is like looking up at breaking waves from the sandy floor of the sea. It is also extremely wet. Birds pipe madly, and if you find the ruins you are looking for, then you slip about a lot on the stones. By early afternoon the storm had blown itself out, I had rescued an inscription from the ditch of a primary school in the village, and come as close as I shall ever get to solving my problem. There was no time for lunch, as I was due at a rendezvous with Takis in a lower village before the sun failed. The village policeman offered me a lift, which I gratefully accepted. Once he had me in the car, he began to cross-question me. He was unimpressed by my passport. That might be forged. It turned out that he assumed, since I admitted having come down from the mountain to avoid a storm, that I must be a partisan. But I had a visiting card, which impressed him, and then Takis vouched for me, so the day ended well. No doubt my file grew a little thicker in Athens. As for what I hoped was an ancient road, it was cut by the villagers themselves in living memory, under the inspiration of a country doctor, just ten years before a new state road put it out of business.

Police files began to be a serious matter. All foreigners are obliged, every so many months, to visit the Office of Aliens in Canning Square, in the noisiest and most abhorrent area of Athens, to have their permit of residence renewed. The files were always in an ungodly muddle, and it took the police several weeks to gather together the material on any individual. With twenty thousand secret informers at work in Athens alone, it must have taken some sorting. If you could avoid the moment when your file was dusted and read, you stood a chance of passing into history as a mere statistic. The dangerous moment was the application for a renewal of the permit of residence. Usually, I would go abroad for a few days and return with a brand new visa; sometimes I simply stayed less long in Greece. But good luck under such a régime does not last for ever.

Amnesty International sent a senior representative to Greece to investigate the rumours of torture and severe repression which were now heavy in the air. I became a member of the organization, at first to translate, then to make introductions and to help in any way I could. The British Embassy, whose policy with George Brown at the Foreign Office was a devious combination of appeasement and commerce, and the British School, which feared for its neutrality and its official recognition, made their displeasure clear. I continued to work at archaeology, and paraded those few friendships I had with Greeks which were neither literary nor with known haters of the régime, but innocently professional. Vanna, for example, was a lady in good standing and a professional archaeologist. Of course she loathed the Colonels. Even her dog went mad if their names were mentioned. But she was a perfectly respectable friend, I supposed. Gustavo Duran was more and more important to all of us. He had taken to singing Spanish republican songs to amuse himself; as I write they still echo in my head. He inspired more courage at that time than anyone else in Athens; he had more common sense, and he went everywhere.

The work of Amnesty in Greece is now a matter of history. What was revealed was awful, but one must remember that much of the very accurate information that began to flow in came from members of the police and the army. The tortures had survived from the days of the Turks, with some new ones, even more revolting, learnt from the Germans. There existed, and probably still exist, judges and prison officials who had kept their jobs since the days of the Nazis. And those who resisted now had resisted the Nazis. Lady Fleming, the Greek doctor who had married the discoverer of penicillin, had risked her life and come near to execution during the war, to save the lives of British airmen. She was now dropped from the Embassy visiting list. I was once in her flat in Athens when two middle-aged New Zealanders arrived unannounced. She had once helped to hide them and to smuggle them home, and never seen them since. Now she was helping the families of the imprisoned and organizing an escape route where it was necessary.

The Colonels had sent witnesses to Strasburg to the European Court of Human Rights, guarded by armed chimpanzees, to maintain that contrary to the prosecution case they had never been tortured. These witnesses had then sensibly defected when an opportunity arose. But the fiancée of one of them at Saloniki was being blackmailed by the police with the threat of renewed torture, to make a statement against her lover. It was necessary to smuggle her out of the country. I played some minor part in this adventure, which had its difficult moments, since the poor girl spoke no foreign language at all and had to travel on a Dutch passport, with an armful of Dutch women's magazines. I found myself at Rome, where I passed a pleasant few days in the museums.

Within a minute of getting back to the British School I was told that the police had been looking for me. They had brought a photograph, and asked where I was. Of course, I assumed that my arrest was a matter of hours, and bolted like a hare to an untapped telephone to make my arrangements. I spent the evening with Takis, whose eyes grew big when he heard the news, and later with Vanna and her husband. I had to promise them never to commit such a folly again. I think it was in those days that I began to realize Vanna's past. As a girl she was in the resistance, which in Athens was communist dominated. She was finally thrown out of the party or left it after being reprimanded for going with a boy, now her husband, who at that time was an anarchist, to look at the sunset over the sea. That was a bourgeois and therefore a politically suspect act. Nikos had killed his first German guard at the age of fourteen, by jumping on him with a knife from the window of a house in the Plaka. During the civil war they took refuge in France.

Days passed; I was not arrested. When the School asked about the policemen I was able to say truthfully I had no idea why they wanted me. In the street I was followed about. At first I took this badly; it is, after all, a disagreeable sensation. But one gets used to it, and quite soon I found many of my friends were more used to it than I was. Curious noises came from the Embassy. At one stage, I left a visiting card or its equivalent on the Ambassador, since we had mutual friends and the poor man had said he wanted to meet me. It was the simplest of social gestures. He never heard of that message. What did happen was a flurry of telegrams between an Embassy official and the Director of the School, then in England. I was in bed with 'flu, and the question at issue was relayed to me. For what political purpose was I attempting to negotiate with the Ambassador? It all seemed to be part of having 'flu.

It turned out that Vanna was the key to this mystery. This same official was carefully cultivating her at the time. He used to ask her many naive questions about the views and the condition of the left in Greece. I was in her house when an elderly cousin warned her not to see him. She was amazed. During the war the resistance in Athens used to meet the resistance from the mountains among the tombs of the labyrinthine cemetery that lay beyond Metz. Vanna used to go there to meet this cousin, who was then a boy in a resistance unit under British control. She took him boots and messages from his mother. Neither of them was twenty. Once she was introduced to his British officer. This same officer was now a mad ex-spy, or for all I know a mad master of spies, at the Embassy in Athens. He assumed that Vanna was still secretly a communist. He must have understood little about life, and little about the sad history of communism in Greece.

My own police followers had an even odder explanation, which I discovered much later. I was, of course, a priest. I had been round the Church authorities in Athens to try to get them all to go together in a body to Pattakos, to get his permission to care for the families of prisoners. Pressure on the families was an important police instrument, but a united committee of churches would have stood a chance. Every single one refused; the most despicable was the Anglican, I am afraid. If I had no witness to that interview I would not believe my own memory of it. But the point I am making is that everyone in Athens knew me as an English clergyman. There was another one, also an archaeologist of some kind, who had a peccadillo. He had a weakness for well-built young soldiers. He had set himself up in a flat somewhere in the city and there, day by day, he had run through platoon after platoon of paratroops and royal bodyguards. In England people often think that sex is at the bottom of political scandals. In Greece I have often observed that the police mind works in the opposite way. Sexual scandal must, they believe, conceal something political. It is a point of view more innocent than ours.

The miserable man was arrested, and held for two or three weeks. He was unable to appeal to the British School or the Embassy, because that would take him, as a clergyman, out of the frying-pan into the fire. At last he thought of a Greek official who could swear to his political innocence, who had known him for years, who could get him out of prison. He went home, and so far as I know he never revisited Greece. I can tell this story now, since he is no longer alive. What the police wanted to know about me at that early stage in our relationship was whether I was seeing any soldiers. As this was fortunately not the case, they let up. But it seemed discreet to resign from the British School for fear of worse trouble. As for the police, we discovered late in the day, from the interrogations that our friends suffered, that they knew almost nothing about any of us. Lady Fleming was caught almost by chance in a ridiculous trap. Vanna never went to prison at all. Nikos got away by the skin of his teeth to France, but even against Nikos they had no evidence until it was handed to them by a prisoner boasting in the dock. What folly.

So I moved to Metz, to what the British call a penthouse and the Athenians a *retiré*. It was one room with windows on three sides and a door on the fourth, with a huge terrace where my landlord grew geraniums and basil in painted petrol-cans. It had a shared bathroom, which was also used for washing clothes by all the ladies who lived below. It cost ten pounds a month. On one side it looked at the pine woods that cover the antiquities on the south shoulder of the stadium, on another at Hymettos and the woods of the cemetery, on the third at the sea and all the islands. On the fourth side it looked down on the old royal gardens and the temple of Olympian Zeus, and straight across at the Parthenon itself and Mount Parnes. I never found a viewing platform so wonderful in all Athens. Flowers were cheap, from the cemetery flower-stalls. Taxis passed two hundred yards away. The police were inactive, and my house had two entrances on different roads. Vanna lived nearby.

My private staircase was the fire-escape. Near the top it was much corroded by bullet-holes from the civil war and swayed gently away from the wall. The house was built by a White Russian, who lived in the whole of it, I think, and used the *retiré* for sunbathing. He disappeared at the time of the war, and my landlord who, I suspect, had begun like most countrymen arriving in Athens as a concierge and handyman, emerged from the war and the civil war as the owner. He was slow, provincial, and exquisitely polite. He had connections with the police, but that worked very well, since I could tell him whatever I supposed they knew already, or whatever I wanted them to know. In fact I misjudged him. The only harm he ever did me was by defending me from enquiries. By that time I undoubtedly had a record. The police called some twenty times; they were never told I was at home.

'I told them you are all over Greece. You are everywhere. No one can find you.'

'But was I never here?'

'Oh yes, often. But I wasn't going to have you troubled by those people.'

The result was a summons to the local section of the security police. I attended with a lawyer, Takis naturally, and an innocent face, or so I hoped. We overwhelmed them with helpfulness, and pressed information on them. We expressed shock that they had no proper file. They denied the existence of any files. We expressed concern that they were cheated of these informative files. It was a triumph. They forgot to ask any questions of substance, though there were some they might have asked.

I loved the terrace room. I shared the heights with a long-distance runner who lived in a triangular chamber like a slice of cheese, which had once been the kitchen to the room I had. He was a friendly, withdrawn lad who had once won a cross-country race as a schoolboy. The army had given him a commission at once, on the condition that he trained every day of his military service at the athletic club beside Olympian Zeus. I doubt if he won any more races. He was no trouble; above all he never used the terrace. There I sat hour after hour, day after day, just gazing at the Parthenon. At Christmas I invited Takis to breakfast there, with proper French coffee and a linen tablecloth, and heaven knows what from Fortnum and Mason.

Christmas in Athens had always been peculiar. At the British School it could be alleviated by hiring a Pontic barrel-organ and taking charge of the drinks, but it was a grim festival. The high point was the glitter of blazing sunshine on northern European Christmas decorations at the street market near Monastiraki, the Athenian equivalent of Portobello Road. But in Metz I came to relish public festivals. I would see a few friends, but otherwise I would shut myself up with a record of flute music by Bach, and plenty of coffee and brandy. The Parthenon was always there. I used to say mass privately, in the room. I had almost deserted the Cathedral, ever since a bad Sunday when I heard a sermon in praise of the Colonels. Religion had become an instrument of government among others. But we all saw more of our friends. When I moved into my room George Seferis and his wife gave me my first box of French cube sugar. When I was ill there, more friends visited me than I can name. Its patriarchal chairs were ones that the Leigh-Fermors had copied in Kalamata from a Spanish model. Its china was an English service from the eighteen-nineties. Its pictures were woodcuts of Jewish heroes by Nikos Stavroulakis. It had the travelling edition of the *Encyclopaedia Britannica*, most of which I read. All the music articles are good, but for general reading I recommend 'S'.

Archaeology in the provinces became even more painful than life in Athens. Fear and suspicion were more intense, and in the country the heavy hand of the police was even more irrational and made of spiked iron. It was improper to encourage any confidence, even where confidence was forthcoming. Stories did break through that barrier, and they could be moving. When Pavlos Zannas was arrested, on an island where he spent the summer with his wife and young children, they knew all day that something was up. People brought them unexpected presents. He dined with neighbours, and as he walked home to his remote little house six armed men burst on him from behind bushes, as if he was a famous bank robber. He was the director of the international trade fair at Saloniki; his offence was translating a foreign news bulletin, I think from the BBC, for an illegal news sheet. There were many of those, and they circulated widely. They were thrust under doors or into coat pockets. He was taken to his house to pack, and his wife walked down with him to a boat that was waiting. Every door, every window in the village was black. There was no witness. As she walked home in tears, every door opened, and from every house the women came out to comfort her.

A poem was smuggled out of the Averof Women's Prison, which I was asked to translate. It never got printed, except in a student magazine, but I believe that Theodorakis has set it to music, though not in this version. It was a long poem, and I can quote only a little of it:

I will send my dreams to disturb their rented sleep.
I will send terror to nest in their hearts without suspicion
and when the official comes for the survey
'escape' the others will say
misunderstanding my death
and only you will know

only you will remember my hands,
the obliterating clamour of the dog outside the prison,
the shouting of the children on the terrace,
the desperation of the Chinese Portrait,
the Greek riddle: What goes up on two feet and they carry it
down in a blanket?
And only you will know
when my body was lost
what became of my voice and sleeplessness,
what are the noises of terror, faces of desperation
'Good God, what had become of the brave men of the world?'
Only you will know.
I will speak this language.

The most terrifying thing about those years was the isolation from a world we consider normal, and the intolerable interweaving of the most ghastly atrocities with everyday life. One of the places for torture was a street behind the National Museum. They tuned a motorcycle engine to drown the noise, but at times you could hear the screaming from the sculpture galleries. I became a close friend of a Greek priest whose life was spent in the docks. He was arrested, maltreated, constantly threatened. One day he was more upset than usual, and I asked him why. An old working man, an assistant in a barber's shop in the Piraeus, had a son who was left wing. The boy fled on the first day of the Colonels; he reached France, but the local police imagined he was still in hiding. Every week or so they interrogated the father. One day they arrested him. His dead body, savagely mutilated and tortured, happened to be washed up by the coal wharf, near his own parish. The priest was sent for by the dockworkers and arrived before the police. When the police came the body was taken away and buried secretly. The family never saw it. The police put a suicide notice in the local paper.

I am a human being before I am an archaeologist or a writer or even, as I was then, a clergyman. It was terribly hard to concentrate on work. And yet work was a great help. It gave more than it got. Madness and outrage could not invade it. In bad political circumstances the avoidance of despair is a privilege that belongs to active resistance, but work is also a solace. I say this as a naturally unpolitical man who prefers his village and his garden and the England he was brought up in, even a natural conservative who would willingly turn back the clock of history five or ten minutes. In Greece at that time it was striking midnight. Almost no political activity was effective. All one could do was to taunt the Colonels, to make their lives a misery and to keep up a steady bombardment of the truth. But that was only the noise of the captive jangling her chains. An American aircraft carrier the size of the whole ackropolis was moored offshore. The future of the Greeks was simply not in their hands. Some of the best became desperate. The curtain between dangerous activity and activity undertaken because danger itself has become attractive, or disaster an easy solution, is subtle and easy to tear.

I undertook a commentary in common with two Greek archaeologists on the first book of Pausanias, which describes Athens. We made some progress, indeed the book was at one time nearly ready for publication. We cleared up the problems that we noticed. We inspected spots in the fields where an inscription had once been found, and isolated churches and antiquities built into them. In one case, it was an inscribed stone re-used as a church doorstep, recently repainted bright green. I photographed every surviving stone of the ancient walls of the Piraeus. I thought it was useless at the time, and I am no great shakes as a photographer, but already today there are fewer of those stones. To some things we came too casually, to others too late. I adventured up a promising track near Eleusis with English friends. It rained heavily, the track became a mountain path, we had to manhandle the car. Once that had been an ancient road. Near the top of the pass, we met a peasant with a horse. I said to the horse, in Greek, 'How are you doing?' The rain dripped off his nose. 'What would a horse do?' asked the peasant. At the top, we found heavy machinery and piles of earth. A new road was being driven through.

Everyone in Athens became terribly tired. If you had the money and could somehow contrive a passport, it was a benefit greater than I can describe to go abroad for a while. This even though you suffered the agony of delayed aeroplanes and a final police check, not knowing who it was they would take back, even when the plane was ready to fly. George Seferis accepted an invitation to Princeton for two or three months. I had the good fortune to meet him there. We sat through a play in which robots destroyed a room in a motel. They tore bibles, wrote obscenities on walls, and a great deal more. That was the play. 'And to think,' said George, 'that these are the people who banned Joyce for obscenity.' In America there was some pressure on him to make a public statement. He resisted that, on the grounds that if he was unable to speak in his own country, he could not speak elsewhere. Something was brewing in his mind. I believe that the distance and the rustic peace of Princeton were useful to him. But when someone asked him a political question at a public reading of poetry his answer was as Delphic as it was devastating.

'Mr. Seferis, how can you, a poet, continue to live in Greece with those filthy Colonels?'

'If I must answer, firstly, I live in Greece because it is my country. Secondly, why do you not rather ask those filthy Colonels how they can continue to live in Greece with Seferis?'

He was conscious of everything that happened in Greece, which is much more than can be said for the British or the Americans at that time. The Americans were so stupid as to believe their own intelligence reports, which showed a massive support for the Colonels. The British were only slightly less stupid, and the best friend of the Greeks in any foreign mission was an American, not an Englishman. One of the nicest Americans was supposed to be the local CIA watchdog. He started out very fierce, but his whole career was a long fall downstairs, bump, bump, bump, to less and less desirable posts, because he always came in his dazed way to sympathise with the natives. From Athens, he was transferred to a jungle.

George Seferis was a merciful and just man, a very rare combination. Now he was free of public office his feelings concentrated on his own country and its plight. He used to say that Greece had lost two generations, in the war and the civil war; it could not afford to lose another, as it was doing under the Colonels. He really loved the young, as they loved him, and he loved his country. When he came back from exile as the Germans were being driven from Greece, he came on deck at dawn and put his arm round the shoulders of Robin Burn, a Scottish Greek scholar who was his fellow traveller. 'Look, Robin,' he said, 'they are still there. They have not taken away a single island.'

When we first talked together about torture I told him I realized the British had done the same. He replied that he knew that. The worst torturer in Cyprus was still a serving officer in the British army. And in Egypt, in the war, the Greek resistance had sent a delegate to the British to negotiate for recognition, I think it was a woman. The delegate was immediately arrested and tortured. A British officer went to George secretly and told him he must intervene. He went at once to the prison and found the victim with a black tongue sticking out of her mouth for lack of water. George Seferis in the late sixties suffered an anguish over his country, and I am certain that it hastened his death. He died of grief, really.

One spring afternoon we had lunch together at a French restaurant near the British School. Afterwards we walked up and down its leafy terrace in the sunshine. I was due to go home to Oxford next day, and he had spoken of some small commission. He now explained that it was a public statement, the first time he had broken silence in Greece since April, 1967. It was pre-arranged that it should be broadcast at the same moment by several foreign stations broadcasting in Greek. I am unable to claim that I carried it, as he had found at the last moment a safer messenger. But I heard it, of course, and read it. It greatly altered the feeling of the whole country. It restored courage and self-respect. He became at a stroke the one person in all Greece who could speak to the young with authority. For the rest of his life, old men would cross the street for the privilege of taking off their hats as he passed, and in the countryside children would appear out of the fields with handfuls of wild flowers. When he visited George Pavlopoulos, policemen dogged him, until they were called off by the officer in command of the district. 'Seferis,' he said, 'is a great man: leave him alone.' It was not obvious at the time of his statement that all this would happen. His words were a headlong challenge to the government, and spoken with the intensity of very great courage:

Some time has gone by since I took the decision to restrain myself from any part in the political affairs of this country. As I have attempted on other occasions to explain, that does not mean in the least that our political life is to me a matter of indifference. So from those years until these recent times I have as a rule refrained from handling such matters. Anyway, what I had published down to the beginning of 1967, and my position since then (I have published nothing in Greece since freedom was strangled) has shown sufficiently clearly, I think, what my thoughts are.

And yet for months now I have felt in myself and all around me more and more urgently the duty to say something about our present situation. With all possible brevity, I would put it like this: It is two full years since a government has been imposed on us absolutely and utterly opposed to the ideals for which our world, and so gloriously our own people, fought in the last world war. It is a situation of compulsory paralysis, in which whatever spiritual values we have succeeded in keeping alive, with toil and suffering, are on their way with the others to be drowned in stagnant and marshy water. It would not be hard for me to understand that damage of that kind would not count very much to certain people. Unhappily, this is not the only danger.

Everyone has been taught by now, and everyone knows, that in dictatorial régimes the beginning can seem easy, but the tragedy is waiting, not to be turned aside, at the end. The drama of that ending tortures us, consciously or unconsciously, as it does in the ancient choruses of Aischylos. The longer the fault remains, the further the evil goes. I am a man with absolutely no political link, and I can claim that I am speaking without fear and without passion. I see before me the abyss into which the oppression that has overshadowed this country is leading us. This fault must cease. The Nation commands it.

Now I am going back to my silence. I beg of God never again to put me under such a necessity to speak.

8

Death is a Pulpit

THE COVER OF my book of poems, *Death is a Pulpit*, shows an enormous tree, high up in the Cretan mountains. Under that tree, by his own wish, Gustavo Duran lies buried. He died of heart failure; the knowledge that he could die when he chose, by merely running across a room, and must die soon anyway, gave his last years a gallantry, and a spirited and responsible courage, that won him the deepest friendship and respect of those from whom he valued it. In Crete he was passionately loved. His consolation in those years was to do everything he could personally, for one remote village. His daughters worked a long Cretan summer, side by side with the villagers, to bring the water of a mountain spring to a tap in the village itself. Gustavo loved his visits to Alones. The mountain-bred bravery, the gaiety, and the thread-bare poverty suited him. It was a small settlement, perfectly traditional and isolated.

During the war every second stone on its mountainsides sheltered a British officer; I have heard a son of the priest of those days praise one of the officers as a good man, such a good and decent man. 'Do you know, he could throw his pistol in the air thirty feet, and catch it by the handle?' Among those lively mountaineers Gustavo was happy. He had a plan to retire to the village, though I do not believe he expected to live long enough. It was a world remote from the Colonels. I do not think the people of Alones realized what a bad lot the Colonels were until one of their sons came of age to go down from the mountains to the nearest local secondary school. Most of Gustavo's time, of course, was spent in Athens. He was a sharp observer and a wise adviser. He kept more than one person out of trouble, his contempt was a tonic, and he was hilariously funny. I remember with particular pleasure his impersonation of the Archbishop of Athens sticking in his hairpins while discussing politics in his sacristy.

Strange little sparks of resistance appeared in unexpected places. A wild and hairy bishop, at the enthronement of a new colleague in Eleia, was so shocked by the military governor, who made a speech in the name of the government on the soundness of the new bishop's views, that he stormed to the pulpit to declare it was the first time he ever heard of the Church asking a blessing of the state. The son of a friend of mine, a boy of about fifteen, got above himself in public one evening and roamed the streets singing songs against the régime. He had a good voice, and the tunes were good. Some elderly people who heard him sent for an ambulance and had him clapped into hospital for the night, to keep him out of the hands of the police. When the Colonels toured the provinces, microphone wires were cut. Potatoes in the exhaust pipes of tanks made havoc of an army parade. When the crowded stadium of Athens was informed by Colonel Pattakos that he was the father of the Greek people, a low, unanimous chanting began and continued for five minutes in accents of irony. 'You are our Daddy. You are our Daddy.'

But nearly everyone I knew was in trouble. After George Seferis had made his statement, eighteen writers, under his influence, challenged the censorship laws by publishing as a book *Eighteen Texts*. The first text was a magnificent and angry poem by Seferis, 'The Cats of Saint Nicholas'. Periodicals were censored before publication, books were subject to prosecution only after they appeared. The government must have felt that any attention drawn to *Eighteen Texts* would be a disaster, at home and abroad. A work of literature could not expect to sell many copies in Greece. There they were mistaken. Many thousands of copies circulated, far more than the publishers admitted. It revolutionized the Greek book trade. It sold and sold. It was needed, and it sold.

The writers included many of my old friends and several new ones. Kay Cicellis, the novelist, was one, Tsirkas another, Takis Sinopoulos, the poet, another. Rodis Roufos, diplomat, poet and novelist, was another. Rodis resigned from the Greek foreign service and devoted himself with skill and energy to the battle against the Colonels. But the inspiring force was Seferis, and the organizing genius, the discreet and quiet negotiator of agreements, was Tsirkas. At least that was my strong impression, and George Seferis confirmed it. It is not as easy as it sounds to produce a united front of so many distinguished Greek writers. Tsirkas went further; he produced virtually a united front among all the important ex-politicans who were rotting away here and there under house arrest or afflicted by the most threatening kind of police surveillance. It was under the Colonels that the survivors of the civil war began to forgive one another. I have been at a dinner party in Athens where people were present who had fought on different sides in the same campaign. The memories they exchanged were horrifying. They are too bad for this book.

Most of the authors of the texts were sent for and interrogated, but none of them was arrested at that time. I would not like to be the policeman whose job it was to shout down Boulis Frangopoulos. That mild man has the appearance of a human bull, and a most formidable voice. He is a good poet who used to be in charge of the government tourist organization. And I would not like to be the lawyer who had to prosecute Arghyriou. He has the clear and subtle mind of an elderly professor; he is one of the best Greek critics. Indeed the government at that time lost almost all its major cases in court. The legal profession was solidly against it, and there are more lawyers in Athens even than there are officers. Whatever could be tried by court martial the government won, but in the courts their authority was whittled away. One of their worst disasters was an attempt to convict an anti-Colonel novelist for obscenity. I have never heard such hay made of prosecution witnesses. One turned out to be a teacher of theology who had never read the book, one was a policeman's brother, and one, if I remember this rightly, failed to turn up altogether.

159

A little before *Eighteen Texts* appeared, I was invited to a congress of modern Greek specialists at Princeton to give a lecture on George Seferis. I did the job as well as I could; I am not sure that my style of discourse about poetry is any pleasure to American academic audiences, but the Greeks liked it, and at the time it was a success. I spoke of his particular tone of voice, the way in which a reader finds himself, through that personal tone, among thoughts and presuppositions that strike the more deeply for being only lightly stated. I discussed the development of his poetry, his authority and greatness. I quoted some poems which refer to real events:

> The economy and the intense power of Seferis' style as it has developed have limited his range. He is not a writer of Shakespearean comedies or of works like Ulysses, nor would that have been possible for a Greek writer of his generation; but the substance of breadth is there, and his writing has not ceased to develop, even at this time. There is a generosity of spirit in his poems that is, if I may say so, very Greek, even when his voice is one of black lamentation.

I ended with long quotations from 'The Cats of St Nicholas'.

Today I am not so sure about any limitation of range. His lighter poems and his children's limericks are only beginning to be valued. I had little idea then that they existed. His fascinating early novel had not yet been published. And although I did notice real events and contemporary history in a few poems, particularly the fall of Crete and the terrible meaning of the cats, I had not realized, as I have done since, how many of his poems have a precise contemporary resonance. When I returned to Greece I took the manuscript of my lecture with me, to show to a few like-minded friends. I had no conception of doing anything more with it. But George Seferis asked to see it and was thrilled by it. Of course I was delighted; I feel ashamed now, as I did on that evening, by his warmth and generosity. I was so pleased he was pleased I hardly knew where to put myself.

Meanwhile Iannis Tsirkas had suggested the lecture might be

given again, in Athens, perhaps at the British Council. The Assistant Director of that organization was a friend of ours. Since the British Council premises rank in some way as diplomatic territory, it was more immune than most places from censorship and police pressure. In the past, when it was staffed with poets and historians of great distinction, it had been a platform for most of what was new and good in the intellectual life of the country. Under the Colonels it was mostly its German equivalent, the Goethe Institute, that played that part. The British were losing their old friends with a spend-thrift energy. Harold Wilson did something to stop the rot by a speech in the House of Commons, but on the whole we were in eclipse. I left the affair of the lecture in the hands of my friends, and went away to the Mani, where I was due to stay for some weeks.

I think that was the time I arrived there at night, in a thunderstorm, with Takis and George Pavlopoulos. The Mani is the weirdest spine of all the Greek mountains, it is the southern tentacle of Taygetos crawling out to sea to die. Its sides are eaten away by the sea. It has deep caves of purple, green and white, small unexpected coastal plains, parched villages, frightening cliffs. It used to be extremely inaccessible, and in the early seventies its only road broke to pieces every winter. Before that wildest of mountain roads was built, the normal route was the sea; on land there was only a narrow and winding stone-paved muletrack. The sea can be stormy. It is the only sea I have ever seen where a rainbow means the weather is getting worse. They have a proverb about it: rainbow out at sea, cats creep into the oven. The numerous surviving cats must have been nestling deep inside the few remaining ovens on the night of our drive.

The Mani has been terribly depopulated. When it was populous, it was the heartland of vendettas. Every clan had its tower, often quite close together, there were villages of towers. From these they bombarded each other from generation to generation. Power in the Mani moved from hand to hand so often and so drastically that the ironic survivors used to say, '*Maniatika, miniatika,*' which means 'It's once a month in the Mani.' Occasionally acts of piracy were committed; the last fling of the old Mani was in the full nineteenth century, when the young men descended on the coastal resort of

Kalamata, and looted every nail, screw and window-frame they could discover. They or their fathers also defeated a full army of Bavarians employed by the King of Greece, 'the majority of the soldiers,' says Lord Carnarvon in 1839, 'owing their lives only to the contempt of their enemies, who sold them, naked and shivering, in the public market-place at the low price of twopence a head.' When a shipload of families from the Mani was settled in the American West they sat in despair in the green pasture. 'What are we to do without stones?'

Our arrival at Kardamyli in the Mani was like a scene from *Le Grand Meaulnes*. We came down very thankfully from the last rutted hilltop, with the sea hissing and heaving below us, the light fading, and the thunder beginning to rattle. In the streets of the village there was asphalt. It was a quirk of local pride. Only inside the village boundaries of Kardamyli the road was civilized. To the north it was a muddy track, to the south a stony track, but inside Kardamyli it was asphalt. I have been in that village once on a night when there was nothing at all to eat anywhere but one big pot of rice with a few herbs and a single thrush to give it flavour. It was my fate that the thrush herself came out on my plate, and I have to admit she was delicious. On this night the wind had gone mad in the trees. It was a wind, as they say, to ring every bell in Areoupolis. Which island is it where the wind is measured by the damage it does outside the cafés: a hat wind, a chair wind, or a table wind? This was worse than a table wind, and then the rain began to fall.

We made our way in pitch darkness with an expiring torch through the olive groves at the far end of the village. I had been to the house before but not for some time, and we got lost. We came on the stone mule-path, the masterpiece of Mavromichaelis Bey, and followed it for a time. I think we were saved by the smell of an olive-wood fire, distinct and strong through the smells of the sea and the storm and of every awakened bush and of the grove itself. We made for it, and came on a wall. The wall was new to me, and the front door of the house had moved thirty yards. We ought to have arrived in the light. But the house and the welcome, the great stone balcony and the mosaic of sea-pebbles, the rain lashing the vine and the warmth indoors in that long library with its carpets and great windows, the music of Mozart, the English suits and ties, since we were not the only guests, seemed suddenly as strange and as moving to me as they did to Takis and to George.

Next morning the sky was clear. The Mani is full of antiquities, though some of them eluded even Pausanias. He records a good deal, all the same, including the rocks where Peleus first saw Thetis, 'emerging breast-high out of the creamy foam', as Catullus says, 'like a film-star in her bath', as the aged don who taught me Latin once remarked. The Mani is Greece on a small scale, the sweetest apples on the most withered, unattainable branch. Because of the isolation of its villages, they have an amazing variety. Even W. M. Leake was impressed. I like Vitylo, the ancient Oitylos, where the Russians landed under Orlov in the eighteenth century, and the stoniest, southernmost settlements that lie beyond it, as severe as Cornish hamlets perched above their coves and inlets of the sea. One would be lucky to find a boiled egg there, or a sardine. Even the churches are stranger than elsewhere. The medieval Mani seems to have developed its own ikonography, which I believe was influential in the Greek settlements of southern Italy. The head-springs of the Renaissance are among mountains like these.

For some reason the English Sunday papers failed to arrive one week. So when in the end I got back to Athens I walked unsuspecting into a situation of some heat. The Director of the British Council, for reasons of his own, influenced perhaps by a curmudgeonly archaeologist of strong conservative views who was also an acquaintance of mine, had suddenly forbidden the Seferis lecture. This news had caused an explosion of anger among Athenian writers, and it had been given to the B.B.C. Ironic headlines had appeared in the British press. The Ambassador had become agitated. One of his first moves was to visit George Seferis, to deplore this attempt to use his name to cause a political commotion. George, whom I saw almost at once, was gleeful about the interview. Did the Ambassador not know me? Oh, but you ought to. He had read the lecture, it was splendid, he was proud of it, he had no objection at all to it. Of course his permission had been asked.

Meanwhile several people at the American Embassy had 'flu, and the American equivalent of the British Council had fallen for a time into liberal hands. Iannis Tsirkas had arranged for the lecture to take place there. This also had been widely reported. The British Ambassador was in a difficult position at that stage. The tougher wing of the American Embassy had risen as one from its bed and resumed control, and once again the lecture was cancelled. Plainly it would do less harm, it could do only good, to the British in whatever game they were playing, if I now consented to give the lecture for the British Council after all, but I was out of contact with Athens. This is the stage at which I returned. I was willing to give my lecture in the Parthenon if necessary, guarded by paratroops with Papadopoulos in the place of Pallas Athene; so the British Council man, a Mr Ball, was ordered that it should take place.

I have never in my life been treated as such a VIP as that morning at the British Embassy in Athens. The telephoning up and down, the exquisite politeness and humility of the messages, the armed guard at the lift, the conniving amazement of my friend the porter, my only friend until then in that building, and then the big study, the grey hair, the enormous, sleepy dog. We got on very well. To be fair to the Ambassador, I think his personal concern really had perhaps been to protect George Seferis, not to insult him. Mr Ball was quickly called to heel. George had refused to advise me what I should do, and commanded all our other friends to leave me to make my own decision. It was not difficult, and when I told him what it was he was extremely pleased. The Greek version of the lecture was produced by Iannis, but George went over the translation with him, and Iannis has told me that was the best Greek lesson he ever had. As for Mr Ball, I thought him mean-spirited and rude when the day came, and so did the Greeks, but we had our triumph. George said of him, 'He reminds me, my dear, of a song the English used to sing in Egypt: Hitler, he only has one ball. Goering, he has two but small. Himmler has something similar, and Goebbels has no balls at all.'

We had the lecture in Greek privately copied in great numbers and distributed to the audience, since I was permitted to speak only in English, though I was allowed to answer questions in Greek.

164

George decided not to come to the meeting, since his public appearance might well lead to a riot and a brutal police intervention. But Maro Seferis came. There were no empty seats; a few young people failed to get in. The police presence was evident in the square outside, but not overwhelming. The public reaction came the next day. It was full page news in every newspaper not controlled by the government. It was their first opportunity to say what they thought about George Seferis, and they used it as fully as they could. I do not know whether that was organized by Iannis, but I would not be at all surprised. I became a minor local celebrity. It was therefore time to leave Athens for another long journey.

Anyway I had to go home soon. So Takis and I took off in his car for a tour of the antiquities of north-western Greece, most of which I had never seen, with the idea of parting at Corfu, where I could take a boat to Italy. Those boats call at Brindisi and Bari and Venice. Arriving in Venice in the spring, slowly swinging and turning through the still water of the lagoon after the open sea, twisting in always closer among the acid green trees and the pink and white brick, must be one of the greatest pleasures that exist for travellers. Takis had served in the civil war in northwestern Greece, and this was the first time he had ever been back. His memories were fear and horror: the panic fear of shell-fire falling very close as he crossed a river, and the horror of abandoned partisan camps, the raw food half-eaten, the poor scattered possessions, the fate of the pursued. At one place droves of twenty or thirty of them at a time had wire twisted round their necks and a small charge of dynamite attached, that removed all the heads together. Beyond us the big mountains of the Albanian border bulked in the sky, covered in white snow.

But the sun shone, and the deep pink flowers of the judas trees blossomed here and there among the rocks. They seem to me somehow the bravest of all flowering trees, against their grey mountainsides. The shrine of our pilgrimage was Dodona, the ancient oracle of Zeus. I had never realized before how utterly remote it is from the classical world. The easiest way for the ancient Greeks to get there must have been from the sea, by a mule-track that still exists. The local people five hundred or more years before

Christ were hardly Greeks. Homer says their feet were unwashed and they slept on the ground. Most of the early pottery that has been found at Dodona, right down to the fifth century BC, came from high up in the northern Balkans. It must have been the poor offerings of wandering shepherds. Even the questions that the oracle answered seem from those that survive to have been the private questions of very ordinary people:

'Herakleidas asks Zeus and Dione for good fortune and asks the god about offspring, whether it shall be from Aigle, the wife he now has.'

'Nikokrateia requests to which god she should best and most excellently sacrifice and be rid of her disease.'

'… if we go to Elina or to Anaktorion and sell the …'

'Lysanias asks Zeus Naios and Dione whether the baby Annyla is now bearing is really his.'

'… whether it would be better and more profitable for me to buy the house in the city and the land.'

'Kleoutas asks Zeus and Dione if it is sound and profitable for him to be a shepherd.'

The shepherds around Dodona must always have been nearly nomadic until modern times. The weather conditions are so extreme, the mountain pastures so desirable in spring, so unbearable in winter. Life is still undisturbed and simple there. We saw old women in their black dresses and embroidery spinning wool as they walked the roads. The local wine was a revelation. In 1979 it was just beginning to be exploited, but until then no one who had not lived nearby had ever heard of it. It is a sparkling wine called Zitsa. I have no idea how it originated or when, from what forgotten French or Italian influence, but Zitsa is the best substitute for champagne I know; in the earlier seventies it cost five or ten shillings a bottle. I remember that we drank ours snowcooled by a roadside, while we were looking for Dodona. The place is more impressive than its ruins, but the ruins are fine. The stone is all lichen-encrusted, the grass is very green in spring, and violets grow in the prodigal profusion which is the reward of mountains and of water. The theatre is late, and not much of a theatre; like most of these monuments, it was several times rebuilt. It first appeared only in the third century BC under Pyrrhos, the ally by marriage of the Macedonians, who tapped the unexhausted power of this distant and wild province to make the last Greek bid for world supremacy. He invaded Sicily and Italy with elephants and an army, and for a time he was a formidable threat to the expanding power of Rome. The oldest surviving building at Dodona is no earlier than the fourth century BC, and by far the most beautiful is the ruined Christian church of the fifth and sixth centuries A.D. Even if it stood alone it would be worth a long journey.

Corfu was thrilling and disappointing. We lived in the town, with its amusing English architecture and Italian colonnades, to be close to the museum and the best of the ancient sites. But the police governed Corfu very roughly. It was an adventure to obtain any newspaper except the government ones that the papersellers called *Pravda* and *Isvestia*. The vintage had been a disaster, and neither of us had ever tasted worse wine in Greece. There were no old-fashioned taverns, only wine-shops in the Sicilian style, in the back alleys. But it was outside one of them that Solomos first heard his Cretan singer, and modern Greek literature began. The caves and the villages that Laurence Durrell had made famous were ruined and vulgarized. Palaiokastritsa was already becoming an insult to the eye. Still, the Corfu cricket club was playing on the gravel, and one could eat a Turkish sweet now rare in Greece called an *ekmek* in the colonnade. I was interested to notice that some of the technical terms of Corfu cricket are Italian, not English. Was cricket an Italian invention?

There are certainly unspoiled corners even in Corfu, but they are mostly owned by the rich or the eccentric or the very lucky. We did visit the absurd palace of the German Emperor, and I did break into the charming park of the King of Greece to inspect the splendid ruins of a temple which are enclosed in it. We made some discoveries about the ancient merchant city of Corfu, which have now been rendered obsolete by being confirmed by excavation. And the Corfu museum must be one of the richest in Greece. But my greatest good luck came by chance, in the search for Edward Lear's lodgings. We were told of a lady who might help us in a tourist office. She was Marie Aspioti, a friend of Durrell and an authority on Lear's letters. She realized from newspaper photographs that I had given the lecture on Seferis, and took me under her wing. Doors opened everywhere, we had a wonderful time.

The most moving and curious survial in Corfu is surely the Readers' Club, certainly the earliest club in Greece, and probably the earliest modern library. Readers' Clubs existed in the eighteen-hundreds all over Europe. They were liberal, co-operative and progressive. Part of their intention was popular education. The roots of the Greek national movement are entangled in them. It was at the Readers' Club in Geneva that the volunteers gathered who went south to the war of independence. The Readers' Club at Corfu has a splendid nineteenth-century dignity. I had little time to read there, but I did find an early edition of a translation of Shakespeare into modern Greek verse. Someone had marked it a little in pencil. It so happens that we know Edward Lear read that translation. He quotes it joyfully in a letter. He particularly liked *Mpaou Vgaou* for 'Bow-wow':

'This place is wonderfully lovely. I wish you could see it; if you came I could put you up beautifully, and feed you on ginger-beer and claret and prawns and figs.' Or again: 'Anything like the splendour of olive-grove and orange garden, the blue of sky and ivory of church and chapel, the violet of mountain, rising from peacock-wing-hued sea, and tipped with lines of silver snow, can hardly be imagined. I wish to goodness gracious grasshoppers you were here.' But in his rooms overlooking the old harbour he was not so happy. He was plagued by pianos, 'jolly jigs', thin walls and floors and, I suppose, open windows. What was worse, the invention of cheap photographs was already making it hard to sell drawings. His view of British influence in Corfu, at a time when the British ruled, was not at all rosy. And 'the aspect spiritual of this little piggywiggy island is much as a very little village in Ireland would be – peopled by Orangemen and Papists – and having all the extra fuss and ill-will produced by a Court and small officials – more or less with or against a resident crowded garrison.'

My principal surprises in Corfu, apart from its antiquities, were the books and the archives. The archives are the most extensive, the most ancient, and the most available in Greece, but for some reason they remain unfrequented by scholars. Their show-piece is a small piece of paper that would fit into the palm of one's hand. It is simply inscribed, '*Touts les fiefs et droits quelconques sont abolis dans cette île. Napoléon.*' But they extend through acres of dusty cellars under the Palace of St Michael and St George. They contain all the papers of the British, the French and the Venetian administrations, all the records of the law-courts, and monastic papers going far back into the Middle Ages. Corfu has a noble history. It has nursed poets and historians. George Phrantzes, who was secretary to the Emperor, and rode with him round the walls of Constantinople the night before it fell, ended as a monk here. This is where he wrote his history and where he died. Nicander who fought for Henry VIII against the Scots came from here. Corfu, under the French not the British, had the first museum in Greece.

But there was a bad surprise. Takis had gone home and I was waiting for my ship. At the last moment I was arrested. The interrogation itself was brief; it was largely a question of identity. What was more unpleasant was the wait while a police captain telephoned office after office on a non-functioning telephone to discover whether it was permitted that I should leave the country. There is a smell of old sweat and stale cigarette-ends about Greek police offices which I find not only repulsive but frightening. The prison of Corfu is a notoriously evil place, and I had no desire to spend a night in it. Of course, it would be a bad move for the Colonels to hold me, or so I told myself. They would look so silly, and there was no charge they could easily bring. My friends in Greece and outside it would break out into an orgy of public indignation. The Colonels would certainly look very silly indeed. But once they put handcuffs on me I would not be feeling so satisfied about that. It is not comfortable to disappear as untraceably as I might have done. The whole episode lasted less than an hour, but I knew then that sooner or later something worse was likely to happen. I accepted that: I had already accepted it.

In those few years I was writing and translating poetry. Those of my own poems that were written in Greece are easy to pick out, if anyone is interested in them. To me it feels a long time ago; life feels like a very long time. I expressed what I felt in this way or that, but I found most of the expressions inadequate or cryptic. I think like many people I reserved the whole truth for some future time of peace. Now I can hardly bear to remember the whole truth. People were being tortured, even murdered. There was extremely little to be done about it, but we exhausted ourselves doing that little. At the back of everyone's fears was another still more awful civil war. That is why those who resisted the Colonels were using no violence of any kind. Almost any civil war is worse than almost any daily dose of horror. Nor is it possible under modern standards of international interference to fight a civil war alone. It has not been possible since Spain, a generation ago. When the ex-King of Greece made his *démarche*, he walked into a carefully prepared trap. He was encouraged to believe the army was loyal to him, but the moment his officers showed their hand they were arrested. He left at once with his family and his dogs. He also abandoned the Greek navy, most of which was anti-Colonel. The arrests and the tortures that followed were sickening. What most characterized that time is the presence of fear, continually punctuated by horror and shock. The fear was not fear for oneself, or rarely so, but fear of consequences.

Yet our pleasures were very sharp. One I shall never forget was a spring holiday in Crete when I went for a walking tour with an Oxford friend. The idea was to walk from end to end of the whole island, but we started out with such a long coastal walk that that became impossible. We set out westwards from Chania, a Venetian harbour town then in its last perfect beauty. It contained my favourite Cretan restaurant, the Crabs, where it used to be normal to find an American writer on a winter's morning writing love-letters in English for the loose ladies who danced at night at the night-club in the old military hut next door. The harbour at Chania sheltered a whole colony of writers and painters. Most of the writers really wrote, and most of the painters painted. None was Greek, some were homosexual, which led to a lot of comedy and one tragedy. An alcoholic, homosexual, non-writing writer had his throat cut by a local boy so thoroughly that when they found him his head was held in place only by his Harvard scarf. He was a friend of mine, I liked him greatly, but he was certainly a doomed character. He behaved intolerably to the boy; what happened was almost predictable. I very much respect the only one of my friends who did what he could for the boy at his trial. At the time of the walking tour I had not been to Crete for years; there was no one I knew at the Crabs except the waiters.

The first night we reached Phalasarna, an ancient town cut into solid rock with the sea pounding in it. It lies towards the north end of the west coast of Crete, at the far end of a long, sandy beach. No one lived there at all except the guardian of the antiquities, in a small house on the beach that sold lemonade in summer, with a little market garden for cucumbers and tomatoes under plastic shelters. He showed us with pride a wooden cross among the sands where there were fresh flowers. It was the grave of an Australian colonel. The body had been taken home he said, a year or two ago, but he still kept the place as it had been, where the colonel had died. It happened during the fall of Crete. One of the last two ships to escape from Chania had limped round the promontory under cover of darkness, but in the morning the Stukas found her. The colonel had disembarked his men, he knew the ship would perish. He was killed by a stray bomb on the beach, and they buried him there.

The guardian served us supper, after which like a Homeric host he asked us the wide-ranging questions that lonely men do ask. He had music of some kind, I think a gramophone. Then he brought in his wife and three beautiful daughters. They danced for us and he invited us to dance with them. I was too old for those capers, but they taught my friend a Greek dance, and he taught them a Scottish dance. Before we went to bed we had an ominous conversation. He would like us to know that in Crete the custom was to take blood vengeance on anyone who wronged a woman. If anyone laid a hand on any of his daughters he would personally be obliged to kill that person, even if he had to travel far to do it. We were then shown with some apology into a cheese-store, a dark and dank outhouse smelling powerfully of cheeses and of the damp. A storm had got up outside, so we nested there.

All the next day the wind raved. Once or twice I was blown over, but the track was pleasant, the gorse was blossoming so that whole mountains smelt of it, and small short-lived flowers were creeping out among the rocks. Was it that day or the next we found bee-orchids, in a field above the sea? We passed silver mines, which explained the otherwise inexplicable existence of Phalasarna. Once it was a seaport, but sea-level has altered sixteen feet, and the rock-cut chambers that the sea enters now are only ruined tombs where rock had once been quarried. There was more to discover at Pharlasarna than we discovered. This region, and in fact most of Crete, was thoroughly explored by John Pendlebury before the war. His death as a soldier in the defence of Heraklion against the Germans, charging too far ahead of his men, and the death of Humphrey Paine from blood poisoning at Mycenae, left British archaeology crippled in Greece. I have very seldom found anything in Crete that advances what Pendlebury had already published when I was a schoolboy.

We spent the next night, wind-battered and exhausted, in a small, white monastery in the south-western corner of the island. It had two goats, one donkey, and two or three monks. The season was Lent, so the food was particularly nauseating. It was at this stage that we began to have fantasies about food; we conducted long dialogues as we walked, in the accents of Irish labourers, about the delights of HP Sauce. Cyril Connolly used to ask for a bottle of Worcester sauce to be buried with him, in case the cooking was not up to scratch in the next world. We were hungrier, and coarser, and far from home. The monastery was called Chrysoskalitissa, the Lady of the Golden Stairs. Among the ninety steps in the rock, one is supposed to be of gold, but no sinner can see it. 'Perhaps it was a treasure,' we were told, 'buried somewhere here; we have all looked, but no one has found it.' We found a few crumbs of Roman pottery where Pendlebury had found more, and we searched for some remnants of a late Bronze Age settlement of fishermen, which existed not far away, but found no trace of it.

On the third night we arrived at Palaiochora, a fine little town with a working harbour. There we settled, to explore the countryside around it. The rocky promontory beyond the town was fortified by the Venetians in 1782 as the castle of Selinos, which gave its name to this entire province. It was ruined by Barbarossa the pirate, in 1593, and even its name vanished. Now it is called the Fortetsa, and the name of the town just means 'the old town'. In 1860 it was nothing but a few warehouses. But underneath its houses lies a classical city. The Fortetsa is a wonderful place, sunny and windswept and full of migratory birds. Somewhere nearby the courageous and invaluable ship *Arkadi*, carrying refugees, was driven ashore by a Turkish squadron in the rebellion of 1866. There are folk songs about her:

> Where are you and you do not come, proud *Arkadi*?
> Midday has past, evening has gone by
> and still your white sails have not appeared.
> Did you not stay in Crete with your children?
> Do you not battle the north wind, sport in calm water?
> Hawk of America, dolphin of Greece!
> Ach! They brought us bitter, poisoned news,
> we run to you in grief across the sands

From Palaiochora the coastal route we were following was impassable. We took to the sea. After a day or two of negotiation, we contrived to travel in a small *kaiki* delivering cement eastwards to Souyia, and to stop for lunch on the way at the isolated shrine of Lisos. It was a perfect morning, with a breeze that freshened our faces and hardly ruffled the water. We tied bottles on strings to cool them in the sea. Someone fished with a line. Lisos is very remote indeed. No road reaches it, and the place itself is nothing but a grove near the sea-shore where spring-water breaks out of the rocks. It was once a prosperous temple of Asklepios. The exact site, which is obvious enough if one knows where to look, was discovered in 1957 by a local peasant searching for the water that cured diseases. He found a hill of broken statues: Asklepios and Health and Plouton of the underworld, statues of children, a girl with pigeons, a boy with a hare, and one golden snake with the inscription Asklas. From that snake's name, which is usually *askalabos*, Asklepios took his own name.

Lisos is quiet and full of birds. It was the day when the flocks started out for their high pastures on the other side of the mountains, so we were invited to a shepherds' feast of home-baked bread and cream cheese and light, delicious wine. It was a scene out of Cymbeline, much more Shakespearean than it was Arcadian. The ruins were beautiful, unexploited, not too demanding. The host had that intense and simple sweetness of one isolated in a cranny of fertility and content. The conversation was a great pleasure. Today I can remember only the accent, not a word that was said; it was about sheep and proverbs and water, the staples of life. A week later we met the same flock with its shepherds, high up in the mountains nearly a hundred miles away. We travelled together for a few hours.

At Souyia when we got ashore, we looked for the friend of a friend who kept a small tavern on the beach. We knew of him through an English officer, from the days of the German occupation; they had fought through it together, moving from cave to cave and village to village in the mountains. Souyia was one of the places where British submarines would creep inshore from Alexandria. Now, like most of those places, it had a highly suspicious garrison of policemen, and one of them was hanging about the tavern. Apparently my name and passport number were on the general wanted list, and I was taken away immediately for interrogation, to a small villa full of policemen with a garden of sunflowers and roses. They let me go after an hour or two, but it was a nasty jolt. Later I apologised to the tavern keeper, but he brushed the politenesses aside. What worried him was an infringement of Cretan hospitality, that this should happen to me in his house. He leaned close over the table to explain.

'They are foreigners, they are not true Cretans. They are not from here. They are jungle animals from Heraklion and Thrace.'

From Souyia we wandered inland, with the intention of exploring the high mountain plain of Omalo and descending the Samaria gorge to the sea. The gorges of Crete are deep and long, with magnificent rocks and trees and birds. They are even better than French gorges. In bad weather the Samaria gorge is impassable. From end to end is a long day's walk, with two or three river crossings. In summer that is a mild adventure, but when the river is in spate it becomes formidable. Rain fell in the mountains, and we called it off. I have regretted that decision ever since. And yet a mountain not climbed, a great gorge where one has never been, can infect imagination as deeply as the real experience can haunt memory. I have walked enough Cretan gorges to know in my bones what that greatest of them must be like.

We returned to Chania by bus, then to Rethymnon, eastwards along the north coast, and inland to Argyrokastro, the end of bus routes and of what most people would recognise as roads. Out of the whole of southern Europe, if ever I had to live permanently abroad I would choose somewhere near Argyrokastro. The eagles are always in the sky over the same mountainside. The pure air, the rushing water, the great plane trees and the enormous valleys maintain a life which is hard and happy. It was at Argyrokastro that the old lady wanted to give me the head of a statue. It was also there that at last we heard 'Erotokritos' sung by an old shepherd, in the tavern on the edge of the village where there was nothing to eat. At the end of his hour all the twenty men in the room were weeping, and so was he. So was I, of course.

We set off at dawn. As we came into a small village at nine in the morning, a large man in a straw hat addressed us in English from his throne on a stone wall. We answered briskly, fearing a Greek American, but he kept pace with us, insisting that we turn aside to see his fine house. It became hard to refuse; then we discovered by discreet compliments that he learnt his English from the British during the German occupation. At half-past-nine we sat down in his house, under a wall full of medals and documents, to a feast of infinite freshly cooked courses, 'just little things, you know, to go with the wine', which lasted until twelve. There was no refusing anything. The third platter of fried eggs, the fourth of thin, delicate cheese-pies, followed their brethren. One of the documents on the wall was from George VI, 'To our trusty well-beloved brother, greetings.' I am not sure what decoration it represented. And there was a letter from Alexander of Tunis.

'In those days we were having gangs. I was having my gang also. One day I made a feast here for all the Englishes. They are under stones, and it is cold, it very cold. So we all ready, wine is ready, table is ready, they are all here. Suddenly a boy came running. Like one come now, when he see you approaching the village. This boy say,

"Germans is coming, very fast. Patrol." Bang, we push English in cellar, under trapdoor, barrel on trapdoor. We have no time. Then in come Germans. In patrol. What is all here? What is feasting. I say, Greek *freund*, German *freund*. He say "*Deutsche freund, ist gut, ja?*" In they come, they eat all food, drink all wine, much wine. Suddenly I see, my God, my pistol. Is under tiles, sticking out, under roof. I make excuse. I move something. I hid him in pot. Phew! Then they go, they make camp, down valley, by Argyrokastro. I take my gangs, we go at night, we shoot all, all every one. Bang, bang, bang. First he eat well, then he die.'

The roars of his laughter still echoed in my head as we staggered out of the village. We were walking now in a sea of little boys. I had given the son of our new friend my compass, and he brought the whole of his age-group to show us our path. This was tiresome, and honour demanded we show no weakness. So we escaped, with the last drip of energy in our veins, by running for half a mile. They flagged, they turned home, we collapsed. In the early evening, we reached Alones, to weep at the grave of Gustavo Duran. His bust in bronze is the first and only monument of that whitewashed village. It stands like a metal head on a flat stone body, on top of a tall tablet with an inscription. The village tap projects from the tablet just about where his private parts would be. It is a curiously moving monument; Gustavo would have liked it greatly.

We spent the night with our friends. We explored the village fields for ancient sites; I have little recollection of what stones we saw; they were obliterated by Cretan wild lilies. These are not the wild Madonna lilies that figured so largely in the art of Knossos, but the white, pure cones with one corner turned down that grow wild only here in all Europe. They stand about two feet tall on single green stems among the grazing grounds. From Alones we crossed the mountains to the south coast, by sheep-tracks and paths. We saw many spring flowers, some of them rare, but nothing so impressive as those lilies. I can recall their delicate smell to this day, and the healthiness of their texture. We passed by a sheep-shearing and met the flock from Lissos. We saw a ruined village where the Germans had murdered those of the inhabitants they could catch by burning them in the baker's oven.

From the great monastery of Preveli, now a police garrison with a very few monks, where we dined on lettuce, rusks and theological conversation, we turned north to Heraklion. The police were not unfriendly at Preveli. The enemy there was a colony of hippies who had been living for years in unutterable squalor, with free sex and no sewers, in the caves further east, and stealing as they chose from the fields and the flocks. The police had a special telescope mounted for viewing the rocks where these admittedly wicked persons used to sunbathe naked. As we were fully dressed and respectably behaved, they were not interested in us. I think we got good marks for theological conversation, an ordeal as fearsome to the police as it was to us, and for interest in Cretan antiquities. The monastic museum at Preveli is fascinating, and we explored an old sub-monastery nearby with magnificent stone vaulting, now a cowshed. The vaulting looked medieval, the museum commemorated Cretan resistance to the Turks hardly a hundred years ago, but it all seemed one world.

The end of that holiday, after a few more days, was a trip out from Athens to Sounion. A big military parade was due to take place in Athens; on that day, above others, we all had the habit of getting away into the countryside. I went with my Oxford friend by bus the previous afternoon. We slept on the sands and made ourselves decent the next morning in a hotel where we had breakfast. By that time I knew Sounion very well indeed. I had almost completed the early pages of my commentary. The greatest coup was discovering a sketch-map by the eighteenth-century French consul Fauvel, in a department of the Bibliothèque Nationale, that showed an ancient building, now vanished, where I suspected one had been; and then the confirmation of that discovery from a heavy block of marble lying close under the cliffs. In the two days with my friend there was a lot to see. We spent half the night as well as most of the morning on our explorations. It was too cold to swim far, but we did everything else.

About noon on the day of the parade George Seferis came out from Athens with his wife and Takis and George Pavlopoulos. Lunch was a feast. We ate in the open air at a little fish tavern on the beach. It was crowded, but our table was reserved and we got excellent, perfectly fresh fish, simply cooked, with that lighter retsina of the far end of Attica. We spoke of limericks, and George confessed to having written one in English. 'If I can remember it, my dear, it was like this: There was a young girl of Naupactus, who had an affair with a cactus ...' Then he noticed that all the tables around had fallen silent. They were listening with baited breath. He refused to go on. I shall never know how it ended, and not for the lack of many guesses. He was happy that day, although there was a black undercurrent of things that we all avoided mentioning. After lunch he became enthusiastic about the landscape at the back of Sounion with its forts and ancient farms, which he had never heard of. He was ill then, but he asked if a road could get him up there by car.

Takis drove his car when necessary as the ancient Britons drove their chariots. He took it up the track behind the Triton hotel, and then two-thirds of the way up a cliff, when it perched. We managed to get George to the top. He was triumphantly happy. It was his last walk ever on such a hill, and his first for a long time. Maro gathered irises and orchids, the gorse was in full flower, and a lesser thorn, *tribolo*, lay here and there in dangerous cushions. I showed George Seferis how its natural shape, made a little bigger in bronze, was the ancient Greek defence against cavalry. One can see them to this day in museums. I asked him the Greek word for gorse. There was some discussion about that. George Pavlopoulos remembered a local name, *asphalaktos*, which had something to do with safety; Takis, I think, remembered the name in another form. George Seferis was sure it was an ancient word, *aspalathos*, that had survived. That night, when Takis called late at his house, he had found his word in Plato. Soon afterwards he wrote 'Epi Aspalathon', 'On gorse' (or 'On thorns') his last, terrible poem. The phrase 'again in the spring season' which occurs in it, comes from a famous song of the war of independence. The rest is clear enough:

(Republic, 616)
It was beautiful, Sounion, that day of the Annunciation
again in the spring season.
A handful of green leaves among the rusty rocks

178

the red earth and the gorse
with big needles ready and yellow bloom.
Far off the ancient columns, strings of a harp still echoing …
Tranquility.

What could have reminded me of Aridaios.
I think one word in Plato, lost in the channels of the mind;
the name of the yellow bush
has not altered since those times.
In the evening I found the passage;
'They bound him hand and foot', he tells us,
'they threw him down and flayed him,
dragged him to pieces, tore him apart
on the thorny gorse-bushes
and went and flung him into hell in rags.'
So in the world below he payed his crimes,
Pamphylian Aridaios, most miserable tyrant.

31st of March, 1971

That was almost the last time I saw George Seferis. He was happy in his friendships and above all in his wife. There was a continual playfulness about him; even though his profound gravity was never distant, the playfulness was like sunshine. I have never known quite that combination in another human being. It was like the surface of the sea. George's playfulness was what I sometimes imagine to be the characteristic tone of Horace. I remember a phone call about Francis Jammes, for whom we shared an enthusiasm. 'I remember Tom Eliot, my dear, was always calling him Francis Jam.' Long, affectionate chuckles. The last things George ever said to me were that I must translate George Pavlopoulos, and take care of that Oxford friend, see that he did not make a shipwreck of his life. We went away home. On the day that George Pavlopoulos published his first book, George Seferis died. Maro cut off her beautiful hair, and flung it into his grave.

9

The End of It

A THENS UNDER the Colonels was a grim city. For years there was no possibility of any massive, popular demonstration against the government except at public funerals. Twenty thousand people followed the coffin of George Seferis. Something like a hundred thousand walked in the funeral of Papandreou, the old prime minister, who died under the dictatorship. Inch by inch, through incessant internal protest and the pressure of foreign opinion, the Greeks won a few small liberties, a little room to manoeuvre. When Lady Fleming's passport was confiscated, we had it returned to her by hand of officer with one letter to *The Times*. All our telephones were tapped, but that was in some ways useful. It meant that one could always let the big brothers know what one wanted them to believe. For a time I had four police followers and two cars; more distinguished figures sometimes had eight. They frequently led to situations of farce.

Everyone knows nowadays there are two quite distinct varieties of surveillance, one when the authorities want you to feel their presence, the other when they want to observe unobserved. The second is even easier to outwit than the first, once one has the least suspicion of it. It was possible, for example, to make three appointments in a morning, all on the telephone. The police would follow you to the first, wait outside with their raincoats and their worry-beads to conduct you to the second, and then as often as not pick you up at the third. Meanwhile, you were free. If they were in cars one could lose them by crossing both lanes of an urban motorway on foot. But on the whole there was no point in annoying them; it was an indulgence. One of mine was a gorilla of a man with a scarred face like a gangster. I have seen him since in a grand suit with a gold watch. Another looked as if he had blisters and stomach ulcers; several times I tried to offer him a drink, but when I finally pinned him down and did so, he just looked sad, and I never saw him again.

It was summer, and I drove south across Europe with another Oxford friend to visit Takis and George Pavlopoulos at Hagios Andreas near Pyrgos, where George lived for the hottest months in a hut on the beach. We took the car ferry from Brindisi. The boat was Greek so our passports were checked at once. Usually, when my passport appeared, the police held me for ten minutes before I was let through, but this time it was painless. We ate a delicious picnic on deck and went to sleep in sleeping bags. During the night the loudspeaker droned on and on. Lowis Pooter, Lewis Piotr, Lewis Patri. It was obviously for me. I went down, with innocence on my face, to see the police. Some small hitch, and would I report before we arrived next morning at Corfu? We were going on to Patras, but Corfu is the technical point of entry even if you are not landing there. I was concerned that whatever happened next should be seen by as many people as possible. I had no wish simply to disappear, and if I was to be refused entry I was not inclined for that to occur secretly either.

My friend knew no Greek at all, he had never before visited Greece. I told him I thought it was just the usual heavy breathing, and he was to wait where he was. I went down again at the last moment. Would I step along to the office on the quay? I would not, who was in charge? Would I come now? I would not, where was the captain of the ship? A mate turned up, and a uniformed police officer from the shore. Would I go now? I was going to be deported. All right, but I wanted to see the order in writing. Would I step along? What about the friend and the car? That could not be be moved. It was at the back of the ship. It would have to go to Patras. In the end I was surrounded by sailors with iron bars, soldiers with machine-guns, police with pistols and some with sticks. Distinctly threatening things were said. I had chosen my position with my back against a big truck, and there I stuck, until the officer in charge really did arrive.

He wore a Savile Row suit, he was small and quiet. As he entered the throng, a pool of ice and silence spread around him. He was a nasty piece of work, that man. I knew him already by name; I am glad to have met him face to face. He showed me the order for my deportation, signed and dated at Athens, and let me take a copy. That was useful, because later I was able to check it with the dates of arrests and other events. The Colonels were worried in the week it was signed about students and anyone who might have influence on them. They foresaw the future better than I did. The senior policeman negotiated with the captain to have the car released, but that failed; I had already, to my pleasure and amazement, delayed the sailing of the ship by an hour and a half. Hence the angry sailors and the threats. It was agreed my friend should be sent back at once to Brindisi, and I emerged on deck, to his great surprise, with a group of armed soldiers, to pick up a few things.

For an interesting hour I found myself under armed guard on the quay at Corfu. The police captain asked me about my political views and I greatly enjoyed expressing them. As they drew a lively appreciation from the crowd, he had the crowd dispersed. I sent a telegram to George from the next boat, which was Italian. Then for ten long days I waited at Brindisi. My friend had been dumped at Igoumenitsa, a grimy beach at the terminal of a motor-road, and it took him that long to get back to Italy. The British Consul at Corfu, a lady, was notably unhelpful, indeed hostile. For all he knew I was in prison; he had last seen me under guard; she assured him there was no need to look for me, though she knew nothing about the deportation order. I record this because it is useful to know the probabilities if one is ever tempted to rely on such a person. It is useful to know who one's friends are.

It was at Brindisi that I really felt like a Greek. I ate in the small taverns haunted by exiles, and observed the flies on the wall as they observed them. I remember a mother who came there once a year to have news of her son. There were worse cases. My own separation from Greece was a comparatively light matter. It made some headlines, for a moment it was on the front page, then I set to work, free at last, to tell the whole of what I knew about the Colonels. I had the impression of some pressure against the publication of this document, but whoever that may be, I was bound to publish soon and negotiations were still taking place when the Greek Embassy in London announced that the ban on me was withdrawn. I insisted on a signed letter and got it. The signature, which was surely genuine, looked like a comic invention. It was E. Stofitopoulos.

So I was back in Greece that winter of early 1973 when the dictatorship began to fall apart. Three public trials, fully reported in the Greek press, marked the late winter. One was the trial of Nikos Panagoulis, whom the secret service had lured back into Greece in a foredoomed attempt to get his tortured and starving brother out of a military prison. He behaved gallantly in the dock as in the rest of his actions, but without much wisdom. His trial was therefore depressing. The second trial was that of most of the committee of the Greek communist party. There were two parties, one Stalinist and based abroad, the other a wounded survivor of many betrayals. These were in the dock. I am not a communist or a Marxist or a materialist or an atheist, but I find those people admirable and very moving. As Gustavo used to say of the anarchists, they are among the noblest human beings I have ever encountered.

They were arrested late in the day, through the paradoxical mistake they made that in a fashionable street in central Athens they hoped to live safely. But at least they had no weapons of any kind; they had broken no law except by party membership. They were therefore bound to be tried in a civil court without reporting restrictions. Their speeches from the dock were long, lucid expositions of the recent history of Greece. They were brilliant. If at that moment they could have opened a recruiting office, half Athens would have joined them. Today, as a party, they hardly exist. But there was nothing they could have contributed to their country and its people so effective as those speeches. The third trial was that of an airforce officer, a war hero retired from service. His contribution, which had cheered us all up for a year or more, had been blowing up parked American motor cars. No one was ever hurt; he risked his life more than once to ensure that. In prison he was worse tortured, I think, than anyone else in the seven years. But he was unbreakable, indomitable. In court his answers were of a resilient gallantry. His trial was the most impressive and the most exhilarating of all.

Before Easter, the first political demonstrations for years in Athens took place. The University of Athens is a dispersed organisation, but the Polytechnic is a coherent unit, on the Napoleonic model. Lectures are compulsory, classes regular, the students know each other, and their morale and intelligence are at least as high as those of university students. The first outbreak was an occupation of the University Law School, a tall, ugly block of buildings in the centre of Athens, where every central bus service begins and ends, a stone's throw from Flocca, a few hundred yards from Constitution Square in one direction and the Place de la Concorde in the other. Crowds blocked the roads outside. From time to time the police charged, but always uselessly. The crowd gave way like water, and I soon saw that those they were after had made a careful tactical study of the area. They always escaped in some unexpected direction, and always reappeared chanting somewhere else when the police were exhausted. The roads for half a mile around were blocked with cars hooting the rhythm of the slogans. I did see one boy trip and fall. An old and fat policeman lagging behind his column kicked him for two or three minutes. All I could do was to approach slowly, staring at the policeman with a disgusted expression. He shambled off; the boy was not badly hurt. But after dark that night there was serious breaking of heads.

The original student leadership were summarily called up into the army; I dread to think what happened to them there. One boy escaped; the police were known to be after him, and Pattakos had personally assured the father, who was a civil servant, that he was interested in the case. At this time all of us, but particularly the bravest and wisest, among whom I rank Vanna, were much concerned by consequences. The rebellion by students was very, very brave, but it was also heartrending. It was going to end terribly. I believe now that morally it was the students who were most responsible for the liberty of their country. Their fate and their courage worked in everyone's mind. At any rate it was a serious time. Above all it was not the moment for stupid personal adventures and self-expressions. But I could not have done otherwise than I did.

A lady I knew, the daughter of a former prime minister, sent me a message to call on her very early if I could, before her watchers came on duty. I went out of mere politeness. The student on the run was near the end of his resources; could I shelter him? I said of course not: my room, which she thought a flat, was highly unsuitable for such games. If he had absolutely nowhere in a week's time, of course I would have him if I must, but I assured her we would both go straight to prison for it. My landlord and the other tenants were curious enough and suspicious enough to ensure that. The police observed me closely. They had recently set up a house or a flat in the street, which we thought they used for some kind of listening device. I hoped I had put her off, but we did arrange a simple code. Such codes, used once only, are unbreakable.

One morning it happened. I arranged to meet him on the edge of my neighbourhood, at a crossroads where one could meet anyone by chance, and where I could be certain that neither of us was watched before I took him home. I nearly gave it all away at the rendezvous. As I sat outside a café a young man came running full pelt down the hill, throwing desperate glances here and there. I got up and he looked at me with relief.

'Can I help you? Are you looking for someone?'

'Yes, 15 Hymettos Street.'

'Are you sure? That's all?'

'That's all the address I was given. I'm late for my lesson.'

When the real young man appeared a little later he was unmistakable. He stepped groggily out of a taxi. He was pale and unshaven. He was too nervous to approach me even though he knew at once who I was. My first task was to calm him down, which I achieved with a bath and coffee and croissants and some Bach flute music. He had a passport, which was English and brand new. It looked perfectly genuine to me. So I told him to his surprise that he was leaving the country at dawn the next morning. That was a nightmare of a day. I managed to fit him up with most of what he needed, including an English briefcase, a gentleman's tie that I used sometimes and a superior shirt, but I had to go and buy him shoes. His passport description was company director, and since his English was imperfect it was essential he should at least look the part. We spent the afternoon reading Evelyn Waugh aloud.

I had given him the choice of train or plane, and he sensibly chose one brief intense anguish rather than the long, dangerous, relaxing dullness of a railway journey. The ticket was a problem, since to buy an air ticket one had to produce his passport, and if he was caught the ticket office could be traced at once, so whoever bought it would be investigated. After some agonising, I went to Takis. I told him little, though he guessed more at once; he had, after all, read the papers. He had an assistant, a law student, who would be impossible to trace, and I knew he sometimes used this young man for odd jobs at agencies and offices. Unfortunately, it was one of the days the assistant chose to turn up three hours late for work. But at the last minute he did turn up, he bought the ticket, and Takis sacked him the same day. The shoes roughly fitted. The intractable problem was spectacles. They were shown in the passport photograph, and the foolish boy had left them in one of the many rooms he had lived in. Getting them back was a fearsome task.

The boy was hard to persuade that he had to dress up. In the end he would have passed muster in a London club, but the question of his pullover was fiercely contested. He must take his red pullover, he wanted to wear it, he was famous for it, he said. He took it hard that I forbade him to make phone calls to say goodbye to friends on my extremely tapped telephone. The business of the spectacles lasted all day. I borrowed a pair but they were hopeless. I tried a doctor who could do nothing. A girl who visited the dangerous room he had just left rang the wrong doorbell and retired in terror from the campaign. Eventually, we made a night sortie like a pair of commandos in a street battle, and called a friend of his from a public phone. We got his glasses, and the friend came at midnight to the corner of an alley, with the parting present of a pebble from a Greek beach.

He got away easily, with his *Daily Telegraph* and his bag. I was left a bit dazed, with a few keys to unsafe rooms and a Greek identity card, which turned out to be nearly indestructible, so I lodged it with Takis. The boy was brave and quite clever. The last warning I gave him was to forget every name he inevitably knew of everyone who had helped him. A few months later, in conversation in Belgium, he was told by others Greeks how impossible it was to escape these days. No one would help any more. He assured them that was untrue. He was challenged and accused of boasting. He told the names, his friend from Greece was arrested on his return home, and under torture named the same names. The lady who sent the boy to me, who was then newly out of prison, was re-arrested and interrogated. She did as we had agreed she should do. I was abroad, so I was credited with masterminding whatever had happened. A message got to me through Paris, and that was the end of my experience of Greece for the indefinite future. I learnt a lot that winter about the archaeology of the Greeks in Sicily. It was a relief to get back to my subject.

Meanwhile when the new university term started, the tragedy in Athens was played out. The students occupied the Polytechnic, a fine neoclassic building with gardens and an iron fence. They broadcast from a private radio station about the freedom of Greece. People flocked to them. Peasants set out in a convoy of tractors from Megara, only to be turned back by tanks. An old Cretan in breeches about eighty-five years old turned up from nowhere to encourage them. People brought food and medicines. The police took up positions on the houses nearby, and one night after dark the shooting started. They shot downwards into an open courtyard. The students were unarmed. There was shooting all around until the streets were cleared. Then tanks broke down the gates, with young people still clinging to them, and the massacre started. The number of deaths has never been certain, but it was somewhere between two and eight hundred. My own conjecture, after lengthy investigations, and based on first hand evidence, would be around three hundred.

Some of the soldiers behaved well. One boy I met had fallen asleep after many sleepless days and nights. Nothing woke him until a Marine in battle-dress with fixed bayonet turned him over. The Marine, with the connivance of his officer, smuggled that boy out of a side gate, and he lived. But the pillars masking the inner courtyard of the Polytechnic carry a neat spray of bullet-holes, and the marble steps of the front entrance show the line of bullets from the balconies, shooting downwards into the crowd. The dead were taken away and buried secretly, in waste ground behind a military headquarters in the suburbs. It was a series of ravines and hollows at the foot of the mountains. A few days later it was levelled by the dumping of thousands of tons of earth.

It was then that the dictatorship came out in its true colours, in defiance of opinion at home and abroad. The Colonels had been challenged and had lost their nerve. Things might have continued longer, but the loss of nerve was crucial. We had always thought that their last card would be a war against Turkey. Nothing else could unite the Greeks under such a government. For some time the Colonels had supported violent intrigues in Cyprus; Archbishop Makarios was their enemy. The original American panic which was so important in bringing the Colonels to power was over the fear of an alliance between Greece, Cyprus, Egypt and Yugoslavia. By now the British were friends to Makarios. I am unable to speak of the American position; I speak only of what I know. The Colonels loathed Makarios. On the day they engineered a coup against him in Cyprus, I happened to have lunch in my club in London. It took us an hour or two, but we predicted every step of what followed. Which shows it was predictable.

The hero was Davos, the general commanding north Greece. He had already shown his mettle, by refusing to let his men be addressed by a colonel. 'He's a policeman,' he said. 'Military law states that soldiers are addressed only by soldiers.' Turkey invaded Cyprus, and the ghastly results are still with us all. The British, having retained their bases in the island for purposes of protection, proclaimed to one another how heroic they were to rescue their own women and children. NATO did nothing. The Colonels declared war on Turkey with a twenty-four hour ultimatum. They painted emergency airstrips on the main roads. They called up the middle-aged to non-existent camps, where they were bitten by snakes and what food there was came in taxis from their families in Athens. They told Davos to march, and Davos gave them twelve hours to resign. And out of the disaster of fascism came the triumph of conservatism, the stable, democratically elected, rather Gaullist government of Mr. Karamanlis. Out of the disaster of Cyprus came the freedom of Greece. All the same, I believe that those who held the Polytechnic and died there are deeply, deeply responsible for the end of the Colonels. They altered the climate.

It was late summer of 1974, and I returned to Greece almost at once. By a freak of chance I had arranged to make a film that summer for the BBC, the third documentary film I had worked on, always with the same producer, Mischa Scorer. But Mischa had been ill, probably luckily for himself, since he had the idea of a film about some remote spot in Scandinavia where the Russian border is nothing but a post in a field, and half the year in darkness. In August he was better, and we agreed at once to make a film in Greece about the lives of ordinary people under the Colonels. We were able at that moment to catch stories told freely for the first time. It was also useful that I knew the language and many of the people concerned. In fact it became embarrassing. Everyone was standing for parliament, even Takis, and most of them got in. Constantine Trypanis, who taught me Greek in Oxford in the fifties, became the Minister of Culture without even needing to be elected. We were acceptable in ministries, helped everywhere. I am not able to express how thrilling it was to see old friends I had thought I might never see again. And the Parthenon was still there. And the Santorini frescoes in the National Museum. And Nikos at Flocca, smiling like a deep-sea whale.

My happiest memories of making that film are memories of Nikos Gatsos, and the most satisfying thing about it was that he really liked it. He wrote us the words of a song for it, to music by the best young composer to have appeared in Athens for years, Loukianos Kilaidonis. I had to translate the words into English for the B.B.C., but I regretted and still regret doing so. The English version, to cover the same music, is dismally flat, I think. The words Nikos wrote expressed what we meant better than I could express it. Here is my flat version of this fine poem:

This night a man is crucified,
O come with me and hear the hammering.

Now on the heavy door
the candles have gone out.
Brother, sister, hear the hammering.
Brother, sister, break the great door down.

Someone is hammered on at dawn,
O come with me and bring a little light.
Deep water covers him,
the secret sun goes out.
Brother, sister, bring a little light.
Brother, sister, the sun is underground.

We spent an evening or two at the recording studios to get the song right. The music was already gripping, but the best part of it was an elderly man in a check tweed coat that would have been extremely smart in its day anywhere in the world. He was an old countryman, the master of the clarina. He took his coat off carefully and played in his waistcoat. The instrument is plaintive and when best played its music is improvised. He meditated a few notes; he understood that this was a lament for the dead; he remained silent for about half an hour. He then improvised such music as I have never heard again. It was the theme Loukianos had given him, in the severe, flexible form of a dirge from his own region of Epiros. It was of a perfect formality, but liquid, spontaneous, unpredictable. Only later did I discover this same old man had been so famous before the war that some of the greatest American jazz musicians used to visit Greece to hear him. He was a friend of Loukianos and of Nikos. Nikos was happy that day, things went well; I recollect him, a huge man with a broad grin, stalking about the musicians' part of the studio with somebody's small white dog on a lead.

We had some dramas too. The funniest and most sinister was when the whole television team got arrested. They were shooting some film of a small grotty-looking military camp in the shadow of the American Embassy. I was away that day, but we had government permission for this scene. A man from the Home Office even went with them to ensure there was no trouble. That camp was where the worst tortures took place in the last years of the dictatorship. In the earlier years there was another, but they moved from it. The BBC cameraman with great presence of mind removed his film and substituted a new one, with which he recorded only the arrest. It was confiscated of course, but after some puffing and blowing we got it back with a personal message to me from the new Minister of Defence. He was sure I would not use it for any purpose against the interest of the army. In fact it was a nice message though a little spine-chilling at the time. I met him once; he writes books and grows the best and most expensive bottled wine in Greece, Robola.

The most dramatic incident of all was at Ligourio, where I found the village had altered utterly. We were filming interviews in one of the new village cafés. Things were not going badly, but nothing very exciting was being said. In came a policeman who stood there looking displeased. We turned off the camera and I did what seemed necessary. I asked him his authority for interfering, showed him our government permissions and insisted on his reading them, and then turned him out. It was the first time, in that village, that anyone had seen what difference a democratic, publicly answerable government was going to make. They warmed up so much that we had to take more film than we could use. One young man calmly and frankly told the village he had been a torturer. He was trained for the job in the most disgusting way, by being subjected to appalling sadism for six months. Then he had to inflict it; the penalty for weakness was to suffer it himself. When he had spoken, he ended by saying he was glad to get it off his chest. He then left alone.

There was still fear and division in the villages, just as there had been when I first went to Greece. In an isolated community the less you say about such things the less trouble you get into. And every régime gives special benefits to its special friends, I suppose. Yet we found very little genuine support for the Colonels even in the remotest villages, and many blistering opinions. The whole of Greece lost children in the massacre at the Polytechnic; no one anywhere could forgive it. The strongest feelings of all were in Crete. There we ran to earth a resistance organisation run by a local squire, a lawyer, a priest as president, a schoolmaster, a motor mechanic and their friends, starting on the very first day the Colonels came to power. Their first action was to let off a few bangs in Heraklion and drive round the town very fast with a first war Luger pistol and a Lewis gun of the same age, letting off this small but noisy armoury into the air. Having concentrated the attention of the police and the army, they made their escape. The aim of the action was to give away hundreds of pamphlets in peace on the other side of Heraklion while it was going on.

In a short time their organising committee had raised thousands of recruits all over Crete. Their security must have been good, because not a word of that reached Athens. At the very end of the story there was no more than a vague rumour of unrest. But their plan was to surround the monastery of Arkadi and to cut its one mountain road, on the day when the King and his minister, in this case Pattakos, made an annual visit to lay their wreaths on the memorial there. The memorial commemorates the blowing up of the monastery by its defenders rather than surrender to the Turks in the last century. The road was to be shut and held, which would be easy enough, a smoke screen layed down, and the King presented with the question whose side he was really on. After that, opinions may differ as to what would have followed. But there was no intention to shed blood. What a very clever idea. Unhappily they were betrayed twenty-four hours before the event.

Television can show, it convinces at once where writers can only explain. Part of the strong impression those men made on me was their simple frankness. There were no heroics. We sat on a balcony in the autumn sunshine eating walnuts in the middle of the countryside. They were old friends seldom reunited. They had nothing to gain and nothing to hide. They would certainly do the same again. The schoolmaster was an elderly man, retired, a little dusty. He said how pleasant a surprise it was when he came out of prison to be the idol of all his pupils for the first time in his life. The others loved him almost best, I thought. I asked the mechanic what was the worst thing about life under the Colonels. There was a pause and a frown.

'The worst thing was the difficulty of getting bullets for the Lewis gun. And morally the worst thing was having to be a burglar, to break into stores to get dynamite.'

'Mr Schoolmaster, if this ever happened again would you act in the same way?'

'Certainly, just the same. I was born a democrat and I am a democrat and I want to die one.'

They were a special group of people, or perhaps all Cretans are special. But heroes are certainly in a special category. The truer measure of events like those in Greece is in destruction, the dislocation of the young, the embitterment of the old. We saw a lot of that, mostly in the cities, of course, but not exclusively. I was struck by a conversation at Anemochori, a village not far from Pyrgos where we recorded for a whole evening.

'How did you get through? What happened?'

'Dictatorship. Dramatic.'

'Were people frightened here?'

'Of the dictatorship, no. Frightened, he says! Ah better that thing should not come back ever.'

'And if it ever did come back, what will happen? What will you do?'

'Oh, at the most they'll smash us up, beat us up, nothing else.'

'We'll leave our bloody reedbeds and run away.'

'We won't just sit here. Why should we sit here?'

'Oh, that such a thing should happen to us again!'

'But if it did?'

'God help us. Holy Virgin, no.'

'We should take the road.'

The village is the only community they know and the 'bloody reedbeds' are the only world they have. Running away would be like the exile that follows a vendetta. They ask for little, they accept less than that little. In making the film I came to understand much more than I had done about suffering in Greece, more even than I had learnt from social anthropologists. I came to read the classics with different eyes. This is not a matter of what the ancient writers say, but of the quality of their acceptance of life, the feelings written between the lines. As I can no longer think of a water-spring without adding to it my experience of thirst, so I can no longer think of a healing shrine without disease, old women, village life at places like Anemochori. These feelings I am stumbling to express are personal; of course they are not unique. It is helpful to re-read Homer as a village poet: that is part of the truth about him.

One of the strongest statements, and the final words of the film, were spoken by George Pavlopoulos. He looked severe and serious, though in fact he was at home in his own house. From the very beginning of his interview he cut to the heart of the matter. He spoke with that passionate gravity I had always noticed and respected in him:

'There is a good deal we could talk about.'

'Yes, there is. We could talk for days and nights, there is no end to what we went through under the dictatorship. Then there are the dead, there are the tortured. Their voices won't let us rest, we hear them all the time, all the time, they cry out to us day and night.'

'Was it like that for seven years?'

'Certainly, we were always hearing those voices, those despairing voices. There were the boys at the Polytechnic, we can never forget them. And the exiles. And those who vanished in that tragedy. Those things have no limit.'

'Did Greece go downhill in those years?'

'Most certainly.'

'Was it like a foreign occupation?'

'I think it was something very much worse. Under the occupation you felt there was a war on, a world war, and we weren't alone in suffering the consequences. But this was the imposition of an intolerable, an inhuman tyranny, that no civilized human being could possibly condone.'

'What advice would you give your son, if it ever happened again in his lifetime?'

'I would say that every action of his and every thought of his should have at the heart of it the idea of freedom. Nothing else.'

Of course it was both interesting and delightful to make a film so much of which was about old friends. We interviewed old Mr Pylarinos, with whom I had shared many jokes and some sorrows under the Colonels. He ran a fish restaurant on the quay at Katakolo. The mullet there is a special sub-species, surely the best in the world. The wine is among the best in Eleia, which is good enough to be getting on with. He was known to hate the Colonels, and to show special favour to anyone else who did, so he was constantly harrassed and fined by the markets division of the local police. The price of a salad was controlled, so when they found two salads on one plate they had him. Like almost everyone else, he was pleased to have his say at last about injustices that had rankled for years. The angriest of all was an old flowerseller with a small shop in Athens. His whole interview was hardly five minutes, but it was devastating.

But in their calmness and their convincing, unhysterical honesty, their steadiness of speech, Kay Cicellis the writer and Arietta the widow of Rodis Roufos, brought to the film a balance it was going to need for English audiences. They both speak excellent English, and it was their naturalness of speech, their obvious sanity, that convinced when they spoke of what they had lived through. Their courage was recognisable because it was so muted, so unspoken; we might have been talking tranquilly on a vicarage lawn. And now, years after the Colonels, Arietta's son Thanos, who was so wildly spirited, who hated the Colonels worse than any boy I knew, whose father dropped his career and died of a heart attack, Thanos has suffered a very serious illness from internal injuries almost certainly caused by a military police beating. There is no limit, as George said.

In 1974, the noise of democratic politics was deafening. On the whole, people behaved extremely well. The old system of patronage and favours in return for votes, the inevitable product of a culture of honour and shame, and the hangover of Turkish Greece – even the word for a political favour, *rousfeti*, is Turkish – had virtually died out. The exiled Stalinists came home at last, and made uncompromising speeches, but they won very few votes. The great mass of voters wanted a safe government, one that would last and be recognised abroad and avoid any repetition of the previous seven years. Gradually, democratic ministers established themselves inside their ministries. A day eventually came when the Minister of Defence succeeded in moving into the grander office that the army were reserving in case the Colonel who used it should come back. Pattakos went shopping and was cornered by a crowd. Someone slapped his face, then they let him go. It is all over now.

When I returned to Greece late in 1975 after the film was finished, it was a new start. My beloved room in Metz had been closed down when I was on the wanted list. Athens was dirtier, busier, more polluted than ever. Many friends of mine were now in public life, but I had no wish at all to take any interest in Greek politics, nor did I favour living in Athens in comparative social grandeur, nor could I afford to do so.

What I really wanted was to bury myself in the provinces and get on with archaeology in a more serious way. Pausanias had suffered a lot in the last few years; I wanted to get back to him. The only scholarship that has any merit, I suppose, is what is useful to other people as well as oneself. The most meritorious of all is what is useful to other scholars, sometimes for generations. I had contrived to put myself in a position where I thought I was capable of serious work, yet I had hardly done any that was useful.

I chose to begin again not at Book One, which would mean living in Athens, but at Books Five and Six, at Olympia. At first I intended to live in one of the wooden houses on the beach at Katakolo and commute on the old railway line, but from Pyrgos to Katakolo no trains run in winter. I ended up in a hotel room in Olympia itself. That village had swollen and become an eyesore, but in winter it was empty, and on my first evening I found the kind of friends I was looking for, a communist master-builder, a farmer, and an old deaf and dumb man called Nikos, full of jokes and high spirits, who had taught the whole village his private system of signs and gestures. We ate together in a small and smoky tavern practically every night.

The village had rhythms of its own. Every morning early the sheep passed through, pausing only to graze on any last flowers that survived in boxes outside the hotels. Evening came slowly, a bus or two, a newspaper, the shutting of shops. All day I was working among the ruins, often with freezing feet where rain or heavy dew hung in the grass. It was satisfying tranquil work: a simple, topographic study to determine as closely as possible to my own satisfaction the original position of every dedication and every inscription. They seemed to have lived in groups and families; it ought to be possible to sort out the history of the whole sanctuary by noticing the date and the succession of these groups, and perhaps by noticing the place of origin that predominated in one group or one period. The Germans have done most of this work already, but I had to check it for myself. I ended the hard work of several months just about in a position to start my commentary.

But it was not quite every day I spent at the site or in the cellars of the museum. Often I explored the countryside, where Pausanias raised a variety of problems. I walked often in the hills and often by the Alpheios. He churned and roared in the winter, endlessly recataloguing his grey and yellow and purple river pebbles. Sometimes I went into Pyrgos to see George Pavlopoulos, usually by train, or he came out to see me. That train was the miracle of his childhood. The school expedition went to Olympia every year in summer, and as they came home at night the whole countryside was a harvest of fireflies. Once or twice I went up into Arkadia, in the evening with a friendly taxi driver, to where lamb gave out and sausages and pork and serious mountains began. Once I went in the afternoon, partly by bus and partly on foot, to the tomb of Koroibos.

Whatever that monument is, it is not the tomb of Koroibos. Ludwig Ross, the tough old German or Dane who excavated it in 1845, gave it that name on a day when he was badly confused, as well he may have been in those resounding valleys. Pausanias puts the tomb of Koroibos on the far side of the river. The place is beautiful. Within a few miles of each other all the greatest rivers in Arkadia meet. At that meeting place the stripling Alpheios becomes a bearded hero. Ladon and Erymanthos in spate are almost too mighty to be called tributaries. Perhaps they are best seen from the mountain road towards Bassai, high up on the south side of Alpheios. I walked down into the gorge from the north side, from Aspra Spitia, a village which is just as its name says, White Houses. This is not a road I would recommend to any motorist, though I have seen vans and even a bus speeding along to Aspra Spitia, sending the gravel flying into the gorges.

Below the village a track goes down to what they call the Tomb of Koroibos, a small green hill like a pudding-basin. From the ruined fortifications on the summit, you can see and hear Ladon falling into Alpheios. Frazer describes the hilltop as 'partially excavated', which is a polite way of expressing the havoc. There is no doubt that tombs and weapons were found there, but the hilltop seems to have been used at very different dates. In the fifth century BC it was a frontier post of the Eleians; it overlooked a grazing ground by the riverside. In the late Roman empire or the early Middle Ages it must have been a simple village. The frontier no longer mattered, the river was a defence and not a threat, the grazing ground and the fertile hillside still existed.

As for Koroibos, he was the legendary winner of the first recorded Olympic games, in 776 BC The records were compiled in the fifth and the fourth centuries, and since he was called Koroibos of Elis it seems likely that he was a famous champion from local mythology, and that the tomb, wherever it was, existed before his legend began. The tomb may easily have been a mere mound. Pausanias tells us that Eleia claimed the tomb of Koroibos as the furthest limit of their own frontier. He makes it plain that it lay beyond the Erymanthos. What the Eleians were claiming in that case is that they had rights on both banks of Erymanthos. That is a wild and wonderful bit of country; I am not surprised that the tomb has never been found. Allen's Grave, on the far side of the Roman road from the village of Stonesfield where I live, must once have meant something similar; it is quite unidentifiable today.

Much of my exploration was to find the roads Pausanias used, and the places on those roads. In Eleia, which is a rich, lush province, that is curiously difficult. I did decide in the end that Pyrgos itself must be the ancient Letrinoi. That city has never been found elsewhere, and Pausanias puts it on the road from Olympia to Elis 'by the plain', which would suit Pyrgos exactly. In his day almost nothing was left of Letrinoi, only 'a few buildings and a statue in a temple'. The statue was Alpheian Artemis, which is also right for Pyrgos. 'This is how they say the goddess got her title. Alpheios fell in love with Artemis, he knew she would never accept him so he was bold enough to try a rape. He came to a night festival at Letrinoi where the goddess sported with her nymphs. But Artemis suspected, and covered her own and everyone's faces with mud, so Alpheios was foiled.'

Pausanias puts a lake close to Letrinoi, and once again that fits Pyrgos. Most of the lakes have been filled up in the last ten years, but they were famous fishing-places for generations. Maybe we shall never know the truth. Maybe the mud that Artemis used to plaster her face has covered Letrinoi once and for all. The only evidence I know that Pyrgos was a classical site is a single unfinished marble statue of a Victory which is now in the Olympia museum. Pyrgos can hardly have been a marble quarry, so an unfinished statue suggests a temple or a workshop. Why not the muddy-faced or muddy-bodied goddess that the river Alpheios loved? Strabo, who wrote about geography a little earlier than Pausanias, puts the sanctuary of the goddess at the mouth of the river. That would not be on the way to Elis, nor would it be a likely or safe site for a city. Frazer puts Letrinoi at Hagios Ioannis on the way to Katakolo, and I suggested in the Penguin Pausanias he must be right. But now I recant. I put my money on Pyrgos.

The sun melted like honey in the pine forests. On the main road down from Arkadia tough-looking old men trotted past me on donkeys. The air smelt of snow. I had plenty of time to think about ruins, about the difference between early medieval and late Roman pottery, about the extent of the racecourse for horses at Olympia, about the quick mountain road to Elis. In the evening we ate eggs or, if we were lucky, a chop. The elderly postman, who for most of his life walked and ran forty miles a day, six days a week, and the old gardener to the German archaeologists, sat usually at the next table. Conversation was village conversation. One day I got some fish from Pyrgos. We ate them like schoolboys eating food from home. I learned the history of the village. Sometimes Nikos danced. He was old, ragged, deaf and dumb, but at charming the tourists he had no equal.

At lunch I sat with the police in the only restaurant that cooked at midday. The owner was an old man on his last legs, a former mayor of Olympia who remembered every archaeologist since the twenties. He remembered the big black cars and the important Nazis in the thirties, and the day when an armoured column arrived at dawn to take vengeance here for an ambush in the hills. The last German archaeologist living alone in the dig-house pleaded successfully for the village. Nobody was shot. The police talked as openly about the past as anyone else did. But most of them were too young to remember very much. Their worst act of tyranny was to command a young man who ran a restaurant to shave off his beard for fear it would seem unhygienic to the tourists. One of the policemen solved a problem for me in the ruins. It was a piece of red marble I was unable to place. Given the date of the monument, it ought not to be African or mainland Greek or Italian, but it must surely be one or the other. He had served in Rhodes, and he knew the quarry it came from.

Maro Seferis and Arietta Roufos came to stay for a few days. Maro comes to Olympia as George used to come, for the spring flowers and the peace as much as for the monuments and the museum. The new museum is an ugly building, the locals call it the chicken factory, but it is immensely rich. Its collection of early bronzes is unique and thrilling; it extends solidly back into the eighth century, into the lifetime of Homer. With Maro and Arietta, we climbed in two cars into the high mountains whose snowy peaks had dazzled me at sunset all through the winter. As far as Andritsaina, the road was exciting and highly pleasurable. On the way up to the temple of Bassai it was too dramatic to be pleasurable. There was snow lying everywhere up there, the rocks were black and running with water, the road surface was packed snow and the signposts were down. We got lost for a time, on a track that led nowhere except into the drifts. The temple under snow was green, slippery, perfectly silent. Then the clouds rolled apart and a long beam of mountain light reached down on it. The snow made the blue of the sky mysteriously purer. Then it darkened again, and rain fell.

At Andritsaina we ate bean soup. The wine was better than I remembered it. You could still buy the pelt of a mountain fox or a whole shop full of sheep-bells. We had each of us our own memories of the town; none of us thought it had altered much. I payed a visit to the bell-tower where I once slept. It looked extremely uncomfortable and rather dangerous, a kind of mountain village crow's nest. But the return journey down to Olympia was magical: it was full spring down there, the sun shone powerfully in village squares, people were sitting out in shirtsleeves. The pine trees smelt as they would in England only on the hottest day of summer. It was a day to sit in the garden and read Shakespeare, which I think is what I did. My Shakespeare is full of old Greek bus tickets.

Athens was back to normal. It was a great capital city again, and I began to re-explore what was left of my old haunts. The seven stones of what was once a grass circle on the level ground below the south slope of the akropolis are still in place if one knows where to look. They are all that is left of the theatre of Aischylos. The water still runs in the strange cave in the akropolis rock which was once a Christian baptistry, and before that, longer ago, the holy water-spring of Asklepios. The little line of stones below the Propylaia which are the last remnant of a gate-tower built before Perikles was born still bask in the sun. They have never been properly published; I was once in trouble with a guard for measuring them without permission. It seemed a very long time ago.

Iannis Tsirkas published a new novel that brings the story of his world down to the first moment of the Colonels. It was reviewed by two brothers, one in the communist journal, the other in the equivalent of *The Times*. They were both respectful, both over-critical. It is hard to bear the truth in the form of fiction. Athenian intellectuals found it irritating that to Iannis much of what happened seemed predictable. But I remember that he did predict it. Both as novelist and as historian he has spent his life understanding the history of his world; he is a specialist in consequences, and the history of Greece in his lifetime has not been at all inconsequential. There have been English writers who thought it was. That is a cockney colonialism of the spirit, it is a vulgar and superficial mistake.

In Oxford I had more and more work. The year that followed was a difficult one. I found that I was not able to do enough to justify my existence in any of my roles in life. I could not call myself a satisfactory priest or a satisfactory scholar, and I resented a kind of charlatan's success which was overtaking me, above all the way in which my life was becoming more public. I was very doubtful about my personal heart or soul, or whatever it should be called, and still more doubtful about the institutions to which I owed loyalty. I therefore decided to scrap my life and begin again. So I left the priesthood in what I hoped was a decently obscure manner and by due process of church law. With my religion, which had not altered, under one arm so to speak, and my books under the other, I started again. I was very much in love and had been for years, so we got married. So far as I can see we shall live happily ever after. It seems an oddly simple solution.

The reader must forgive elements of autobiography in this book. But Greece has twisted itself into my skeleton like a climbing flower. I find it impossible to disentangle myself from what I want to say about the Greeks and about Greece. It is time to write it down; the present so quickly becomes the past. I did visit Greece once more in the spring of 1977, on my own just before our marriage. I went to the hill above Katakolo where Takis has a huge vegetable garden on the cliffs. He drives there from Athens through the night at a fearsome speed, and works all day among his vines and his artichokes. The only hazard of this road is the enormous fruit lorries covered all over with coloured lights like a fishing fleet in the Channel. We slept up there in someone's holiday house, and I spent the next morning watching quails in the long grass. A few days later I caught pneumonia somehow, so I came home to England a little shaken.

We planned to go to Greece the next summer or the next winter, but the time never came, we were obsessed with our own village house, and our own garden, long and green under the churchyard wall. Then there was work, the university term, the school term, everything that impedes you as it does me from wandering away into the Balkans. We made our journey at last in the autumn of 1978. That summer George Katsimbalis died. It was the end of a generation and the loss of someone I greatly loved. At the end of his life he was rich and ill. He had a large car and a chauffeur. He had come to detest the Colonels on the eccentric grounds that wherever he was driven in Attica his favourite places were full of military camps. He was, when I last saw him, still the most hilariously funny story-teller. I think of him in the sea during the great fire of Saloniki in the First World War, with his cavalry breeches so full of gold sovereigns that in the end he had to take them off to swim away. Or in bed with the lady who believed her dead husband's soul had entered into her pet chameleon. I remember him one evening out with the Captain; it was a terribly noisy table and Katsimbalis was happy. The old sailor, the subtlest of Greek poets, scribbled something on a scrap of his paper that I happened to see. It was: 'Maybe I am the silence.'

We read about his death at Thonon, a little lakeside holiday town that Proust must have known, on the French side of the lake of Geneva. With my wife, who had never been to Greece before, and a step-son aged eight who was crazy about fossils, I was on my way to Athens. I felt as if it were the first time for me also, the first real time.

10

The Hill of Kronos

I^T WAS A long, hard journey through Channel gales, heat-waves, broken roads and mosquito-haunted, poor hotels. The only one of us who took it quite tranquilly was young Matthew. He found his first new fossils on the way to London on the first morning, somewhere in Maidenhead Thicket. After that he never looked back. For us in the consolations of the endless road were Châtillon sur Seine and the Val de Suzon and the old mountain route that leads to Ferny. It was the trees withering and blazing among the rocks:

> *Les grandes forêts qui ont perdu la voix*
> *et les framboises qui rouillent dans les bois,*
> *de chaque été le grand étcéte?ra.*

At Venice we rested for a week and the car rested. What most surprised Deirdre was buildings so much more beautiful than the pictures of them, and the sense which Venice gives of a place of pleasure, to which slowly and gently we resigned. The band outside the café played Gershwin with overtones of Debussy. We counted the colours of stones. My journal became incoherent with delights:

> Greek stones are the teeth of dinosaurs, though they do speak out. San Marco is a leaden bubble bath, an imperial petrified tent. Its stones are re-used, not quarried. Softness and dustiness

of the gold. Stones of apricot, *prosciutto*, lapis, Spartan green, porphyry. Several whites and greys and blacks. It's the details that are moving, it wasn't meant to be a unity. The high galleries where Monteverdi learnt the trick of double choirs.

Under the sanctuary carpet of Westminster Abbey, on what was once the great top step that led to the shrine of the Confessor, lies a floor of coloured stones of the same date, almost more beautiful. I wish it were uncovered.

The first of Greece that we saw was unpleasant and quite new to me, since I had never entered the country by car before from Yugoslavia. Once again I was arrested at the border. There is a doggedness about Greek police files which is almost admirable. The Greek Foreign Office, the prime minister's office, and a long series of highly placed individuals have tried to have my card removed from the 'unwanted' file which is kept at every border post, but uselessly. After an hour we got through, and drove through a sombre, darkening landscape to the great urban blot of Saloniki. Once it was a whitewashed town full of minarets. But the seawall was pulled down in 1866 and today the last pathetic seaside villas of the nineteenth century are overshadowed by ambitious blocks of offices. The best that has survived is in a few splendid Byzantine churches, and the last white tower of the old sea wall, built by Venetian architects for the Turks in the fifteenth century.

We slept for ten hours, and waking was like walking into a dream. It was a misty autumn morning; the quiet water of a harbour stretched away from below our windows; the white tower sparkled in the early light. I hardly felt yet that we were in Greece, but little by little I relaxed, the border crossing drifted away like a nightmare and daily life spoke with authority to all of us. The last neoclassic villa still crouched between bigger buildings under a pine tree older than itself. Tankers were wallowing in the heat. Seventy-year-old waiters ambled across the promenade to their work at a quarter to seven in the evening. Children fished and rode their bicycles. One day we drove out to Hagia Triada, an empty beach full of fuming light, with two or three quiet cafés and a string of coloured bulbs. Matthew and I found a hermit crab in the sea. We ate our first Greek seaside lunch, fresh sole and chips, salty cheese, sweet grapes. The wine was unremarkable. We began to feel at home.

Our first place of serious pilgrimage was the museum, where the treasure of the tomb of Philip of Macedon, the father of Alexander the Great and first conqueror of all Greece, had just been opened to the public. There had been an earthquake earlier that year, some hotels were still closed, some people were living in tents in the public gardens, and the museum was guarded by armed commandos. Even in Greece I do not suppose that is a permanent arrangement. But the newly discovered treasure is one of the most impressive displays in the world. There have been arguments about whether the tomb it came from was really Philip's, but there remains no doubt at all in my own mind. The arguments are too technical to discuss at length, but it seems to me this was a king's tomb, and the king was Philip. He was lame: the personal armour in the tomb was made at the right date and made for a lame man. There was a wreath of oak-leaves and a wreath of myrtle in blossom. The richness and grandeur of what was found with him are already a powerful evidence. But what is so moving about it all is that these things are unique both in grandeur and in beauty. The wreaths of golden leaves are blushing in a perpetual last sunlight; they speak about immortality as a king might conceive it. But the small box for his ashes is terribly small; its ornaments are terribly restrained.

In the same museum I solved part of a problem that had preoccupied me for five or six years. When did old coloured marbles begin to be cut up and re-used in the west? The porphyry tombs of the kings of Sicily must have come somehow from Byzantium. But the re-use of old marbles spread swiftly all over Italy. When monolithic marble columns were re-used, they dictated a new height of buildings, in the Cathedral at Messina for example. What of the work of the Copts? What of the Arabs in Sicily? Cosimo Medici's tomb is a huge circle of porphyry, a slice of a very big column. A perfect circle of re-used stone let into a floor must indicate that an ancient column was sliced like a salami. Who first cut up coloured marbles into patterns of carpets to make floors? The answer is that the late Roman emperors were already doing it.

There are some coloured marbles from the palace of Galerius in the Saloniki museum that had been re-used to make a floor. Such an invention, such an economic piece of magnificence, was certain to be imitated. Even the poet of *Beowulf* knows about floors of coloured stones.

That night our mood was shattered by another earthquake. I have been in a number of earthquakes, enough at least to have a feeling for the livid, stormy atmosphere, thunderous without thunder, that announces them. Then the world shakes slightly or one's bed rattles and the windows quiver. But this was much worse. The wind sang one continuous buzzing and whistling note all night long. The treetop disappeared from outside our window, the tree was bent horizontal. In the morning the sea itself was catastrophic. The water was black, with white horses and the same disturbing wind. The shock itself was only 2.8 on the scale, but the tremors were sharp and serious. Out of doors the trees were in hysterics. The diabolic whining of the wind and the sea's deeper anger drove us out of Saloniki as soon as we could go. That earthquake did no serious damage; it had been predicted, though not to us. Still, it was a nasty surprise. Greece has always, in one way and another, been a surprising place.

We drove south through the vale of Tempe, Apollo's autumnal gorge, where the twinkling rocks and water-springs are as wonderful as the dense and glittering leaves. Its name means the Woods. Deirdre was so much exalted by Tempe I could hardly understand why. It turned out that she supposed this was a mere foretaste, and that the whole of the rest of Greece from now on would be just as beautiful, just as perfect. For me the chief excitement of that day was Olympos, the mountain of Zeus. Why did the ancient Greeks believe that the gods lived on Olympos? Olympia in the south is named after the Olympic gods, but Olympos itself was their Homeric heaven. It was remote, and very high. Its god must be powerful. You could see Olympos from a ship at sea, you could see it from Pelion to the south. Prehistorians are inclined to think that the first Greeks must have lived below Olympos before they moved south into what became their world. I am more inclined to imagine a god of the weather, a god of wandering shepherds, and a rumour of his distant mountain that took root. The mountain is certainly very grand indeed. From the distance it was a pile of vast blue rocks as ragged as clouds.

The road was fine and lined with tall aspens, like an old French *route nationale*, only that this was better constructed. The only eyesores were the hotels, which seemed to have been flung down here and there by an infantile giant. But the endless plains of Thessaly are still unspoilt. The only difference in ten years is that now you see tractors and the fields are greener. How amazed any prehistoric people would be at the sights of a modern cultivated field. Even in my own lifetime in Oxfordshire the stoniest of fields that were only good for sheep pasture have learnt to carry crops. The region inland from Volos, where we were now travelling, nourished an earlier people than the Myceneans. They were neolithic farmers, but I knew almost nothing about them; the excavations that revealed them were relatively recent, and I had never seen what was found. But as we crossed that fertile, muddy country my mind turned to them. In those fields classical civilization seemed a disturbance.

Slowly we folded ourselves more deeply into Greece. Volos had altered but not essentially; the railway no longer ran in the street, and there was even more industry, but Volos was soon behind us. We arrived in the early evening at a tiny seaside village on the Gulf, where plane trees stretched themselves in a little square. Behind the village the foot of Mount Pelion was buried under its olive groves. The sea was level water with mountains beyond it and an island. It was to harbours like this that the sailors came home from 'many glittering seas and many shadowy islands' in the days of *The Odyssey*. There is a sense in which any poem, but particularly epic poetry, is created or recreated by those who need it, by the way in which they use it. I like the small scale of *The Odyssey*. The scale of our village, Kala Nera, the good water, was even smaller. It was full of jasmine and geraniums. It smelt of well-watered growing things and charcoal fires and bakeries. But the sea was infested with small pink jelly-fish, and the lavatories of the hotel were a monument to a hundred years of disease. Still, we slept and rested and were happy.

Next day, we adventured further along that small coast, to

Aphyssos. It was like an island village. Vines had engulfed the wires of the telephone system. The square was like a stage with many entrances, old crones wandered across it, a farmer rode down some steps with a bunch of flowers at his mule's saddlebow and a led donkey. Children played badminton over the electric wires. Our village hotel was spotlessly clean and simple and full of flowers. It had *art nouveau* bead curtains and it was called the Alexandra; to our surprise, the lady who ran it suddenly addressed Deirdre in English. In Greek, she could have been an ambassador's wife, her appearance and manners were perfect, even noble, but she had learnt her English in Noo Joizy. We liked her enormously. In the hall of the hotel she had a thermometer or a barometer on a key-shaved stand with the following inscription: 'After all the real key to success – SAVING. The Downtown Trust Co., East Jersey and Third Street, Elizabeth.'

We did little in Aphyssos but watch the gentle dramas of the village square. All day a wandering mule made a series of clever raids, and every so often he was chased away. An old man on a horse rode in with honey. He had twelve hives and five hundred olive trees, that was his life. The saddling and unsaddling, the chasing of the mule, even the choosing of a chair, were performed with deliberation, like a liturgy where every gesture counted. It is a kind of liturgy, I suppose, but it covers the countryside and it stretches far backwards in time. Maybe in the landscape around there is a satisfied, well-tended god. It has its bees and its olives. In the afternoon we swam and slept in the shade of the trees. The sun went down in an apricot stew and left a tomato sauce blush in the sky, and a gigantic evening star. I began again to write poetry in Greek, which is always a good sign with me. Here is an English version of that poem:

> Where the village ends, where nothing begins
> love cries out, he is a priest of grass,
> monotonous songs, the light monotonous.
> Here dwell dogs, mosquitoes, we
> and a donkey in love.
> We kiss, we are like birds,

we learn about the soul inside the mouth,
our own gods and their songs
monotonous and grave as mosquitoes.
Others go to the music, to the girls,
we are dying in all seriousness
our life becomes rhythm

That night a bus full of tourists from Athens on a weekend expedition was expected at Aphyssos. It never arrived, I think it simply broke down, but the conversation about it sounded like a medieval chronicle. 'They suffered hurt at the Burnt Rocks.' 'Ugly? What did they suffer?' 'Who knows? No wounded.' A notice in the garden of our hotel proclaimed, 'Hours of general rest, 11–7 and 2.30–5.' Even Greek English is a pleasure. 'Water Lilly Snack Bar Restaurant Soft Music.' One understands at once what they mean. We drove back into Volos to the museum. Above the road near Aphyssos every shady patch, every stony patch in the olive groves was swarming with autumn cyclamen. The thistles were white skeletons, but the tough little rock-ferns were still dark green in the walls. How suddenly a mood or a landscape can alter. We were tempted to stay in Aphyssos much longer, we thought of driving back there from Athens. Time seemed infinite.

Yet it was already too late in time to revisit all the places and the people I had been so enchanted by fifteen years ago. In those days there would have been no hotel at Aphyssos, the rich lowland farms would have been poorer, what industry there was more ramshackle. And now even inside the heart of Greece we already wanted a refuge, our own secret place. Perhaps it was middle-age, or the happy company of a little boy collecting beach pebbles. Or perhaps it was the experience of all our lifetimes, in which so many landscapes, so many village lives have disappeared that the surface of the earth has taken on a sad quality of transitoriness, a new impermanence. That has certainly sharpened my own interest even in the country world of my own boyhood. What was once ordinary has become precious. In Greece we fell automatically into similar feelings, but with more intensity, because of the innocence, the movingness, the wildness of what has survived. These feelings have nothing to do with classical antiquity; they have more to do with the nineteenth century and with prehistoric life. I am not much ashamed of them.

We did go back, luckily for us, to the museum at Volos. It had altered greatly, and my memory of it was also faulty. How can I have forgotten or perhaps neglected its big collection of Roman and Byzantine sculpture? Perhaps because it was in the garden, under the pine trees. Matthew and Dierdre played football there with pine-cones while I gaped at the stones. Indoors in the coolness I attempted to draw, but Matthew's eye was on me and in the end I gave up. The painted tombstones were as interesting as ever, but since I was first in Volos their technique has been thoroughly studied by an art historian, so they no longer raised the same old questions. This time what I liked was a woman at an altar in a garden. She was like a modern Athenian lady on a summer island, cooking out of doors: a green dress in a green shade. But the greatest excitement was for Deirdre. I drank it in from her. She has a passion for prehistoric terracotta statuettes of village goddesses or village women. In a new room at Volos she came on the whole wealth of neolithic Thessaly. These figures are so subtle and tense, so brilliant, so alive, and in some cases so humorous that they change even an educated view of neolithic Greece. They are unique, I think. They compare well with anything else in the world of their date and style. If these people were among the ancestors of the Greeks, then what flowered in the sixth century was an inherited skill. I suppose that the three most thrilling museums in Europe for prehistoric art must now be Copenhagen, Lipari and Volos.

The discoveries of archaeologists have a short life as news, but in Greece they accummulate into a vast wealth which even a professional scholar would find it hard to sift year by year. In the last ten years or so alone the Santorini frescoes have altered our ideas about the power and purity of Minoan art; the sanctuary of Brauron in Attica has thrown a new light on the classical age; some new archaic marble sculptures have modified the history of ancient techniques, and the great painted tombs of Macedonia have transformed the study of ancient painting. The neolithic discoveries now housed at Volos are as important as all these others, and almost as recent. All this is in Greece itself. But the other day in a tomb of the sixth century BC, not far from Stuttgart, Chinese silk was discovered. In the same tomb there was a bronze cauldron ornamented with Greek bronze lions. The reader will understand me if I say that my subject is inexhaustible. I have somewhere else written that every tourist is slightly an archaeologist at heart, and every archaeologist slightly a tourist at heart. I find that in myself both passions are constantly renewed.

We climbed away out of Volos by the mountain road to Portaria, a nineteenth-century merchant village among water-springs and chestnut forests that lies close below the summit of Mount Pelion. As the road shook itself free and started to mountaineer, yellow roses and yellow lemons spilled over garden walls. In a field below Hagios Theodoros we spotted waxen yellow autumn crocuses; I think they were *sternbergia lutea*, but at Portaria the same variety had been planted in gardens. Wild flowers do survive like that, just at the moment when they begin to be rare. The village smelt of apples, of elderflowers, mules and water and stone. It had huge, untenanted houses, and even buildings only a hundred years old had already taken on the stark, overgrown beauty of old age. The best of the houses have stone tiles like the Stonesfield slates that do so much for the villages of the English Cotswolds. Inside the church, which was handsome and innocent and almost empty, the priest was chanting vespers with a boy, and sadly and gently correcting his mistakes.

We loved Pelion. We liked the stone paths and the constant roar of water. We liked the mountain plane trees, the huge shade of the Spanish chestnuts, the waterfall above the village that the city of Volos is soon likely to drain dry. The sun was lost in the infinity of leaves. My journal is full of scraps of poetry, and somewhere between the pages of a book I pressed a deep crimson flower called *agriostemma*, like an eccentric autumn pink, that I had never seen before. The highest plane tree we could observe, high up on a cleft of bare mountain side, was already exploding into solar yellow and beginning to lose its leaves. The single apple tree in a mountain field that we passed every day was full of fruit. Its branches were propped up in six places, that tree was so old and beaming and fruitful. It was a fountain of pink and green. You could smell it from the path fifty yards away. The whole of that region was as if one had never seen these colours, smelt this air, heard this water, since first childhood. I had forgotten what it was like to walk home in the dark, hearing the odd dog and the odd 'goodnight', under that sounding wall of mountain.

We would have stayed on for a long time on that mountain, but nothing goes on as you expect. Matthew fell in the hotel and hit his head on a marble floor, Deirdre was also unwell, and I contracted a raging toothache. Matthew was soon better, but my face swelled up monstrously, and we fled through the very worst of the heatwave towards Athens. No photographs from the Volos museum, no more mountain shadows, no more pure air and cool water. The drive was appalling. 'God,' said Deirdre, 'stayed in Italy. He stopped at the border. Those little silver toys in the churches are meant to attract him, but God is listening to the band playing Gershwin outside Florian's. That's why they have to say he's on top of Olympos. He's at Florian's, he's just slipped out of St Mark's for a minute or two.' The fields were tawny yellow or burnt black. They were a fine cobweb of dead thistles and dead grasses, extending a day's walk in every direction. There was no shade, and the disaster of the approach to Athens lay before us like a case of failed surgery abandoned on a battlefield. I have never seen anything in Greece so ugly as that road has now become. After dark the air of Athens slapped warmly against our faces like a hot flannel soaked in diesel oil.

We were only in Athens for the dentist, and I remember little else that we did. Somehow we contrived to have lunch with Nikos Gatsos. Deirdre fell for him headlong, at once. She loved him within five minutes as much as I do after so many years. She liked his smile and the way he stood and the way he walked. She discovered many thoughts and feelings in common with him. She was bowled over by his courtesy, by his parcels, by his niece, Agatha. At four in the afternoon we slipped out of the city. It took only half an hour to get clear, with one startling lightstruck glimpse of the Parthenon through the fumes. We were on the road to Pyrgos, past Megara where the Colonels used their army to massacre the olive groves for an oil refinery or a shipyard. Nothing has been built, and no compensation has yet been paid. Greece owes as much to Karamanlis as France does to de Gaulle, but he has not been able to wave a magic wand over every problem, and I doubt if I would personally vote for him. But the mountains and the islands showed their clear lines between the pale blue wash of sky and the dark wash of the sea. The air was suddenly clean again. We bought Matthew a straw hat at Loutraki and ran in and out of the waves that were breaking over the promenade.

A night in a hotel at Corinth is not to be recommended to anyone. I have done it twice, both times it was a disaster, but on that evening the more distant hotel we were aiming for had declined steeply and Corinth was the nearest refuge. Our first choice was wind-whipped, its concrete was cracked, factories had crept up all around it, a herd of goats patrolled the garden. The proprietor cursed us ritually for not booking a room. The night at Corinth was much disturbed by the hooting and grinding of lorries, the infestation of mosquitoes, and in my case the troubled dreams that come from antibiotics. The morning was calm and pure, the streets were full of schoolgirls. By the modern road Patras is not far from Corinth. I used to like the slow train that stopped among hens and old crones and lemon trees, but seen at speed the mountains and the sea are even more magnificent than they were through fly-stricken windows. After Patras, which has one of the best restaurants in Greece, the road southward is more rustic but none the worse for that. It begins to smell of basil and rigani with a deep undertone of mule. In October the lemons were yellow everywhere, but the oranges were still deep green and small. Why do thunderstorms in those mountains always smell so of wild lavender?

George Pavlopoulos was wearing his best suit. We went for a drink in the town café that looks towards the sea from the hideous new square of Pyrgos. But there are still pine trees, the stone steps where he played as a child have survived somehow, the sea is the sea, George is the same. My journal for that day is full of Greek names for grapes, which he must have told me: *phileri*, which is a wine-grape; *moschostaphylo*, the low-growing musk-grape; *korinthi*, the currant-grape; *tourkopoula*, a plump grape; *aïtonychi*, eagle-claw;

asproudi, a white grape; *boidomati*, cow-eye, a dark grape; *tinachtoroyi*, the shaker; *roditis*, the sweet pink grape of late summer; *rompola*, which makes Mr Averoff's admirable wine, I suppose; and the light-growing *sabbatiano*, the sabbath grape. There are many more: *tsirichi*; *probatina*; *fraoula*, strawberry, which is crisp and dry; *ephtakilo*, a long dark purple grape; *kerino*, the best of the yellow-greens; *kokorarchido*; sultanina; *tsimpimpo*; avgoustiati; *kardinalios*; *violeti*, which is American; *razaki* and *santameriana*, named after the Baron de St Omer, who held land near Pyrgos in the Middle Ages. I find this a fascinating and comforting list.

We stayed in the best Pyrgos hotel in rooms looking away from the road and the sea at a grove of birch trees and some hens. At breakfast next morning a German lady from the last tourist bus of the season was capering excitedly about with a flash-camera to record a framed travel poster of the Hermes of Praxiteles. I am not sure how she came to miss the original, but maybe she wanted both. We were already house-hunting, with constant help from Takis, who wasted days on us. The S.P.A.P. hotel at Olympia would be too expensive for a long stay, but we had the idea of settling in some sort of nest somewhere near here for most of our time in Greece. I had memories of a wooden house with a rose-garden on the beach at Katakolo near the fish restaurant of Mr Pylarinos. Or there was the house on the cliffs near Hagios Andreas. But already on that first day I see that I wrote down the names of three villages: Leventochori, Skourochori and Korakochori—the village of heroes, the grey village and the village of crows. They lie a little inland from the sea among small hills a little to the north of Hagios Andreas.

We chose Korakochori. George's wife had cousins there so we stayed in a room on their farm. It was a peaceful smallholding, a few crops, a few flowers, a few animals. We ate our first lunch, and many more after it, out of doors in the shade of a mulberry tree, with a treefrog chirping in the leaves. I learnt a new proverb that day. As the farmer's wife handed out knives she said to Takis, 'He that has the knife eats the melon.' We came to know and expect the peace of that place, the crows and the pine trees, the reed-plumes seen from the road and the morning glories. Lemons came fresh from the tree, eggs came fresh from the hens, the baker's van hooted at the gate. Whenever we tired of country life we moved to the S.P.A.P. hotel at Olympia for a few days at a time, but most of our excursions were day excursions. As the sun went down we were usually on the beach or in the sea at Hagios Andreas. Matthew found the bones of some big sea creature fossilized in rock.

But Mr Pylarinos was closing. We found him on almost his last day of work. The Colonels and a life of vigorous labour and anxiety had undone him: he suffered a stroke, from which he recovered, but it was a warning sign and he was shutting his restaurant. He had children in Canada, and he was going there. One last time we all hugged each other and ate the most splendid fish I have ever eaten even there. As for the beans, however, it was Mme Pylarinos who cooked them; it has taken Deirdre a year of thought and experiment to discover the secret. It was only two days ago, for the first time, that she achieved the true dish of runner beans *à la* Mme Pylarinos. One of the serious problems was to know whether she used basil and how much. It was a disaster for us as well as a personal loss that they closed. From that moment we were refugees. The local restaurants are not wonderful, and at that season they are often shut. Deirdre cooked on a camping gas stove a series of soups that I remember still with joy. Near the end of our time we found a small place on the unlighted beach of Katakolo that opened only at night to cook fish.

We explored Olympia stone by stone. I think that I saw it then more freshly than before. Often I found that Deirdre amazed me by seeing what I had noticed when I first looked, and later forgot, but often what we saw together was quite new. I am inclined to believe one ought always to have a friend, one ought always to compare notes. But most of my journal at Olympia is about flowers. I had never realized that judas trees have an autumn season. I had never seen so many varieties of crocus. Even the cabbage-headed roses in the hotel garden with their heavy mouths and their inward blackness were new to me. They were almost terrifying, so heavy and dark as one would never see in an English garden. One morning at Olympia we found ourselves reading Tennyson in bed. Deirdre remarked that she felt transported in the spirit to Reid's

Hotel in Madeira, she could feel bridge coming over her. Olympia is a huge glen, I suppose, an endless variety of green tones. It was surely constructed by God for horse-races. The Olympic games were a kind of highland gathering. But as for the hotel garden:

> The Lotos blooms below the barren peak,
> All day the wind breathes low with mellow tone.

What goes on nowadays among the ruins is another matter. I spotted a fattish German in early middle-age with a silver trident on his chest crowning a young German girl with daisies. They were as near to naked as you could be in a remote corner of those mighty monuments, stroking one another with daisies a foot long. Later on she had so many daisies in her hair they looked like a bathing cap. I wish them no harm, and none to the young men with their first moustaches measuring themselves inwardly against the stripped, fragmentary marbles. But Olympia is, or has been, more serious than that. All art is disturbing, ancient art in particular, but here it has a certain sanctity. Is it only a matter of the great stones and the pine trees? Hardly so, because the same holiness stares back at you from the earliest bronzes. Can it be some quality of crispness, certainty, vigorous weight? This is a problem I am not able to solve, but I believe it has something to do with Zeus.

At Korakochori the tea-roses faded from apricot to blanched cream, and the oranges were turning colour. The morning had silver tones, the dusk had yellow tones. At Olympia old Athanasis from the lunch-time tavern was fading away like a dream in the day-light, his son had grey hair, the master-builder had moved away. Only the postman looked as well as ever, younger than ever. Old Nikos the deaf and dumb man had a splendid new suit. His business is cleaning cars, and the first morning we found him waiting beside ours. The hugs and capers and the sparkling car mattered more to me than the welcome Odysseus got. At that hotel there was always a noise in the morning that I took for the murmur of the plumbing or the wind in the pine trees. I discovered it was the bees in an ivy bush twenty-five feet high, with yellow clusters of blossom, and some blue flowers of morning glory breaking out at the top.

Our life moved mostly between Korakochori, Pyrgos and Olympia. It is important to stress their relative size. Korakochori is a tiny, untouched settlement of farming people. From there the distant view of Pyrgos was like a mirage of Manhattan in a Bob Hope film of the nineteen-forties. The road to Olympia wound through big villages growing bigger every year. Olympia itself was a big, self-important village. Apostolos, the son of Athanasis, was preoccupied with the election of a mayor. He was still a very loving young man, with that combination of purity and book-learning which belongs to his generation in Greece, and he will be mayor himself one day.

Here is a scrap of village conversation: 'I always soap my tomatoes and then I put them in the fridge…Twenty doctors said he must die…I gave the doctor a hundred pounds, I slipped it to him, and…' Here is another poem written in Greek at that time, at Korakochori:

In the waters of the sun
the mountains and the apples change colour
and the seas transform
and the skin of the moon is whitewashed;
slowly the oranges are changing,
slowly the great snakes are dying in the grass.

Even our small farm began to alter with the season. The coldness and glitter of the mulberry tree still covered us, but yellow dry leaves dropped out of it, it began to smell faintly of mulberries, the treefrog fell silent. The goats strayed on their long tethers among shoulder-high coltsfoot and the hens made sorties into the mountain of drying maize. The farmer's wife and her son, who had lost an arm as a boy, playing with a stray hand-grenade in the fields, spent most of the day sawing and welding at a metal cabin for their little open van, to make it warmer in the early mornings of the winter that was coming. When we drove south to Pylos and south to the enormous fourth-century fortress of Messene, we were caught in thunderstorms. Messene is a whole landscape fortified. In the rain on that broken road it was more menacing than any

219

photograph shows it: the stones were black, the raggedness of the walls savage, the tall ruined gate belonged to the storm.

On one of the last afternoons of heat and silence I climbed up alone to Pontikokastro. It has all been rebuilt more than once. Round towers rise from square bases, with tiles between the stone blocks. But there are still dusty squirts of ancient pottery bleeding from the hillside. I put my hand on a dead tree under the walls. It was swarming with black ants. Someone had painted a socialist election slogan on the battlements. It had once been a slogan for Takis, I suppose, but now it was only an element of a very old, ruined castle. The whole hillside was overgrown with coltsfoot, reeds, dittany, larkspur, sunflower-headed thistles and every kind of thorn. It had its dignity. On other days we made expeditions into Arkadia; once we came on a newly excavated site that I had looked for years ago. I had come within half a mile of it, on the other side of the hill. Its name is Nea Skillountia: the place where I searched is Palia Skillountia, also called Mazi. If the village had not been moved because of an earthquake, the place would still be undiscovered. Once we ate our lunch in a little pine wood of almost Chinese beauty, above a stream, but we suffered a siege from indignant dogs. They were bigger than we were, so we gave ground.

We compared notes with Takis and George about the better provincial restaurants. There are two categories. In one the Greek friend who knows the place says, 'Sit down and keep quiet, I'll tell you what you eat here.' In the other, which may have many good things, the owner takes over. When you say, 'Could my chop not be overdone and not have too much salt?' he becomes indignant. 'Are you ill? You should go to a hospital, not a restaurant.' Or if you drive all the way from Athens, and then ask for a second plate of some particular fish-soup, he is offended. 'I give people as much soup as anyone needs the first time.' We were happiest in the small, rather secret fish-tavern on the sands. One night it was full of very young sailors, dancing together and singing the sad words of a song by Nikos Gatsos. 'Where are they taking the boy, swallow in a cage? Where to, what do they say to him, and his brothers weep?' The sailors must have been boys from the islands. We had never seen young men so innocent. They played very happily with Matthew's toys.

220

Terribly heavy rain and high winds suddenly lashed the farm. Winter came very early that year. We abandoned an expedition to Phigalia and Lykosoura at the mere sight of those furious clouds and the mountains compounded of mist and darkness. The hills where I once set off to walk there were still like basking whales, but now they were black, and rivers ran prodigally over the roads. Big flocks of sheep were moving everywhere, to winter quarters I suppose. On the lower and better roads to which we kept we suffered only the skirts of storms. A Roman aqueduct glittered in the rain. The banks were full of cyclamens, darker than before. The end of autumn made its last attempt to quench the sun in foliage. Little owls hooted in the vineyards an hour after dusk like mountain trains. Matthew began to make maps of the castle and the villages. The nearest village was marked four hours away, or by mule about ninety hours. One was marked, 'Quickest way by car sixty hours.'

Not far away from our own village we found our way to the monastery of Skafidia, lost among unchartable tracks. It stands by the sea; in its essential origin it was a fortified house of the fifteenth century, a monastic keep round which a monastery has grown. The hideous Miramare Hotel is quite close, only a beach away, but fortunately that is hardly visible. The chapel has fresh paint and floors scoured by nuns. A few antiquities sleep in the courtyard, some fragments of grey specked Egyptian granite and some stone bases without inscriptions; they could have come from anywhere. A schoolroom clock ticks away time. The ikons are of every age. The most thrilling was the baptist, whom the Greeks call Prodromos, the Forerunner, painted in 1783. The saint himself could still be early medieval, but the soft air of the Ionian islands has wafted in some other influence. His gilt and austerity are just at the point of melting into a yellow sunset with mountains and lakes. The geometric vegetation has become realistic and independent and very dark green.

As we threaded this way and that through the countryside we came on houses of great beauty, many of them ruinous, some empty, and on sunstruck farms, great groves of reeds and of trees, a mile-long avenue of thistles as formal as Versailles. The crests of the hills were crowded with cypress and olive. No road led where one

221

thought it did. It was among these tracks and villages that George Pavlopoulos used to ride as a boy, high up on his horse because his lameness made the stirrups useless, galloping for hours until he was known by sight for miles around as the mad boy on the horse. But not all our journeys were idyllic. One of the worst was very high up in a Mexican landscape of mountains and heat between storms, among villages striken by earthquakes. Buzzards were hunting there. That night we wept and the mosquitoes bit us round the eyes; we were so tired.

When we were most tired, we sat as quiet as stones among the ruins at Olympia. Afterwards we played pine-cone football in the ancient stadium. Or there were suddenly twenty or thirty goldfinches in the fig tree at the farm. You heard them before you saw them, an extraordinary bubbling music, very loud and sweet. Or we walked down to the sea, by a path haunted by every variety of butterfly and moth, tan and charcoal, tan and lemon, peacocks, admirals, pink and charcoal wings, dark yellow wings. Or we climbed on the Hill of Kronos. We drowsed there to the noise of sheepbells from the seventy sheep that come down from Drouva. On that amazing hill under the pine trees there was always quietness and fine air. Underfoot in the glades of the hillside the grass was starred with cyclamen. They grew profusely in drifts and torrents and cascades. Pines sprinkled the sky and cyclamen sprinkled the earth. The trees created huge spaces below them and between them, the sky was an extension of their space. It was a natural hermitage of glistening green and huge shadows, carpeted with wild cyclamen.

Kronos had no festival day at Olympia, no month was named after him in the Olympian year. Only the young women raced on his hill, it was outside the sanctuary, the sacred wood of sanctuaries. But it towers above the oldest temples and the oracle, a great cone of motionless pine trees. The days of Kronos were the good old days. The tower of Kronos was distant, holy, glorious. Is the Hill of Kronos not perhaps the first form of his tower? Did it stray to the world's end in the developed, rationalized mythology of the later Greeks, just because something so wonderful must be infinitely remote? Was there a time when this was really his seat, where he lived on in the company of the just and brave? Elsewhere he survived as a private god or a country god. On his feast he received two cakes, one in the form of an ox or a bull. In mythology he survived as one of the bad old gods, with a whiff of violence and remote antiquity. In the anthropology of Sir James Frazer he was the King of the Saturnalia, the keystone of the ancient world. I prefer to think of him as a tired old god, confusing and confused, but numinous, inextinguishable.

Pindar captured his quality. His hillside was the perfect place for us; we still have dreams about it. Pausanias does say Kronos had a shrine at Olympia on his own hill, but it was built by the people of the golden age before Zeus was born, before the first wild olive trees grew in Greece. 'Some say Zeus wrestled there with Kronos for the throne of heaven, but some say he held the games as a celebration of his triumph.' But the older gods are not necessarily the gods of an earlier age. They are often only an explanation of the gods we have now. In an age when all explanation was narrative, the germ of a story would grow backwards as well as forwards through unmeasured time. Of course, every myth is a version of some other people's myth. I have found it possible to prove that the God of my ancestors is a cousin of Zeus; their relationship can be established through the myths and legends of the Canaanites. One would be a fool to take that sort of thing seriously. In the great days of the Olympic festival, Kronos was a remote and happy god, and I think he still lived on this hill.

It was cool there. One day in Pyrgos we found some bottles of Zitsa; we climbed into a glade on the hill under big straggling oak trees, more straggly than the sun's rays. The cyclamens were every colour from mauve to paper-white with vivid lips. White crocus grew among the pine-needles. We found holly-oaks, myrtles and ferns. A gentle wind blew. The solemnity of the pine-boughs relented, the shade was checkered. As for the flowers, these are not the flowers that sprang up where Zeus lay with Hera in *The Iliad*, but Kronos must once have slept with Rhea in these glades. I doubt whether the flowers or even the trees have altered much. More pines perhaps and fewer oak trees. When we got back to England we had lunch one day with beloved old E. R. Dodds, a veteran classical scholar and a friend to poets. He was in the last few weeks of his life. When we told him about our magical hill his eyes kindled. 'I still have cyclamens from there,' he said, 'at the bottom of my garden, from before the war.'

The time had come to set off homewards. We had not yet seen Athens or Delphi and money was running out. We had some trouble with getting it through Greek banks, and it was then that I learnt from Takis a new and invaluable Greek word, *jemenfoutismos*, which displaces in my affections even the word for hooliganism, *teddyboyismos*. I also learnt from the newspapers 'amok', which has a life of its own in Greek. It is a condition you can be found in, or a stroke of fate that can possess you. 'Amok had struck him.' We did see many more of the antiquities of Greece than those that have already crammed this book, and we came at last to the Parthenon, tiny in the distance in a haze of pink soot, and then suddenly close, and huge, and very white. The approach to Athens was by a road lined with shops and courtyards full of smashed vehicles, smashed shapes of smashed vehicles, cars broken on rooftops, cars on end leaning against walls. There was one tiny shop called European Technology selling modern religious art of horrendous nastiness, with a dreadful foodshop under the same crumbling façade, so small that its enormous owner could hardly fit into it. He had to sit outside with his feet in the traffic. We felt somehow that we were back in modern Europe.

We sat every day with Nikos Gatsos at Flocca. He was as tranquil as Kronos, preoccupied with the difference between the English words 'wood' and 'forest'. He wanted to know everything possible about Stonesfield, where we live. He touched the chords of literature like the keys of a piano. His conversation was full of jokes. It was as if we had never been anywhere else; it always is. On the twenty-eighth of October, snow fell all over northern Greece. In Athens, gunfire ushered in a holy day. The artillery was just behind our hotel, it sounded through a torrential thunderstorm. By mid-morning a double rainbow hung in the sky. The air was stripped pure and smelt of snow. I have never seen the Parthenon in a stronger, clearer light. Other days it was broken-backed, solemn. We pondered the mystery of its survival. Sometimes it brooded high up above the streets where we climbed. Sometimes it was clouded under a 1914 fog. At times the sun seemed to be exploding inside it.

At this time I was writing poems to Deirdre, but we wrote together a postcard to a friend: 'Gardening stops at the Alps, God stops in Venice, milk stops in Yugoslavia, only the Greek language never stops. Now the car is full of fossils and we have no money and few plans.' The sight of the only British aircraft carrier in existence paying a brave and friendly visit to the Piraeus cheered us up, but not enough. Snow came near to catching us on the way to Delphi. There the pine-wood fires and the smell of pines and olives consoled us, but not permanently. It was simply time to go home. We chased through Yugoslavia, through the early winter gorges, with snow imminent, and on a lonely, unlighted road at night, just before the Austrian border, two plainclothes policemen stepped out of the shadows and flagged us down. It was only a normal check, because the border was unmanned, and they were quite pleasant about it, but it did bring back memories. One more day of terrifying mountain tunnels and of valleys of unbelievable beauty brought us gasping with amazement and relief to Salzburg, the city of the purest pleasure and the most unexpected beauty either of us had ever seen.

All the way home we remembered our goodbyes at Korakochori. 'I have lit a candle for you to Saint Demetrios. For your long journey. To the good may you go. All things good may you find.' Maybe that saint sweeps away snow with his beard. Maybe to other people our journey would not be so great an adventure. We also were younger once. To us it was an adventure of many kinds. At night in October in central Athens, the smell of orange trees and lemon trees was stronger than the smell of petrol. At Olympia, on the Hill of Kronos, what must the smell be at night? On our last day in Athens we saw an old taxi with the female figure of Speed from a Rolls-Royce bonnet stuck on its nose. She was fitted with red plastic wings. The original of the original of that figure, I suppose, in the sixth century BC, might easily have had coloured wings. Then what about the two priests in the Hotel Grande Bretagne, with hats like industrial chimneys and beards like polluted rivers? We saw far too much for me to write about all of it. No one understands everything about Greece, except maybe Nikos Gatsos. I think of him smiling.

Poems

1

An Angel sat on a tomb-stone top. He sang
a country song.
The wine is in the pine tree, shepherd,
that hums so pleasantly: and your flute is pleasant
the angel said. Shepherds talk in the shade,
a half-remembered story, how a nymph
loved Daphnis, and he died in a crowd
of mortals and immortals, and the lions
howled for him in the hills, and lurking bears
dropped hot tears for him. Sing you shepherds
said the angel, Sing when the thin cicadas
chir in the heat, and the thickets have their leaves.
Autumn is coming that will pick them clean.
Winter is coming with his claws of ice
to break the flute and bend the pleasant pine.
At the year's end stands Christ in a pillar of fire.

2

When poisoned Socrates,
blinded, with stiffening knees,
died and grew cold,
it was the young were with him, not the old.

Young passionate Plato heard
and honoured every word,
mastered his mind,
knew what he knew, was blind where he was blind.

His mind with a strong wing
hawk-hovering, questioning,
thought it no rest
to build in fabulous truth his tree-top nest.

Plato mapped the air,
what winds were foul, what fair,
at last grew fat,
fluttered his feathers on this wind and that.

He nested in dark trees,
forests of mysteries,
took playful flight
in skies ambiguously day or night.

With the old it's always so,
their fancies come and go,
attract, repel,
with death in sight and life, heaven and hell.

It was with irony
that old man claimed to see
his godlike One;
mystics, and not believers, claim the sun.

There was one scorned to be wise,
grew old with sober eyes,
drank with profound
religion poison, while the young stood round.

3 Digenes Akritas

vos exemplaria Graeca/nocturna versate manu ...

That hero was strong,
outlaw and captain:
but shaggy Charon
forced his body down
wrestling with him.
Streaming blood, he despised his fears,
and the ghost of Plato sang in his ears.

But he was wise too
in his mind, he was one who
committed his passion, master, to you,
the simply good and true,
knew proved in his own body what he knew.
The mind's courage exists in isolation,
committed reason is a hard passion.

Mortal passion
is felt in common,
reducing men like the action
of lust in any whore's conception.
When blood ran in a river down his chest,
Plato's wise ghost understood the test.

In three days it was over,
and that black wrestler
had forced him lower with a heavy shoulder.
He died, lonely huntsman and gardener,
clear-tonngued, taking the Sacrament with tears.
And still Plato's ghost sang in his ears.

4 For Poets in Prison without a trial

All day teaching in some classroom
I can hear your maddened pens,
scratch, scratch, where human foreknowledge comes home,
O images of violence,

O condemned poets, O dead who write
with iron pens in your unresonant cells,
and into mere blackness of the wasting night
drift out like solemn cries of ruined walls,

O dying poets in your terrible rooms,
breathe out your useless messages, your fact
to the inconsequential gaoler when he comes,
the inevitable beauty, passionate and abstract,

and O if some confusion of daylight
drops in the end like leaves on your faces,
then make your eyes star-purple, planet-bright,
like natural forces, echoless voices.

5 *for Peter Hacker*

These quiet autumns hide despair
old rhetoric, my mental state,
day after day through misty air
the dry echoes reverberate.
Now climber on his cliff, too scared to climb,
I search from rock to rock, misted in time.

Gardens and roads when I was three
first lured my wandering sense to spin
these crystals of maturity
to expose imagination in.
Winter brought dusk, autumn released in rain
the dropping leafage with its dying stain.
Then in the pages of school-books
I found stories about my life;
the masters gave me curious looks,
I fiddled with a small pen-knife;
all savage pleasures, and that pain and shame
vanished in moon and mist when autumn came.

The antique writers, the dead style,
horrific symbols, bleak comments
seemed altered in a little while
to a nervous kind of ornaments,
or roughened shells or craggy rock faces
worn into shape by cold autumnal seas.

All those philosophies have gone,
since pleasure, doubt, the sense of death
teach schoolmasters their own lesson
in voices tangible as breath,
and adolescents, studying what I write,
note the dead foliage and the dying light.

Now an intense reflective rage
by seasonal rebirth and loss
rips away words, page after page,
ringing eros on thanatos;
I study bare landscape, question the dead,
listen to cold rain falling in my head.

6   *Pancakes for the Queen of Babylon*

Ten poems for Nikos Gatsos

I

Branches of green in trees of darker green

they ran barefoot
they have thrown away their shoes.

Footprint of a star.

I was hungry all night;
I was thirsty all night.
One of them will bring water in her hand,
another will bring berries in his hand

the desert
stirring again
the dust of revolutionary wars.

Sleeping sometimes in the foliage of the vineyard

The darkness hand in hand with the darkness.
I am a secret mountain
tenebrous, flea-bitten by starlight,
my eyes are gone:
then when you cut my throat it bleeds coffee
with a trickle of alcohol.

I am unable to wake
in the vine's thin foliage only fumble
for the dregs of night at the breast of the darkness.

And one hoof of a star printing the dark
is ringing like a nail of a new metal.

II

Midnight wrings out its withering sunset
I clutch my violet, it smells of garlic
and sleep heavy.
Confusion is bluer than violets.

The law is already an antique:
it is always older than when you woke,
you are unable to say how you know it;
the law is older
                is a given thing
                         and when I wake
waking will be as deep as the dream was

Waking is walking,
is to wake to find
a cold violet coast in a green waste,
where a black horse in bud and a white horse
are chewing down the piebald rose-bushes.

My law is this confusion:
if it were not obscure how could I wake?
The law is an old question
which was over before we were awake.

We woke to find
a white boat rocking on black water
a black wind rocking on white water
a white boat rocking on black water

III

To speak about the soul.
I wake early. You don't sleep in summer.
In the morning a dead-eyed nightingale is still awake in you.
What has been done and suffered
with whatever is left to be suffered
is in the soul.
Oracles are given elsewhere. Their speech is associated with
  bronze.

In the early morning
you see women walking to the sanctuaries:
a light touch of sun on the whitewash:
a light touch of fire burning the oil.
You tell me nothing.
This is the desert I will write about.
The desert is not an island: the island is not enchanted: and
  the desert is no habitation for men.
The bird with the burnt eyes sang sweetest.
a desert further off
One small simple cloud. Heat at midday. A little constellated
  handwriting. Heat at midnight.

You never say.
To be woken by hearing
the voices of the enchanted birds
and the voices of disenchanted birds.

Say what is like a tree, like a river, like a mountain, a cloud over
  the sun?
My memory has been overshadowed
by that live light and by that dying light.

The soul is no more than human.

The rising sky is as wide as the desert.

IV

Two hours after waking
and the air already overgrown with coarse grass.
Catch me the little foxes.
Stones and places vary.

These stones and these places
are unattractive to lovers
in the deserts of my imagination poetry is the naked exercise
    of the entire man

its people are not inarticulate
no animal ever leaves a footprint

Light streaming headlong, rivers running sand,
the sweating heads of black and white horses
are beginning to speak.

I was hungry for horse-blood and for horse-sweat.

But listen. They are beginning to speak.
Wild archangels on storming horses trouble
the entire blue canopy of the air.
Music is to be out of tune with them.

The fire and stone-eyed horses shudder their flanks
and speak in gentle, articulate words.

To God, and to the air.

To familiar stones, to familiar places.

V

Flowers in sand.
There are no footprints in the level sand.
The dune-grass is a rough and hardy green.

Cooling coal smokes on the charred tongue.
The dune-flowers are stiff-looking and white.
Blue coal his dead breath in the freezing mouth.

She is this sand.
One of her hands will hold a reaping-hook.

The sand-flowers are too thin to trample.

Now he is cold;
a stub of candle on one rib.

His mouth is full of burning tobacco.
She heaven-like dissolving into sand,
more stars than sand, more stars than birds,
more birds than rain. It has been raining.

Intermixes with the breath of the sea.

That sand shifting about
will still support a few frail flowers,
bluer than the bluest shadow in her body.

And when I have stood living in this ash
and when I shall stand living

VI

At night they sleep straight out like the dead.

Their voice is like the black swarming of bees

overlooked by hill forts
among the wild, soft barrage of foothills,
discovered early high on the skyline
drowning in the wet, dim purple.

Squeaking birds rouse them in ruined gardens.

and whom the spirit persuades to the wilderness,
or whom the wilderness persuaded to the spirit
persuaded in the wilderness
with others whom the wilderness persuaded

When dusk scattered its handful of grime
they stream down in the rivers of red flags

Between bones of the sky the sun hangs
and pure and golden
he sharpens up his long blade on the rock.
They glitter in the integuments of brass.

They are shadow-scabbed. The brass is curdled.

who have not been confined
into the elements that wasted them,
rust-riveted weapons, discarded whistles,
and bugles in the thick tangle of grass.

You see them always moving. Winter sun
sprinkles the air with solid black and white.

not understanding fortune in the end

fishing for bream contriving their future

and in autumn in the bewildered woods
they lapped the yellow water of the sun
with certain dying stars which ran together
in the dark fields of my nativity.

coarser than a leaf, more lucid than a bird,
not very green

Something is always shifting in the universe.

They are in flight,
dwarfed by the processions of enormous cloud

a lonely motor-cyclist in the sky
look down on cities
stone neck, disproportionate bodies,
unkempt roses, unharvested apples

she offers her big breast without waking

what is the drum-beat of retiring time?
Harshly, loudly, and in the strictest time.

water be clear running over gravel
lead statues absolutely motionless.
He is the only human left alive,
runs with one arm free, swings his lighted
head like a danger-lamp, red in one hand.
This dreadful bird was shrieking in the trees.

Moving about together in the trees.

    In the congregation of young hares at moonrise not a curlew
utters and no other creature can keep awake. A night train
scatters sparks. Landscape is black and motionable. Dog-bones
are mossy.

their voices carry through the afternoon
they are always learning.
                    they disappear
one by one

                    into the circles of the universe,
possessed by forces I have never understood.

They are familiar with cave-journeys and snow-falls.

most dawns are misty

    by evening it has rained, the disillusioned priest and the
workmen settle down, black stream obscures the sky

they are moving there

    many ages of faith and some of reason went underfoot to
make this breeding-ground.

who came to life under cheerful rose-coloured heavens
and under the rose-coloured and grieving heavens of morning
whose boots were soaked through with field-dew

and the hell of fire will not alter their thoughts

she heaves her green swellings
she trails her brown and yellow kite of vines

in livid metal like a thundercrack
inlaid with yellow and with white metal

and hell of metal will not alter their thoughts

who alter like the season
whose courage is unnatural
the hell of water is less deep

Look, the liquid movements of a water-rat.

These wood-birds in their winter occupations.

VII

Under the white stone in the black river
dismembered, waiting for the coming voice

Justice is the beginning of my words.

When the aether was burning in mid-heaven
and every other heaven beyond heaven
had burned itself away,
a drift of cooling soot would cover over
the desert and the burnt-out desert birds

the Law is in flower

small newly given laws are lost already
in a chaos of flowering

And now on the highest, barest hill
the mountain sheep are grazing the sky blue.

No water is fresher or more alive

The Law was never given
but young men
                and children were found reciting it
their mouths are full of foliage.

Its voice is rocks, wind and the tearing apart of elements.

or you discover
heavy fruit in a multitude of leaf
        and
the sky is raining soot

Mountainous landscape was not in my words.

God is the Law
and has been newly given
and is in leaf

Powder-crackle
                fire
                        reverberation
are music to my words.
Poetry is burnt out.

It is necessity to speak.

VIII

A city built in darkness and cold air

            cold fire

the cold rattle of sparrows and milk-bottles
and early feet already in the street

Towering tomorrows
wade ankle-deep in a groundmist of gardens.

in any man in his life in the meditation of his heart

        your body, my body

There are five pure colours
and one impure religion.

Darkness.
Far away the mountains are snow-speckled.
The shadow edges forward,
it marks the giant doors of the bus station.

    Dressed in blue canves the nightwind dispeses a smell of
rain of diesels and of sleep. This flurry is colder than the last.

wrapped in a heavy coat my younger brother
vanishes quickly in the smoking fog.

The city is a matter of darkness.

uncertain if my brother evers sleeps
what my life is or does what my life is

Fumes of a dying nest of newspapers,
upstairs alone in an abandoned house.

at other times
when the horsechesnuts lighted their candles

clamour of metal in the snow and mist.

their bodies are like water their life summer,
the sunlight will be rumpling everything

We have come back.

Handfuls of leaves are painting a whole street.

                       and in the nettles where
alleys of shadows and humidity
step downward into ranker water-scenes

The stone itself is
the stones are beginning.
The trees have broken into their new youth.
Houses overhanging rivers
                    suddenly
break out into

Ragged red banners are appearing.

  Your body and my body.

Last week, at the railway station,
you said. Do you remember.
There wasa kind of smoky smell of sun.
For us, to whom nothing has been promised.

I can believe in nothing but in God.

my life is in this belief

my life is in this city

IX

I was asleep in heaven

Now it is evening
and shall we swallow the cup of our life?
I am always thinking about early morning
these woods have been much ruined and confused

The unatural wilderness of this rock
and loud the echo whistling in the rocks.

Who can consume nature? Who can
consume his nature?
                          That prophet
lies down beside his universe

there are no echoes whistling in the rocks
and light as breath lighter than death it
is magnified by mist and water-spray
sprinkling a green fire and blue scented fire

hardly touches the harsh air into leaf

Empting out your nature you shall find
a sky that has been hot has been early

is evening how and a certain blackness
is running on the edges of my life

It will be early. I shall wake and hear
and sweet nit-witted chattering of birds

and loud the echoes whistling in the rocks

X

Thousand on thousand spirits in the sun

   I am at the beginning

the blushing birthday roses in my garden

I cannot keep proverbs out of my voice

guttering in the deeper, deeper air

white the sandflowers sprouting among rocks
whose heavy smell is virgin in the rocks

I cannot keep my life out of my voice

one came back from the Asiatic dead
dragging a mass of Asian foliage:
and those with white faces
who rose early, who soberly rehearsed
some few words that had broken greater sleep.

Storm-clouds were cannonading in mid-air.

horses through the mist
                        serpents in the dust

We have drunk dry the voices in the well.

wild fruit
        fresh water
                those long-legged boys
the nightstick of the sun will batter down
shouting and swearing, stonily

  But underfoot some kind of new grass with a dusky breath.
Moisture, whole threads of aubergines. Yellow and purple, ripe,
  ripening.

Or a handful of sparrows at daybreak
coupled again in the rusty scaffolding
break down at night to iron and to stone
the wireless we heard crying in the sun

children's games, lover's mutterings.

  This spirit was in me.
  I will live in the wind

one who said:
I will eat herbs in the meadows of Glaukos
and live among the dead under the sea,
will feed on honey-cakes and sea-berries,
death and the sea shall herd me with his conch.

Hooters rebounded from Mount Pelion.

Caves will crack and the sea fly apart.

The universe has once been magical

a grain of sugar for the kettle

one who came back
naked under his bronze and linen
his face scarred by planets

this freedom is my theme

green and white comet-tails of fire and ice
trailing into extinction in his eyes

the foxes running on the dead terrace

Daybreak has washed away the dog's print from the dew
these letters from the sand

and shall arise

the second death is deeper than my life

and shall arise
and the moist ringing of a bird-whistle
alleluiando in the blackened trees

and shall rise

This freedom is my theme.

7 for Joan and Paddy

Fifty years ago I might have died.
Nothing is growing in the villages
but scraggy wheat: *ploutos* repurified.
The children are in leaf darker than trees.
I think there are bare voices in the stars.
The mutterings of those cold fires are wars.

Something died and has come alive in us,
it withers cobble stones and old railings;
beautiful poverty was victorious,
I am fighting the coherence of things.
All my true-seeming words will shake to pieces
when my lamp dies and the dawn cold increases.

Labouring all night on the moon's dark side
I built an iron train: that train is full;
but might have died where Agamemnon died
slowly threshing the water like a gull,
and am in love with cuttings in the rock
where the muse cuckoos like a cuckoo clock.

I have built nothing in thirty-five years
except five wooden gates into a wood.
I sweated mist, beach pebbles were my tears,
red and white dawns which I have understood
broke into cold, and dried up in the end.
The people have no flag left to defend.

There is nothing in providence but leaves,
there is nothing in my heaven but stone;
no one in mountain villages believes
what I believe when I am alone;
the hammer strikes again and again,
it is the gold and silver age again.

Men are like birds and have their building times,
a man's wing will be free and his cheek red,
birds in his hand, not anything that rhymes,
sparkshowers shadows metal compacted,
a note so true that not one bird can sound it,
but whole ages of years stand still around it.

8

The sky cleared and we came to an island
fresher than daisies greener than sunshine
the mountain spouted fire, it was God's land.

We saw a virgin standing in the cave
greener than daisies fresher than sunshine
her shadows and that fruit are all we have.
The storm has not cleared. We are in the storm.

One day was clear, the evening gilt and green,
shooting long shadows, it could mean no harm,
the sea will be where the island has been.
It is dark now. We use life in the storm.

9 *Kapetan Michalis*

He has gone, leaving written papers.
To many houses, all stone and sky,
some green growth in summer, some deep snow in spring.
Thousands of words of dream scribbled on a bedsheet.
This man tore down the fruit from solitude unripe.

In these woods, in the first leaf of the elm
when stone becomes shadow
the most tormented mind is motionable
it will be stony,
can settle among trees like an enormous butterfly
and shadow becomes stone.

Has gone away through the woods.
Where you hear birds now and then.
Small bodies, shrill voices,
a hundred juliets in balconies of branches.
Indoors at night the yellow globe
illuminating nothing.
Words written in the light of death.
It measures time, ripens without falling.
By now has gone a long way through the woods.

He is above the snowline,
in yellow and white clouds swirling marble
coughed out a star a tiny speck of blood.
You cannot know. You only know that he went on.
Am in this poem like a monastery
inscribing words on air and on darkness,
with the texture of rocks and villages
and the sea's unripeness.

Which is neither mine nor his, but in common.

10 In Memory of George Seferis

1

A sandy rock, my one name crusted over,
and I do not remember my father's name.
Was scything widely in a league of grass
ten days with the long tongue in balance,
it will be sharp in the black of greeness.
I have trodden down flowers without names.
I shall invent, sweat, I shall not speak.
    Building in limestone
with a construction differs from a tree:
or when the airy clang may be in flight,
invisible, the stone will be breathing.
While my long scythe will bite and whistle in
the wizzened regiment, it falls in line.
                        I shall begin
with the sky open morning and evening.

2

The horizon is green ink and blue ink,
and the trees inky colours,
except for the wild cherry which is white.
Then death is nothing, a dark edge:
but the spirit, the moral, the absurd?
It is an absolute of majesty.
Then love's a bed, purple and white and grass,
no star so purple and a water-shoot.
Who can believe in the God of nature?
Is nothing, nothing, a dark edge:
it hangs in the air like a smell of snow.
And reading in the book's memory I
can prophesy pages by pages
and can labour in the words of a song,
and can begin.

3

Who thought deeply, loved also what was living.
Virtue was in the mountains, in the stony villages,
magpie in meadow,
swiftly the shade, swiftly the afternoon.
The shepherd sees the city it is in his eye.
The oracle is water. Stone shall prophesy.
I am lost in this deserted extent.
Eagle his eye so brilliant in air
he will consume away the shepherd's eye.
There is succession of times in God,
but my identity is seasonal:
aspires, is blood and feathers, mows mid-air,
nor do I live for what is living,
I am frightened to awaken those who sleep,
or brush their eyes with nameless flowers.
In sleep the soul recovers its nature.
But virtue is in the mountains, in the stony villages.

4

So black as is midnight.
So strong as is the wind.
You hear the creaking of the iron gate
seeming to move on mountains,
the moon stone-footed in the sun's eclipse,
hopeful of green and white. You will go back,
eat honey in darkness, tread down clover,
lie in cress and in grass.
Today there is no moral only mountain wind,
tomorrow's snowy outline will visit
the air as lightly, in sleep as lightly.
It is the ruins, you will live in them.

5

Should have been what the dark is
and imitate fruit trees extend shadows.
Turkish roses sweated in shadow.
Chill and wet in my grandfather's linen
I see trees and woods how they extend.
The knocking of the axes of daylight.
Chill and wet in the leather on my feet.
Poor as a pebble. Stars were foreign armies,
they never whistled morning or night.
I do expect that motion like a star
was once familiar to the darkness.
Now should be dark
and should extend in the grain of a tree,
but that my mouth and hands are like a star.
Poor as a pebble.

6

On this rock the fineness of ivy
painted with suns or shadows
and valleys, airs, the coarsest lavender.
Wordless, and to begin again.
Iris, anenome, long grass:
what has been lost is never in nature,
it is not to be found by the snow-horses
that I can hear in the bones of my head
nor in the absolute difference of the sea.
At night this bone is frozen,
they scatter frost and ice,
champing the glitter of fragments and the mist.
Outside, uncovered, in the wind and mist.
The dead trumpet was shrieking, it has blackened.
Grief is the principal leavings of time.

May-December 1971

11

The sun of twenty years ago in mist
lemon-coloured in a sweat of weakness:
and a tree of rain in a twist of thunder,
a withered chirping and a tree of rock.
We shall never come through again.
There is something old-fashioned in our eyes.
A wind without words has been blowing.
How many bones makes a Parthenon?
The world being a system of seed
a sheet of rock is the end of the dead.
A rain of sun in a forest of stone
will ripen nothing but a wordless wind.

12 *(The Law School Riots, Athens, 1973)*

A kite a blue scratch on a blue sky:
scatter of white snow on a screen of rock,
and the sun pouring away into the sea
greener thinner and colder than honey.
A new stem weeps or sleeps between rocks.
I am dreaming my head is broken rock.
Everything fresh is breathing in one stream:
the breath of rock when we are free in dreams
cracks a bone open, courage is this shock,
scatter of white snow on a screen of rock.

About the Author

Peter Chad Tigar Levi was born at Ruislip, Middlesex, in 1931. The contrast between that most English of birthplaces and the exoticism of his baptismal names mirrored the interplay between his upbringing and his roots that was to be the decisive influence on his life and his writing.

On the one hand, he appeared to embody a strand of conventional if Victorian Englishness that was to lead him through classical scholarship and the Church to the post of Professor of Poetry at Oxford. Yet his Levantine nature – impulsive, frivolous, restless – was forever tugging at his gown, whispering thoughts of escape and fulfilment in some Aegean adventure. For Levi, England was bramble and winter light and duty; Greece was myrtle and summer heat and pleasure.

His grandfather, Moses Levi, had been a dealer in indigo, or carpets and coloured textiles, in Istanbul. Having removed himself and his trade to London, he would return to Turkey once a year to beget another child of his long-suffering wife, Sultana. Ultimately, her patience wore thin and, having piled her 21 offspring and numerous servants onto a steamboat hired for the purpose, she too sailed for England. Undeterred by the lack of an address for her absent spouse, Sultana moored in the Thames until he had been run to ground by Maples, the department store.

From his mother's family, the Tigars, Peter Levi inherited Sephardic blood, but both his parents were practising Roman Catholics. Raised devoutly, even narrowly, Peter and his brother and sister would all eventually enter the religious life. First, however, he was educated by Jesuits, at Prior Park and then at Beaumont, to which he had demanded to be sent as it had better provision for the teaching of Greek.

Such precociousness, even preciousness, was characteristic; at this stage in his life the culprit was Oscar Wilde, whose declaration that the Gospels in Greek was the most beautiful of all books led to what would prove an important introduction to the language. More formative still was illness. At 16, Levi contracted polio, and then while up at Campion Hall, Oxford, reading Greats, he was struck by a car. Both these misfortunes bred long periods of enforced leisure that allowed him to read exceptionally widely for one so young. As well as sparking his desire to be a scholar, these literary encounters also prompted him to begin writing poetry.

Having decided to seek a vocation as a Jesuit priest, Levi taught for two years at Stonyhurst, a school run by the order. He engaged his pupils' interest in Latin by having them translate the popular science fiction of *Quatermass and the Pit*.

With his rather romantic looks and somewhat fey manner, Levi did not fit the traditional image of the theology student, and his fellow ordinands at Heythrop, the Jesuit training college, later recalled that his study was as likely to contain half a bottle of champagne as the works of the divines. Levi used to render the text '*Beati immaculati in via*' as 'Blessed are those not caught on the way out.' His frequent breaches of the Society's rules, and his own querying of his vocation, led to his ordination being postponed until he was 33.

By then, he had experienced another revelation. An attack of catarrh, and the intention of translating Pausanias's travel books, led Levi to spend the spring of 1963 on an archaeological walking tour of southern Greece. As described in *The Hill of Kronos*, what had hitherto been a chaste love affair carried on at a distance now became a full-blown passion. Levi's new intimacy with the country awakened emotions that had hitherto slumbered inside him, while his friendship with its contemporary poets, especially George Seferis, had a similarly profound effect on his verse.

Levi's early poems had often been studies of the English weather and landscape. Now, in a radical departure, he began to form poems around words chosen for their associative effects, most notably in *Pancakes for the Queen of Babylon* (1968), probably the only poem to derive its title from a diatribe by the Reverend Ian Paisley.

By the mid-1960s, Father Levi was a familiar if peripheral figure in Oxford's academic life. He taught at Campion, was friendly with Maurice Bowra and Lord David Cecil, and also with literary London. When he journeyed to Afghanistan, it was with the young Bruce Chatwin as his travelling companion. His account of that experience was written up as *The Light Garden of the Angel King* (1973), and not always to Chatwin's advantage; Levi too might have been self-regarding, but not self-seeking.

As a conversationalist, his capacity for flights of fancy spiced with abstruse learning put his admirers in mind of Harold Acton, while his imaginary dialogues between Dickensian characters, delivered in Victorian cockney, were positively Byronic (albeit in the tradition of Robert, rather than George Gordon).

To Patrick Leigh Fermor, at the height of the Colonels' dictatorship in Greece, he wrote letters in Latin, further encoded as elegiac couplets, so that his criticisms of the junta might evade their censors. Levi, who always sided with the downtrodden, as befitted a priest, played an active part in the opposition to the regime. Deceived by the nonchalance with which he dropped names into his writing, his critics characterised him merely as an intellectual dandy and dilettante, but if he sometimes skittered across the surface of things he also possessed a good store of integrity and a sense of indebtedness to Greek culture.

Levi's detractors, however, were increasingly supplied with goads with which to jab him. Shortly before his ordination, he met and fell in love with Cyril Connolly's wife, Deirdre. Their closeness, though never unseemly, soon became apparent to all, including the jealous Connolly. Once, sitting downstairs talking at his home, the pair were startled by the appearance of Connolly's spectacles in their midst. Looking up, they saw him hanging bat-like from the balcony above, straining to hear what was passing between them.

In 1977, three years after Connolly's death, they were married and Levi left the Jesuits. Though there was no pram in the hall, his new domestic responsibilities demanded more of an income than could be supplied by part-time classics teaching at St Catherine's, Oxford, and he began to accept commissions for books. Like many who have to write for their living, he probably wrote too much and too quickly; by the end of his life, he had published some 60 books in less than 40 years.

His output was highly varied, both in range and quality. There were works on the classical world and its writers, on travel, and translations -- even (in the case of *Marko The Prince*, 1983) from Serbo-Croat. Among the biographies he wrote were those of his fellow philhellene Edward Lear, Horace, Tennyson, Milton and Pasternak, whom he thought the best European poet and whose poetry spurred him to learn Russian. Other books included an anthology of Christian verse and a history of monasticism.

Some of this writing was brilliant, especially in its confident command of European civilisation, but it could also appear insufficiently considered, and Levi out of his depth. Like a sprinter, he was best in short bursts. When he entered marathons, others delighted in tripping him up. His translation of the Psalms, which relied overmuch on a faulty Hebrew crib, was brutally reviewed, while his claim in 1988 that he had found a new poem by Shakespeare had to be withdrawn when it was shown that the 'WS' in question was probably the less celebrated Elizabethan poet William Skipwith.

The best that could be said of Levi in these moments was that he never took himself too seriously, having a capacity for self-parody that more than matched that for self-delusion. Though a tall man who could occasionally appear intimidating, he liked to induce mirth and he had a broad if not conspicuously displayed fund of kindness. Among his finest poems are elegies for friends, including that for his fellow poet David Jones. He could also be generous: the sum he sponsored his stepson for a charity swim at Eton was far larger, and perhaps less affordable, than that given by much richer parents.

In 1984, Levi was elected Professor of Poetry at Oxford, a five-year tenure which demanded little beyond one lecture a term and which brought him not so much an income but, as he called it, 'an enormous tip'. He had always been frail, and now ill health and blindness began to overwhelm him.

Having retired to Frampton on Severn, Gloucestershire, he continued to write almost to the last. 'A blank piece of paper,' he once declared, 'is the only thing in the world I have a serious ambition to control.' He died in 2000, aged 68.

James Owen
July 10, 2007

ELAND

61 Exmouth Market, London EC1R 4QL
Tel: 020 7833 0762   Fax: 020 7833 4434
Email: info@travelbooks.co.uk

Eland was started in 1982 to revive great travel books
that had fallen out of print. Although the list has diversified
into biography and fiction, it is united by a quest to define the
spirit of place. These are books for travellers, and for readers who aspire
to explore the world but who are also content to travel in their own
minds.

Eland books open out our understanding of other
cultures, interpret the unknown and reveal different environments
as well as celebrating the humour and occasional horrors of travel. We
take immense trouble to select only the most readable
books and therefore many readers collect the entire series.

All our books are printed on fine, pliable, cream-coloured paper.
Most are still gathered in sections by our printer and sewn as well
as glued, almost unheard of for a paperback book these days.
This gives larger margins in the gutter, as well as
making the books stronger.

You will find a very brief description of all our books on the
following pages. Extracts from each and every one of them can be
read on our website, at www.travelbooks.co.uk. If you would
like a free copy of our catalogue, please telephone, email
or write to us (details above).

ELAND

'One of the very best travel lists' WILLIAM DALRYMPLE

Memoirs of a Bengal Civilian
JOHN BEAMES
*Sketches of nineteenth-century India
painted with the richness of Dickens*

Jigsaw
SYBILLE BEDFORD
*An intensely remembered autobiographical
novel about an inter-war childhood*

A Visit to Don Otavio
SYBILLE BEDFORD
*The hell of travel and the Eden of arrival
in post-war Mexico*

Journey into the Mind's Eye
LESLEY BLANCH
*An obsessive love affair with Russia and
one particular Russian*

The Way of the World
NICOLAS BOUVIER
*Two men in a car from Serbia to
Afghanistan.*

The Devil Drives
FAWN BRODIE
*Biography of Sir Richard Burton,
explorer, linguist and pornographer*

Turkish Letters
OGIER DE BUSBECQ
*Eyewitness history at its best:
Istanbul during the reign of Suleyman
the Magnificent*

My Early Life
WINSTON CHURCHILL
*From North-West Frontier to Boer War
by the age of twenty-five*

Sicily: through writers' eyes
ED. HORATIO CLARE
*Guidebooks for the mind: a selection
of the best travel writing on Sicily*

A Square of Sky
JANINA DAVID
*A Jewish childhood in the Warsaw
ghetto and hiding from the Nazis.*

Chantemesle
ROBIN FEDDEN
*A lyrical evocation of childhood
in Normandy*

Croatia: through writers' eyes
ED. FRANKOPAN, GOODING & LAVINGTON
*Guidebooks for the mind: a selection
of the best travel writing on Croatia*

Travels with Myself and Another
MARTHA GELLHORN
*Five journeys from hell by a great
war correspondent*

The Weather in Africa
MARTHA GELLHORN
*Three novellas set amongst the
white settlers of East Africa*

The Last Leopard
DAVID GILMOUR
*The biography of Giuseppe di Lampedusa,
author of* The Leopard.

Walled Gardens
ANNABEL GOFF
An Anglo-Irish childhood

Africa Dances
GEOFFREY GORER
*The magic of indigenous culture
and the banality of colonisation*

Cinema Eden
JUAN GOYTISOLO
*Essays from the Muslim
Mediterranean*

A State of Fear
ANDREW GRAHAM-YOOLL
*A journalist witnesses Argentina's
nightmare in the 1970s*

Warriors
GERALD HANLEY
Life and death among the Somalis

Morocco That Was
WALTER HARRIS
*All the cruelty, fascination and
humour of a pre-modern kingdom.*

Far Away and Long Ago
W H HUDSON
A childhood in Argentina.

Holding On
MERVYN JONES
*One family and one street in
London's East End: 1880-1960* Red Moon &
High Summer

HERBERT KAUFMANN
*A coming-of-age novel following a
young singer in his Tuareg homeland*

Three Came Home
AGNES KEITH
*A mother's ordeal in a Japanese
prison camp*

Peking Story
DAVID KIDD
*The ruin of an ancient Mandarin
family under the new Communist order*

Syria: through writers' eyes
ED. MARIUS KOCIEJOWSKI
*Guidebooks for the mind: a selection
of the best travel writing on Syria*

Scum of the Earth
ARTHUR KOESTLER
*Koestler's personal experience of
France in World War II*

A Dragon Apparent
NORMAN LEWIS
*Cambodia, Laos and Vietnam
on the eve of war*

Golden Earth
NORMAN LEWIS
Travels in Burma

The Honoured Society
NORMAN LEWIS
Sicily, her people and the Mafia within

Naples '44
NORMAN LEWIS
*Post-war Naples and an intelligence
officer's love of Italy's gift for life*

A View of the World
NORMAN LEWIS
*Collected writings by the great
English travel writer*

An Indian Attachment
SARAH LLOYD
Life and love in a remote Indian village

A Pike in the Basement
SIMON LOFTUS
*Tales of a hungry traveller: from catfish
in Mississippi to fried eggs with chapatis
in Pakistan*

Among the Faithful
DAHRIS MARTIN
*An American woman living in the holy
city of Kairouan, Tunisia in the 1920s*

Lords of the Atlas
GAVIN MAXWELL
*The rise and fall of Morocco's infamous
Glaoua family 1893-1956*

A Reed Shaken by the Wind
GAVIN MAXWELL
*Travels among the threatened Marsh
Arabs of southern Iraq*

A Year in Marrakesh
PETER MAYNE
Back-street life in Morocco in the 1950s

Sultan in Oman
JAN MORRIS
*An historic journey through the still-medieval
state of Oman in the 1950s*

The Caravan Moves On
IRFAN ORGA
Life with the nomads of central Turkey

Portrait of a Turkish Family
IRFAN ORGA
*The decline of a prosperous Ottoman
family in the new Republic.*

The Undefeated
GEORGE PALOCZI-HORVATH
Fighting injustice in communist Hungary

Travels into the Interior of Africa
MUNGO PARK
The first – and still the best – European record of west-African exploration

Lighthouse
TONY PARKER
Britain's lighthouse-keepers, in their own words

The People of Providence
TONY PARKER
A London housing estate and some of its inhabitants

Begums, Thugs & White Mughals
FANNY PARKES
William Dalrymple edits and introduces his favourite Indian travel book

The Last Time I Saw Paris
ELLIOT PAUL
One street, its loves and loathings, set against the passionate politics of inter-war Paris

Rites
VICTOR PERERA
A Jewish childhood in Guatemala

A Cure for Serpents
THE DUKE OF PIRAJNO
An Italian doctor and his bedouin patients, Libyan sheikhs and Tuareg mistress in the 1920s

Nunaga
DUNCAN PRYDE
Ten years among the Eskimos: hunting, fur-trading and heroic dog-treks.

A Funny Old Quist
EVAN ROGERS
A gamekeeper's passionate evocation of a now-vanished English rural lifestyle

Meetings with Remarkable Muslims
ED. ROGERSON & BARING
A collection of contemporary travel writing that celebrates cultural difference and the Islamic World

Marrakesh: through writers' eyes
ED. ROGERSON & LAVINGTON
Guidebooks for the mind: a selection of the best travel writing on Marrakesh

Living Poor
MORITZ THOMSEN
An American's encounter with poverty in Ecuador

Hermit of Peking
HUGH TREVOR-ROPER
The hidden life of the scholar Sir Edmund Backhouse

The Law
ROGER VAILLAND
The harsh game of life played in the taverns of southern Italy

The Road to Nab End
WILLIAM WOODRUFF
The best-selling story of poverty and survival in a Lancashire mill town

The Village in the Jungle
LEONARD WOOLF
A dark novel of native villagers struggling to survive in colonial Ceylon

Death's Other Kingdom
GAMEL WOOLSEY
The tragic arrival of civil war in an Andalucian village in 1936

The Ginger Tree
OSWALD WYND
A Scotswoman's love and survival in early twentieth-century Japan